SIMEON OF DURHAM'S HISTORY OF THE KINGS OF ENGLAND.

SIMEON
OF
DURHAM

A
HISTORY
OF THE
KINGS
OF
ENGLAND

Translated from the Latin
by J. Stehpenson,
and first published
in 1858 in the
Church Historians
of England.

Facsimile reprint, 1987,
Llanerch Enterprises,
Felinfach, Lampeter,
Dyfed, Wales.

PREFACE TO SIMEON OF DURHAM.

§ 1. RESPECTING the personal history of Simeon, monk and precentor of Durham, we have very little trustworthy information. The only fact connected with him upon which we can speak with confidence is, that he was present at the disentombment[1] of the body of St. Cuthbert, in the year 1104, at which time he was an inmate of that cathedral church. There is reason to believe that he died shortly after (A.D. 1129),[2] at which period his chronicle terminates. He had probably been connected with the church of Durham from an early period of his life. These chronological details, although scanty, harmonise with the statements which are contained in his writings.

§ 2. A rubric, however, which occurs in the only known copy of Simeon's chronicle, disturbs the chronology noted above. It informs[3] us that Simeon flourished in the year 1164, or as the rubricator expresses it, four hundred and twenty-nine years after the death of the venerable Beda, an incident which, as we know, occurred in 735. If this statement be correct, it involves the inquiry in some difficulties. It leaves unexplained the fact that Simeon's chronicle ends thirty-five years before his death ; and by implication it throws doubt upon many of his statements, which claim to have been written by a man, whose life could not, in the ordinary course of things, have extended to the year 1164.

§ 3. These two statements stand so far apart as to be nearly irreconcilable ; and we are compelled to accept one of them, and to reject the other. We must decide whether the history is to be interpreted by the rubric, or the rubric by the history.

§ 4. The former of these alternatives was adopted by Selden,[4] who, in his preface to the Decem Scriptores, does not scruple to accuse Simeon of wholesale plagiarism, and of having perpetrated an extensive literary fraud.[5] Selden's theory is, that the History of the Church of Durham is the work of Turgot, prior of Durham, and eventually bishop of St. Andrew's ;—that upon the death of Turgot, (which occurred at Durham, where Simeon was at that time a monk,) his unpublished work, then existing in a single copy, fell into the hands of Simeon, who prefixed his own name to it, and

---

[1] See the present volume, p. 779. [2] Id. p. 617.

[3] Id. pp. 425 and 617.

[4] As early as the year 1618, Selden ascribed this work to Turgot. See his History of Tithes, p. 276. The Decem Scriptores did not appear until 1652.

[5] "Omnino credendum est opus integrum. . . . a libri primi initio usque in finem quarti. . . . antea diligenter compositum fuisse a Turgoto. . . . audax nimium facinus."—Selden's Præf. p. iv.

claimed it as the production of his own pen. By this process
Selden reconciles with the year 1164 the various chronological
statements which are scattered throughout the narrative ; and the
external and internal evidence are thus brought into harmony with
each other.   Selden's name invested this theory with an authority
to which its own merits did not entitle it, and for many years
Simeon was known only as a detected plagiarist, and as such held
up to general reprobation.

§ 5. Such was the state of the question from the year 1652 to
1732, at which latter date a dissertation by the Rev. Thomas
Rud, librarian to the dean and chapter of Durham, (prefixed to
Bedford's highly creditable edition of Simeon's History,) did tardy
but ample justice to the character of our historian.   Selden's false
reasonings, unwarranted assumptions, and forced conclusions, are
exposed and corrected in this masterly essay ; and Simeon was
restored to that position in our literature of which he had been so
unjustly deprived.   It is unnecessary for our present purpose to
conduct the reader through the different steps of the argument ; it
may suffice to state that the conclusion is based upon evidence
which is amply sufficient for its establishment.

§ 6. The existence of Simeon as an independent English historian being thus established, we have now to inquire into the
character and value of the writings of which he is the author.
Translations of the following histories are here presented to the
reader :—

§ 7. " Simeon's History of the Kings."—This consists of two
divisions ; the former extending from A.D. 616 to 957 (p. 483),
the second from 848 to 1129.   Prefixed to the entire work is an
account of the martyrdom of SS. Ethelbert and Ethelred,[1] which
being of Kentish origin has no immediate connexion with a history
which treats of the affairs of the kingdom of Northumbria ; nor does
there appear to be any obvious reason why it should occupy the
prominent place here assigned to it.

§ 8. This document, the History of the Kings, is of varied authority.   From its beginning until the death of Beda, in 735, it is con-
fessedly a compilation from the writings of that author, and from
a few other sources,[2] some of which are specified.   At A.D. 846[3]
Asser's life of king Alfred is largely employed.   Florence of Worcester is afterwards copied at some length, and William of Malmesbury
is cited.[4]   Two portions, however, of the History of the Kings
appear to be original ; that, namely, which extends from A.D. 735 to
802, and from 1119 to the end : both of considerable value, more
especially for the history of the northern provinces of England.

[1] The legend in its present form is earlier than Simeon's time, for it speaks of
the bodies of the martyrs as still deposited at Wackering, (see the present volume,
p. 730,) whereas about A.D. 990 they were removed to Ramsey. See Capgrave,
Nova Legenda Angl. f. 143.

[2] It may suffice to remark that Simeon's copy of the Anglo-Saxon Chronicle
corresponds with no existing manuscript of that document.

[3] There is a blank in the narrative from A.D. 803 to 846, with the exception of
a single entry under the year 830. A comparison with Hoveden's text during the
same period leads to the inference that the copy which he had before him was
defective at the same point.   [4] P. 843.

§ 9. It is not probable that both these chronicles, which constitute the History of the Kings, are the work of Simeon of Durham ; or, indeed, that they are to be ascribed to one and the same author. They contain statements which are contradictory the one to the other, and they vary in their chronology. It might be doubted, were we disposed to be sceptical, how far either of them is the production of the author whose name the whole now bears. They give no prominence to the fortunes of the church of Durham,[1] or the individuals who were connected with it ; whereas the history of Hexham[2] and its bishops is detailed at considerable length, so much so indeed, as to lead to the inference that the author was an inmate of that establishment.

§ 10. Only one manuscript copy of this chronicle is known to be extant. It is preserved in the library of Corpus Christi College at Cambridge, No. cxxxix. in folio, written in double columns upon vellum by a hand of the twelfth century. From this source it was printed by Twysden in his Decem Scriptores, the only complete edition which has yet appeared. The portion from the beginning as far as the year 978 is given by Petrie and Hardy in their Collection of English Historians. The present text is a translation from these two authorities.

§ 11. "Simeon's History of the Church of Durham" gives a detailed and connected account of the fortunes and migrations of the monks of St. Cuthbert, from the introduction of the Christian faith into Northumbria until the year 1096. Although professing to deal with ecclesiastical history only, it furnishes us with many important illustrations of the secular affairs of the northern districts of England. Simeon—for we have no longer any room to question its author—was well informed upon the incidents which he narrates, although it must be admitted that he is sometimes betrayed into serious errors.[3] He loses no opportunity of magnifying the dignity and importance of his patron saint by recounting incidents which draw largely upon the credulity of his readers ; but these narratives for the most part so well illustrate either the history, or the manners, or the faith of the age to which they relate, that we are no losers by their introduction.

§ 12. Of this work there have appeared two editions. The first of these is contained in the collection of English historians known as Twysden's Decem Scriptores. It is formed upon two MSS., the Cottonian MS. Faustina A. v. (apparently contemporary with Simeon himself), the other in the public library of the University of Cambridge. This edition, although executed with considerable care, is now entirely superseded by the publication of Bedford's volume,[4] which appeared in 1732. The great value of this later

[1] This remark does not apply to the portion extending from A.D. 1119 to the end.
[2] See A.D. 781, 788.
[3] For instance, in his assertion (p. 659) that king Alfred lay hidden for three years in the marshes at Glastonbury, for which he apparently cites the Historia de S. Cuthberto, printed by Twysden, col. 67, (cf. col. 71, line 23,) or some common authority.
[4] The full title of this satisfactory work is as follows :—"Symeonis monachi Dunelmensis libellus de exordio atque procursu Dunhelmensis ecclesiæ. Cui pre-

edition is, that it faithfully represents the text of a manuscript, (now belonging to the public library of the University of Durham,) which, as Rud has satisfactorily proved, is Simeon's autograph. With such an authority as this before us, supported by the Cottonian copy, Faustina A. v., any further reference to manuscripts [1] becomes a work of supererogation. It is from this text that our translation has been made.

§ 13. Appended to this History are two Continuations.

The former of these (p. 712) embraces a period extending from 1096 to 1144, and gives an account of the episcopate of Ralph Flambard and Geoffrey Rufus, and of the troubles which occurred during the invasion of the see by William Cumin. The anonymous writer, apparently a Durham monk, was an eye-witness of many of the incidents which he recounts, and the whole of his narrative is valuable and interesting. It occurs in the Durham manuscript without any distinct title, and is written in a hand somewhat later than the remainder of the volume. Other copies are to be found in the Cottonian manuscripts Titus A. ii.,[2] and Vespasian A. vi.,[3] some extracts from which are printed by Wharton in his Anglia Sacra.[4] The translation here given is from Bedford's edition; Wharton's text and the manuscript copies mentioned above have been consulted, but without affording any important results.

§ 14. " The History of the unjust Persecution of the first Bishop William." (p. 731,) is also a document of much historical value. It possesses the additional interest of placing before us a vivid picture of one of the struggles which took place between the civil and the ecclesiastical authorities. Its professed object is to give an account of the circumstances which led to the banishment of William Karilef by William Rufus, and its anonymous author, probably a monk of Durham, has executed his task with considerable skill. Bedford's text, which is here translated, is formed upon two manuscript copies, that at Durham, already so frequently mentioned, and another in the Bodleian Library.[5]

§ 15. "A short History concerning the Intruder during the time of Bishop William the Second," next follows, (p. 751.) This account of the invasion of the see of Durham by William Cumin, is here given from Twysden's edition; the manuscripts which he followed differing, at this point, from Bedford's text. As each fur-

---

mittitur rev. viri Thomæ Rud erudita disquisitio, in qua probatur non Turgotum, sed Symeonem fuisse verum hujus libelli auctorem. E codice MS. perantiquo in Bibliotheca publica episcoporum Dunhelmensium descripsit ediditque Thomas Bedford. Accedunt, præter alia, ex eodem codice, historiæ Dunhelmensium episcoporum continuatio, et libellus De injusta vexatione Willelmi I. episcopi, nunc primum editus." 8vo. Lond. 1732.

[1] The Cottonian MSS., Vesp. A. vi. of the fourteenth century, and Titus A. ii. of the fifteenth, have been examined, but the results are unimportant, tending only to confirm the value of the Durham copy.

[2] This manuscript ends imperfectly, with the words "contra episcopales" (Bedford, p. 278, l. 20), corresponding with the present edition, p. 724, l. 21.

[3] This copy is complete, and is followed by the History of Geoffrey of Coldingham. These two manuscripts agree closely with Bedford's edition.

[4] i. 705.

[5] MS. Fairfax vi., a folio volume upon vellum, written at Durham in the fourteenth century.

nishes an independent account of the same transactions, both are included in the present volume.

§ 16. "Simeon's Chronicles of the Angles," (p. 757,) supply us with a brief outline of the history of the kings of Northumbria from the time of Ida until that kingdom merged with the other states in the formation of the realm under Ecgbert. Thence it is continued until the end of the reign of Henry the First. This is translated from the text furnished by Twysden,[1] which is derived from the manuscript in Corpus Christi College at Cambridge, already mentioned (§ 2).

§ 17. We are indebted to the same source for "Simeon's History of the Siege of Durham," (p. 763.) No other manuscript copy than that which was used by Twysden (MS. Corpus Christi College, see § 2) is known to exist.

§ 18. "Simeon's Letter to Hugh, the Dean of York, concerning the Archbishops of York," (p. 769,) is printed from Twysden's volume. The succession of the occupants of that see extends to Roger, who ascended the archiepiscopal throne in the year 1154.[2] But this list is carried beyond Simeon's own date. A copy contained in one of the Cottonian manuscripts continues the succession no further than Thurstan (A.D. 1119—1139).[3]

§ 19. The object of the Appendix of Documents which follows (p. 775) is twofold. It not only furnishes some documents, highly valuable and interesting in themselves, which illustrate the period of history embraced in Simeon's writings, but it affords us the means of testing his accuracy and credibility as a writer. A comparison of Simeon's narrative with these writings—themselves of indisputable authority—strengthens our general confidence in him as a truthful and an honest historian.

[1] Prefixed to his edition of Simeon's History of the Church of Durham.
[2] Hardy's Le Neve, iii. 100.
[3] Id. iii. 98. The MS. here referred to is Titus A. xix., which, though of comparatively modern execution, undoubtedly represents an earlier and better text than that of the Corpus Christi copy. As there were two deans of the name of Hugh about this time, we gain no help from the letter being addressed to this individual.

J. S.

Leighton Buzzard,
    15th April, 1855.

SIMEON OF DURHAM'S

HISTORY OF THE KINGS,

HERE begins the history of Simeon, of holy and pleasant memory, Monk and Precentor of the Church of St. Cuthbert, of Durham, concerning the Kings of the Angles and Danes, and their numerous wars, pillages and burnings; from after the death of the Venerable Beda, priest, to within a little of the death of King Henry the First, son of William the Bastard, who conquered England; that is, during a period of four hundred and twenty-nine years and four months.

Here begins the Martyrdom of SS. Ethelbert and Ethelred, youths of the royal lineage.[1]

IN the year six hundred and sixteen from our Lord's incarnation, which is twenty-one years after the blessed Augustin with his companions was sent here to preach the Gospel, Ethelbert, king of the men of Kent, after having with great renown occupied an earthly kingdom for fifty-six years, entered upon the eternal joys of the kingdom of heaven. This king was the son of Irmiric,[2] the son of Octa, the son of Oiric, whose father Hengest, with his son Oisc, first entered Britain at the invitation of King Wirtigern, as Beda[3] has related in his luminous history. Eadbald, the son of Ethelbyrht, then assumed the reins of government. He begot two sons,[4] Eormenred and Erconbyrht. King Eadbald, departing this life, transmitted the sceptre of the state to Erconbert. He was first of the kings of the Angles who commanded the idols in the whole of his kingdom to be forsaken and destroyed, and likewise ordered the fast of the forty days [of Lent] to be observed by royal authority. To him was born a son, named Ecgbert. Eormenred had two sons, Ethelbert and Ethelred, to whose life and triumph of martyrdom it is right to give a place in the commencement of our history, and to show forth the glory of their holiness.

---

[1] The legend here incorporated is of doubtful authority, and the statements which depend upon its unsupported assertion should be accepted with caution. Another recension of the narrative is contained in MS. Bodl. 285, apparently the production of Gotscelin, an abridgment of which may be seen in Capgrave's Nova Legenda Angliæ, fol. 142 *b*; from which a few variations have been gleaned.   [2] More correctly, Irmenric.   [3] Hist. Eccl. ii. 5. § 101.

[4] The existence of a third son, Ecgfrith, unknown to Beda and the author of this legend, is proved by a charter of Eadbald, (if it be genuine,) Cod. Diplom. i. 9.

For king Ethelbert was complete in the rule of the glorious power,[1] when mightily attracted by the words of divine knowledge, he was washed in the baptism of salvation. By his care or wise assistance the condition of the churches of God was everywhere strengthened, and, by contribution of their property, the assembly of the faithful was strengthened. The government of the kingdom being in consequence very ably arranged, to the best of his ability, called by the goodness of the Just Rewarder (for in all things He had caused him to follow Himself), he was set free from earthly things, and raised to reign with the saints in the height of heaven. His son Eadbald succeeded him in the administration of affairs, as before stated ; to whom were born two sons of the royal line, Eormenred and Erconbyrht, the younger of whom, by his father's arrangement, assumed the sovereignty of the kingdom. After the death of Erconbyrht, his son, named Ecgbert, governed with great power ; but the elder, Eormenred, continued through the changing course of this frail life without the rule of empire. To this pious man were born of his very pious wife two sons, who having been brought up in the courts of their Master, the King of Heaven, were in various ways enriched with the royal blessing of eternal glory. The one became renowned by the name of Ethelred ; the other shone under that of Ethelbyrht. For at their sacred nativity we may well suppose, that all the orders of blessed spirits in heaven rejoiced to perceive that those whom they then beheld destined for earth, would return to them strengthened by the severe trials of this life. The height of the earth rejoiced in feeling itself adorned with the grace of a twofold gift, and because, oppressed by the exceeding malice of adversaries, it hoped to be for ever bettered by such aid. Moreover, holy Mother Church was joyful in being enriched by her Spouse with so great a dowry, by which she might shine the brighter in the light of good works, and might always be growing towards the highest point of holiness and righteousness. For, delivered to the womb of this preeminent teaching (not to speak in the choice phrases of scholarly learning), first of all in the calm sanctuary of its holy study, they were washed in the bright font of saving water, in the seven steps of which pure fluid they obtained the seven gifts of the Holy Spirit, were sprinkled with the episcopal blessing, and anointed with the holy chrism.[2] Most excellently supported on every side by these gifts, they strove to live virgins; and carefully preserving a chaste body, in seven courses of days that increased seven times seven and one[3] added, they hoped to gain the enjoyments of one jubilee, that is, the year of endless felicity. For, marked by a singular beauty of holiness, bound in the closest yoke of charity, rich in the duties of meek humility,

---

[1] An allusion, apparently, to the dignity of the Bretwalda.

[2] Allusion is here made to the custom of giving unction immediately after baptism, which is said to have been introduced by pope Silvester the First. Illustrations of this rite may be seen in Martene, de Antiquis Ecclesiæ Ritibus, I. xv. § 2; Durant, de Ritibus Eccl. Cath. I. xix. § 33.

[3] Beda (Opp. vii. 52, ed. fol. Basil.) enlarges upon the mystical meaning of the numbers forty-nine and fifty; affirming that the latter of these typifies the state of our resurrection to eternal life. See also the same volume, p. 60, col. 2, line i.

blessed with the distinction of unconquerable patience, adorned with the inmost grace of unwearying prayer, they were fulfilled with abundant reflections of the goodness of the Father of spirits. Having thus, according to our ability, given a foretaste of those plants of virtue naturally rooted in them, we will now attempt to give a brief account of the way in which they were called, through the crown of martyrdom, to the inheritance of the joys of the kingdom of heaven.

Both of their parents, then, being delivered from the misery of this life, while as yet they were in the helplessness of childhood, they were handed over to their relative, king Egbert, the king's brother,[1] in order that they might be educated in the exercises of sound learning, and might receive that training which human weakness renders necessary. But such good intentions were opposed by the envenomed weapons of iniquity and hatred, which the sons of unbelief always employ against the children of God. For in the royal palace was found a certain man of sin, and son of perdition, a limb of Satan, and of the house of the devil, who, puffed up with the empty pomp of the world, and graced by the munificence of the king, neither feared God nor regarded man. He, as by his exceeding craving after honour, entered above all into the counsels of the ruler, so was he vainly exalted by the rank favour of human levity; Haman was excited to put Mordecai to a cruel death on the gallows, on which he, bound in an unexpected way, was himself afterwards hanged. This man moreover was appropriately named Thunur, which means "Thunder," for he was unceasingly tormented by deadly furies of wicked spirits, by whose hideous tumults he should be sunk in the pit of hell.[2] Seeing then those happy whom we have before stated to have lived in so blessed a manner, defiled by the foul itching of corrupt thoughts, he began, in the filthy sty of his ungodly mind, to deliberate by what vile contrivances he might put them to death. Therefore, as with the tooth of a dog, he presumed to gnaw at their good fame in the presence of many of the courtiers, and in his mad detraction of them, to propound to the king such things as these : "Since, most gracious king, by your active mind and dexterous management, by the strength of your ready talent, and the able equity of your government, the very large extent of the kingdoms subject to your majesty is ordered with a most wise balance of justice, it is equally important, not only that the sceptre of the realm should be guided and directed by the firm rod of power, but also that the glory of a sound peace should protect your renowned race. For, in the case of yourself, you would not be so much harassed by the clouds of anxiety, were it not that you are blessed with noble specimens of sons, the illustrious successors of your dignity. Wherefore we consider it necessary that

---

[1] About A. D. 664, in which year Ecgbert succeeded to the throne, on the death of his father Earconbert, the uncle of these two martyrs. See Beda, Eccl. Hist. § 172.

[2] From these and other expressions it is not improbable that Thunor was a heathen, and that his hatred of the royal youths arose from their Christianity. It was not until the reign of Eadbald, that the old pagan Saxon idols were destroyed in the kingdom of Kent. See Beda, Eccl. Hist. § 172.

the path of tranquillity should be rendered easy to them, so that the
state of which they are to have the charge, may be shaken by no
stormy waves, and agitated by no grievous discords.   May all happiness, abounding in all good things, smile on them ; may constant
joy flow on them, filled with continual delight.   But I seem to perceive that great injury to this happy state may arise from yourself,
in consequence of your cherishing with care those who will some
day presume to usurp to themselves the highest dignity of your
kingdom, and to effect a revolution.   You grant such things to
them as are prejudicial to yourself and your posterity.   I speak of
those offshoots in your dignity, the youngsters Ethelred and Ethelbyrht, who are promoted rather to the hurt, than the advancement
of you and your children.   Therefore, having examined how far
this my intimation of an obvious calamity be correct, let the speedy
decision of reason be put in force against them.   I believe that
your common advantage would be consulted, either by your
ordering them into a long exile from the country, or by speedily
permitting me to put them to death."

The king winked at these things, not asserting that he was averse
to either plan ; and Thunur earnestly urging him to assent to the
deed, and often recurring to this, whilst the king coldly and weakly
opposed it, he strove in desperate audacity for their destruction.
Oh, the cunning craftiness of the treacherous against the guiltless !
Oh, the fierce rage of the deceitful against the innocent ! No gentle
affectionate feelings of kindness, no bowels of mercy are there in
them.   All their thoughts are bitter, and all their device is like
poison.   But why need we dwell on this ?   The same destroying
fury is armed against himself by the deadly malice with which, in
the absence of the king, he proceeded to stretch out his hands
against the necks of the innocent, meekly bent to God.

By this plan of the malicious persecutor the martyrs of Christ
were crowned with the palm of victory, and being received by
Christ into the inheritance of eternal life, rejoice with the angels of
heaven.   But the precious bodies of these noble champions were
ordered by him to be interred in the earth in a disgraced part of
the royal courts, supposing that what the invention of senseless
wickedness had effected, by the infamous malice of the murderer,
would long be concealed from all.   But though bewailed by no
sigh heaved for them, by no sounding service of ten-stringed instru-
ments, no stately honour of Ambrosian hymns, nor Gregorian
organ uttering sweet harmony, yet there were not wanting bounties
of manifold power from the highest Deity.

For, in the dead of night, there appeared from God a glittering
pillar of light shining over the hall of the king's palace, which by
its unwonted illumination aroused many of the king's household ;
and they in their great astonishment uttering loud cries, the king
was awakened, and, ignorant of what had occurred, arose from his
bed, and set out to go to the hymns of matins while it was yet
night.   On leaving the house, he saw a globe of extraordinary
splendour burning with a white flame, the origin of which proceeded
from the aforesaid wonderful seat of light.   Greatly astonished

indeed at the sight of so strange an appearance, the anxious king became agitated with trouble of mind, both as to where they were whom he had seen the day before, and concerning the conference which the servant of iniquity had formerly held with him respecting the destruction of the martyrs.   Then, the author of this enormous crime being speedily summoned, he inquired at what distance from the country his relatives were placed, of the great happiness of whose beautiful presence he was deprived.   The villanous murderer, turning a deaf ear to these pricking questions, and growling out with the voice of Cain—and worse than he in haughty pride of heart—that he knew not, the king, as one terrified by the brightness of the divine light, is said to have addressed him with a threatening countenance in these terms, "You always spoke evil things to me concerning them; you talked wickedly and abominably of their exile and their death; you uttered many outrageous slanders against them.   You, O wretch, must make me fully acquainted as to where they are to be found, whom you persecuted with intense eagerness of hatred and evil intention."   To this replied that vile and foul sink of iniquity, "Their dead bodies lie under the site of your dwelling."   What could the king do?   For struck with a paroxysm of fear, he stood stupefied and grieved to the utmost, because tormented by the sting of conscience that he shared in the infamy; since he had not strongly resisted the enemy of goodness, and because he was unable to avenge what had so wrongfully been perpetrated.   At the first dawn of day, summoning the earls and chiefs of his kingdom on whom he then depended, with the bishops, among whom was the archbishop of Canterbury, a man of great blessedness, Deusdedit by name,[1] he hastened to the spot where these innocents were laid, dug up the earth with a spade, and uncovered their sacred bodies, murdered and dishonourably buried. Alas, how dead must have been his feelings if he had not wept, when he saw the innocent children of his uncle slain!   How hard must have been his heart if he had not been overwhelmed with grief, when he saw his near relations dyed in their innocent blood! What showers of tears must he have shed, when he saw such rare flowers of nobility consigned to an untimely grave!

To the funeral solemnities of man were added mighty works of the everlasting God; for though they were crowned on the throne of the kingdom of eternity, He deigned to visit them, even here, with the wondrous working of his power.   These things happened in the royal vill called, in the common tongue, Easterige.[2]   When, therefore, the most precious bodies of these holy innocents were to be deposited in the bosom of the earth, it was intended that, being carried to the city of Canterbury, they should be buried in the monastery of Christ; but they could not be moved from the place in which they had been laid.   They proposed to carry them to very many and honourable places, but the arms of those who laid

---

[1] Gotscelin, and from him Capgrave, here speaks of archbishop Theodore, instead of Deusdedit, and apparently more correctly, since Deusdedit died in 664, the year of Ecgbert's accession.

[2] Now Eastry, near Sandwich.

hold of the coffins became powerless. At length a better design being discovered, that they should be carried to the famous monastery called Wakering,[1] they were then raised with such unexpected ease and swiftness, that there seemed no difficulty in the carriage so long desired. On their arrival they were received with rich chanting of hymns and sweet melody of psalms, with full-sounding chorus and jubilant cymbals, and were admitted to an honoured burial behind the high altar. For many years after they had been laid here, the Most High God, who has respect unto the lowly, but beholds the proud afar off, was pleased to enrich them with frequent miracles, two of the latest of which I shall make known in this treatise.

It happened that a certain man, coveting his neighbours' goods, carried off secretly a sheep belonging to a poor man, which bearing on his shoulders, with its feet tied, he designed to convey past the monastery of the holy martyrs: but he was not able; he could carry it there, but he had no power to bear it thence. The perpetrator of this crime was at once deprived of the breath of life, and struck dead to the ground, having the sheep alive in his hands, the man on whom the robbery had been committed pursuing him. The guiltless received his own, and left the guilty, cut off by death through the speedy vengeance of the holy innocents. Running forthwith to the porter, he inquired if he had put the robber to death, and learnt that he was slain by no mortal hand. Receiving permission to carry back what was his own, he returned cheerful and rejoicing to his home, giving many thanks to God and the saints.

Having, therefore, to the best of my ability, correctly related the sufferings of the holy martyrs, it remains that I briefly state the manner in which the divine vengeance fell upon the unjust judge, the author of their most sacred death. They had a sister, on both the father's and mother's side, named Eormenburg or Domneva,[2] who became the wife, by lawful marriage, of Mearwold,[3] king of the Mercians. King Ecgberht, sending one to carry his message, invited her to visit him. She was received, when she came, by all the chiefs of the kingdom, with the respectful honour and magnificence which were due to her. The king, therefore, designing to honour her, desired that she might ask whatever she wished within the compass of his power to bestow, if it were a thing becoming his dignity, and she should immediately receive it. The holy woman, in a meek reply, begged that he would grant her only as much land as a doe which she had brought up, guided by divine instinct, could travel over in one day. The king, well pleased, immediately ordered a party of the earls to be in readiness on the

---

[1] "Ad monasterium Wacrinense;" viz. Wakering in Essex, as appears from Gotscelin and Capgrave, who, however, give no account of the manner in which the bodies reached that monastery.

[2] The pedigree of Ermenburga is carefully examined by Henschenius, Acta SS. Mens. Feb. iii. 389, §§ 3, 4.

[3] Merewald was one of the under-kings of Mercia, and ruled over the eastern part of that extensive district (Flor. of Worcester, ad an. 675) occupied by the "Westan Hecani." (Flor. Appen. ii. 396 of this Series.)

morrow, attended by whom he would proceed in ships to the Isle of Thanet. Having arrived there, and she with the doe having made the voyage to the island, the doe pointed out the way, and was followed by the king and the handmaid of Christ, with the military array on horseback. A very large portion being now encompassed, the infamous murderer was moved by spite, and as if out of fidelity to the king, to whom it appeared as if nothing would be left out of his lavish kindness, he began, as if sympathizing in his ways, to chatter in this manner: "Since all your actions are guided by acute judgment, why do you follow, in this devout procession, this brute animal, as if it could perform something wonderful?" As he said this, struck by the bolt of the Almighty, he fell from his steed. Immediately the very wretched Thunor was swallowed up, with his horse and arms, in a frightful chasm of the earth. The king, with all his comrades, seized with excessive terror, hastily ordered his body to be covered with an immense heap of stones, the soul being reserved for everlasting burning in the dreadful fires of hell, of the pains of which it has been said, "Souls shall pass from the pangs of snows to devouring flames." This place is called by wayfarers "Thunerhleap," and it still retains the name.[1] This raging murderer having been visited by the catastrophe of so awful a death, and, instead of pleasure, suffering the penalty of torments, the before-mentioned animal made a path for those who accompanied it, as the will of God permitted, and then stood still, to the wonder of all. The king, startled by the miracle which he had seen, did as he had promised, confirmed it with his own hand, and so returned home.

This woman, a lover of holy virtue and specially chosen of God, founded a church upon this island, dedicated to the blessed Mother of God, Mary the perpetual virgin, in memory of the innocent martyrs of Christ, her brothers, and soon after placed there her daughter Mildryda, a virgin of virtuous disposition, educated in ecclesiastical discipline in foreign parts, and gathered there seventy nuns, consecrated by the holy archbishop Deusdedit. There the mother of the blessed Mildritha, after the lapse of many years, having shown forth many virtues, and edified many souls of men and virgins whom she strengthened in Christ, obtained with the lamp of righteousness to hear from Christ the words, "Rise up, my love, my fair one, and come from Lebanon; come, and thou shalt be crowned."[2] The soul, carried to the court of heaven, received from Christ the incorruptible prize of victory, to reign with Him and his saints in eternal glory. To her succeeded in the government of the monastery her illustrious daughter, whom she had carefully educated, the aforesaid noble Mildrytha, unwearied in the service of Christ, a most holy virgin, greatly embellished with the grace of miracles.

Of these I shall relate one, which undoubtedly proves that God

---

[1] Gotscelin and Capgrave call the place "Thundreshleau," *i. e.* "the tomb of Thuner;" this was probably the reading of Symeon; but the scribe has mistaken the Saxon w (ƿ) for p, an error of no unfrequent occurrence.

[2] Canticles, ii. 10.

had done for her many things unutterable by mortal man ; for at
a certain time, somewhat overcome by sleep, she was resting on a
couch, her limbs wearied with protracted labour, an angel of God,
in the form of a dove, attended her, resting on her head to protect
her from the illusion of evil spirits. This holy virgin, like her
blessed mother, leaving a good example to those who followed, the
Almighty Father of spirits taking her soul unto Himself, amidst
the tears of earth and the rejoicings of heaven, now lives in everlasting happiness, her sacred body receiving a fitting place of
sepulture in the church of the blessed Mother of God, Mary, perpetual virgin. Having thus related the sudden destruction of the
bloody persecutor of the blessed martyrs, and then glanced at the
honourable deeds of their sister and niece, to whom at the same
time to live was Christ and to die was gain, we must haste, for his
sake and by his help, to narrate other events, preserving the order
of history.

In the beginning of this work I have accurately recounted the
succession of the Kentish kings ; I must now set forth that of the
Northumbrians, that we may come to the times of those of whom
there is no history, after the death of the venerable priest Beda.

King Ida[1] reigned eleven years ; after whose death Glappa
reigned one year, whose successor, Adda, held the power of the
kingdom for eight years. He being cast into the lower regions, as
he deserved, Ethelric obtained the earthly kingdom, which he held
seven years. He, going into the depth of hell, left the empire to
Theoderic ; who, after reigning four years, lost at once his kingdom and his life, going into outer darkness, where, bound in heavy
chains, he is compelled to undergo a miserable servitude.[2] After
him Frithuwold held the sceptre for seven years, and, departing this
life, left the monarchy to king Hussa. He, after exercising impe-
rial authority for seven years, learnt in his own experience the truth
of the saying,

> " High glory death despises ;
> Upon the lofty and the lowly head
> He falls alike ; bringing to equal level
> The high and lowly born."

Eighth in the kingdom shone Ethelfryth, the bravest of kings,
who, after a reign of twenty-eight years, lost his life and kingdom.
To him succeeded king Edwin, who, receiving the faith of Christianity, earned the reward of heaven as king and martyr, after
having reigned in honour and dignity for seventeen years. After
him, the most christian king Oswald received the kingdom of the
Northumbrians, which he held eight years ; and when he, who
sought the joys of a better country, that is a heavenly, had

[1] The succession of the early kings of Bernicia, as here given, differs from that
adopted by Florence of Worcester ; to which, however, it seems preferable, when
we consider the relative opportunities of the two authors for obtaining trustworthy information.

[2] These all died in heathendom ; hence the expressions used by Simeon.

ascended thither, king Oswy succeeded to the cares of state for twenty-eight years. On his removal from earth to heaven, he committed the earthly kingdom to Egfrid, who held it fifteen years. He was slain by the Picts in an unjust invasion of Ireland, and in his stead, his brother Alfrid reigned nineteen years. To Alfrid succeeded his son Osred for eleven years. He being slain, Coenred held rule for eleven years. Osric succeeded him in the kingdom for eleven years. Ceolwlf the brother of Coenred succeeded Osric for eight years. To him the historian Beda dedicated his History of the Angles. In the fourth year of the aforesaid king Egfrid, a noble monastery was built at Wearmouth, [1]and in the seventh year of his reign the great Beda was born. How this was brought about the truthful Beda tells in his life of his blessed abbot Benedict, and of Ceolfred, which he has narrated in pleasing style, and copies of which are to be found in most places. This place was built and consecrated in honour of Peter, the chief of the apostles. Moreover another monastery was built in reverence of Paul, the teacher of the Gentiles, at the place called Et Gyrvum.[2]

Having stated these things, we must now insert in this work some of the events which occurred in the days of those abbots, that those who have not read their lives, may hear how great a light of Christianity shone at that time in those regions, as Beda narrates in his treatises.

[3]There was a man of holy life, Benedict by grace as by name, who, from his very childhood, possessed the discretion of an old man, for, passing the flower of his age in virtue, he gave not one thought to pleasure. He was born of a noble race among the Angles, but raised by the no less nobility of his mind to the well deserved fellowship of angels. At length, when he was the minister of king Oswy, and had received by his gift an estate suitable to his rank, he set light by the perishable possession, that he might gain the eternal. He despised earthly warfare with its corruptible rewards, that fighting for the true King he might earn an everlasting kingdom of heavenly bliss. He left his home, his friends, and his country, for Christ and the Gospel, that he might receive an hundredfold, and inherit everlasting life. He rejected earthly nuptials, that he might be able to follow the pure Lamb, in the glory of virginity, in the kingdom of heaven. He refused to beget mortal children in the flesh, having been predestined by Christ to bring up for Him, in spiritual learning, sons ever abiding in a heavenly life. Leaving his country, therefore, he went to Rome, bent on worshipping at the tomb of the blessed apostles, with love to whom he had ever been inflamed ; and afterwards returning to his country, he ceased not earnestly to love, to honour, and to inculcate on whom he could, those institutes of ecclesiastical life which he had witnessed. He journeyed again to the gates of the holy apostles, in the time of Pope Vitalian ; and, going thence, he joined the convent of

---

[1] The following thirteen words occur on the margin of the MS.
[2] Namely, Jarrow.
[3] This narrative is based upon Beda's Lives of the Abbots of Wearmouth and Jarrow, which have already been printed in this Collection.

monks in the island of Lirins, received the tonsure, and after remaining there two years, again yielding to his love of the blessed Peter, he determined once more to tread his sacred threshold. At this time the apostolic pope sent bishop Theodore and abbot Adrian, with the man of God, Benedict, to the Anglican nation. Who shall declare how many divine volumes, how many relics of the blessed apostles or martyrs of Christ, Benedict brought over? King Egfrid at that time held the kingdom of the Northumbrians under his pious rule; in whose sight he found such favour of extreme kindness, that he very soon bestowed on him, out of his own estates, a possession of seventy hides of land, and enjoined the first pastor of the church to found thereon a monastery at the mouth of the river Wear, on the left bank, A.D. 674, in the second indiction, but in the fourth year of the reign of this king. After this he obtained masons, and invited glass-makers, and abundantly supplied all that was necessary. He five times, as the history of his life shows, crossed the stormy waves of the ocean; he brought so great gifts and offerings of every kind that they cannot be recounted for multitude.

King Egfrid, then, highly delighted with the virtue, diligence, and piety of the venerable Benedict, when he saw the land which he had given to build the monastery so well and beneficially applied, had the zeal to add, in his royal bounty, a further gift of forty hides. Oh, gracious kindness of Christ! Oh, kindly piety of the king! who not only willingly bestowed his goods upon the good, but had the disposition to increase it, in fulfilment of that which is written, " Did not his heart burn within him?" [St. Luke xxiv. 32.] Woe to the enemies of Christ! Woe to those who destroy and burn up the temples of God! They themselves shall be burned, where the worm dieth not, and the fire is not quenched. But of them let us now be silent, and speak only of matter of rejoicing. In the course of twelve months, about seventeen monks were assembled, Ceolfrid being appointed as their provost and priest.

But Benedict the servant of Jesus Christ, by the advice, yea even command, of the aforesaid king Egfrid, founded another monastery, in honour of the most holy apostle Paul, not far from the former; for this purpose, namely, that between the two places peace and concord alone, and the same intimacy and kindness, might ever be kept up; so that as, so to say, the body cannot be severed from the head by which it breathes, nor the head be forgetful of the body, without which it cannot exist, so no one should attempt, by any effort, to create discord between these monasteries of the chief apostles, united in motherly alliance.

The man of God, Benedict, finally appointed the most reverend Ceolfrid over the monastery of St. Paul the apostle; and Eosterwin he preferred as abbot in the convent of St. Peter the apostle. But Benedict did this in order that a guardianship according to rule should always be kept up, lest on account of the increase of his labour, the rule of holy discipline might be indifferently preserved. And even the great abbot Benedict himself, as the holy pope Gregory tells of him, appointed under himself twelve abbots, without any loss, nay to the increase of love. Eosterwin then received the charge of governing the monastery, in the ninth year of its foundation, and remained in it until his death, which occurred four years afterwards; a man noble in worldly rank, but using external nobility not, as do some, as a matter of vainglory and to the despising of others, but, as becomes the servant of God, converting it to the greater nobility of the soul. For he was the cousin by the father's side to his abbot Benedict; but so great was the simplicity of both, such their utter contempt of worldly honour, that neither did the one who entered the monastery suppose that any honour was to be sought by him on account of regard to relationship or rank, nor did the other think of offering any, but the well-disposed young man gloried in observing strict discipline in all things in equal measure with his brethren. And indeed, although he had been the minister of king Egfrid, yet, worldly affairs being once relinquished, his arms laid aside, the spiritual warfare taken up, he remained so humble and so like the rest of his brethren, that he delighted to winnow and thrash with them, to milk the sheep and heifers, to be employed, cheerfully and obediently, in the bakehouse, the garden, the kitchen, and all the labours of the monastery. But also, after taking the title of abbot, he preserved the same disposition towards all, according to the admonition of a certain wise man, " They have made thee a ruler, be not puffed up, but be amongst them as one of themselves." For he was mild, affable, and kind to all; and although, when occasion required, restraining offenders by strict discipline, yet still more, by natural earnest intercourse, careful to warn them against the desire to sin, and so to hide, under the cloud of their iniquity, the clear light of his countenance. Often in travelling anywhere on the business of the monastery, when he found the brethren at work, he was wont at once to take part in their labour, either guiding the plough, or shaping the iron with the hammer, or brandishing the winnowing-fan in his hand, or doing any other work of the same kind. For he was a young man of great strength, and pleasing in speech; cheerful moreover in disposition, full of kindness, and of an agreeable aspect. He always, when at home, lived upon the same food as the rest of the brethren. He slept in the same common dormitory which he had occupied before he became abbot; so that even when seized by death, and conscious, by unmistakeable tokens, of his own departure, he yet lay two days in the dormitory of the brethren. For, five days before the hour of his departure, he removed into a more private dwelling; there, one day, leaving the house and sitting in the open air, having summoned all the brethren, he, according to his kindly nature, gave the kiss of peace to them as they were weeping and mourning over the departure of so good a father and pastor. He died on the night of the nones of March [7th March], the brethren being engaged in chanting the lauds of the morning psalms. He was twenty-four years of age when he went to the monastery; he lived in it twelve years; seven years he discharged the office of the priesthood, during four of which he held the government of the monastery; and so, leaving the earthly body and its perishable members, he sought the heavenly kingdom, there to be crowned with a twofold diadem, according to the import of his name, that is, Easter and Wine, he being noted for his participation of the true passover, which is the true triumphal song. But having briefly premised these things from the life of the venerable Easter-wine, let us resume the thread of our narrative.

He being appointed abbot of the monastery of St. Peter the apostle, and Ceolfrid ruler of that of St. Paul, not long after, Benedict, the courageous soldier of the Lord, travelling for the fifth time from Britain to Rome, returned as usual enriched with innumerable donations of things useful to the church.

And soon after this, the blessed Benedict began to sink under an attack of disease; and his health gradually failing for three years, he was disabled by paralysis, and became altogether deadened in the whole of the lower limbs, the upper part of the body alone, without whose vitality man cannot exist, being kept alive for the exercise of virtue and of patience. Both abbots, Benedict namely and Sigfrid, were always, in their trouble, earnest in thanksgiving to their Maker, and occupied themselves in the praises of God and in brotherly exhortations.

He held many conferences with the brethren, and was wont earnestly to impress upon them this charge : That in the election of an abbot they should not imagine that regard ought to be paid to nobility of race, but that they should consider purity of life and doctrine as the chief requisites. But when both abbots, worn out by long-continued sickness, perceived themselves on the point of death, and unable to rule the monastery in so great weakness of the flesh, the strength of Christ was perfected in them. On a certain day, desiring to see and converse with each other before their departure from this life, Sigfrid was carried on a litter to the chamber where Benedict also lay on his couch, and being laid together in one place by the hands of their attendants, their heads rested, a mournful spectacle, on one pillow ; and they had only so much strength remaining, that they could join their lips, placed close together, in kissing each other. Benedict, entering into sound consultation with him and the whole of the brethren, sent for the abbot Ceolfrid, whom he had placed over the monastery of St. Paul the apostle, a man related to him not so much by human alliance as by fellowship in virtues ; and, all agreeing and considering it a most advantageous measure, he appointed him father over both monasteries, considering it in all respects wholesome for the preservation of peaceful unity and concord between the places, that they should always have one father and ruler ; often mentioning the example of the kingdom of Israel, which always remained indestructible and inviolate by foreign nations, so long as it was governed by single rulers, and those of their own race ; but afterwards, when, on account of their previous sins, it was torn asunder by fierce internal contests, it perished by degrees ; and, shaken from its basis, was destroyed.

At length, after they had completed all that concerned the

things of God, after the lapse of two months, first the venerable
abbot Sigfrid, beloved of God, having passed through the fire and
water of temporal tribulation, was taken to the enjoyment of
eternal rest, and entered on his abode in the heavenly kingdom
with offerings of endless rejoicings.

Four months later, Benedict, the conqueror of sin, subdued by
weakness of body, approached his latter end.   Then he, so admi-
rably accomplished in virtues, shone at the period of his departure
by his utter defiance of the bands of the enemies.   He so fought
the good fight of holy faith, so employed the talents committed to
his charge, so preserved the fruit of rare chastity, and kept the oil
within the secret chamber of his heart, that he was counted worthy
to enter into the holy of holies, and to receive the liberty of the
year of jubilee.

> " Chill night comes on with wintry blasts,"

soon to give place to a holy day of eternal blessedness, peace, and
light.

The holy servant of God received as a viaticum, at the very hour
of his departure, the sacrament of the Body and Blood of his
Lord ; and so that holy soul, long tried and purified by the flames of
blessed suffering, left the earthen tenement of the flesh, and sped,
free, to the glory of supreme felicity.   This pious confessor rested
in the Lord in the sixteenth year after he had founded the monastery, on the day before the ides of January [12th Jan. A.D. 690].

The abbot Ceolfrid, in all respects illustrious, a man acute in
genius, bold in action, mature in mind, fervent in religious zeal,
pious, as I before said, by the command and with the assistance of
Benedict, founded, finished, and ruled over the monastery of St.
Paul the apostle for seven years, and then presided for twenty-
eight years, with able rule, over the two monasteries ; or, to speak
more correctly, over the one monastery of the blessed apostles Peter
and Paul, situated in two places ; and all things which his predecessor with admirable and pious pains had commenced, he took
care diligently to complete.   He built, therefore, many altars, he
made oratories, he augmented vestments of every kind, he procured three copies of the Bible, two of which he left to the two
monasteries.   He received from pope Sergius a charter of privileges
for the monastery, which, being brought and laid before the synod,
was confirmed by the signature of the great king Alfrid.   But when,
after great observance of strict discipline, after incomparable diligence in prayer and praise, after wonderful vigour in restraining
the evil and gentleness in comforting the weak, after abstinence in
meat and drink, and poverty of clothing unusual in rulers, he perceived that, growing old and full of days, he was no longer able,
either by his teaching or his living, to set before those under him
a rule of spiritual practice ; giving for a long time much thought
to the matter, he decided that it was expedient that, a mandate
being issued to the brethren according to the statutes of their privilege, and according to the rule of the holy abbot Benedict, they
might choose from among their number a father who should be

more suitable than himself. What the devout father desired was
done, though all at first resisted, and with tears and sighs bent their
knees in repeated dissuasions.

Hwetbyrht, therefore, was elected, a good and just man, who had
been a disciple of abbot Sigfrid, to whose consecration bishop Acca
was invited, who admitted him to the office of abbot with the usual
benediction. The holy man Ceolfrid set out for the gates of the
most holy prince of the apostles ; but, before he could arrive there,
he was attacked by the illness of which he died. But the discharged
soldier reached Langres about the third hour of the day on the
seventh of the calends of October [25th Sept.], as we have said,
and took up his quarters in the meadows of that city. And it
so fell out, by the will of God, that on that day, about the tenth
hour, he departed to the Lord. His sacred body was buried in the
church of the holy martyrs Speusippus, Eleusippus, and Meleu-
sippus, where many miracles and works of healing are witnessed,
the gifts of Him who is wont to assist his saints militant here, and
to crown the victors hereafter.

These accounts we have extracted from the writings of the
blessed Beda. We must now say something of him, recalling the
memory of his holiness, and grateful for his labours. For, speaking
of the annals, that is, the records of each year, he says :—

> " Let him peruse this work, who longs to know
> The chronicles of years, watching the tide
> Of age and waning life. Time governs all,
> Leads all in triumph, changes in their turns
> The elements and seasons; days and nights
> Alternate lengthen. The flowers have their time
> To show their beauties, the harvest has its season
> To yield a bounteous increase, when the plains,
> Clothed with rich store of grain, rejoice and sing.
> Seasons there are of gladness, and of grief.
> Life has its period, so has bitter death ;
> Time's hour glides on, ages in moments fly ;
> Time all he gives, inconstant, takes away ;
> Spring, summer, autumn, winter come and go."
>   These lines of truthful eloquence proceed
>   From the smooth pen of venerable Bede.

I shall here insert the verses which he composed for bishop
Acca,[1] on the " Day of Judgment." Yet I shall not do this with
strict accuracy ; and as I do not know in what position to place
them, I beg the indulgence of the learned.

> " Seated alone upon the flowery turf,
> Beneath the branches of a shady tree
> Which rustled in the breeze, sad and oppress'd
> With heavy thought, I sang this mournful song;
> Remembering with deep grief, the sins and stains
> Which mark'd my life, the dreaded hour of death;
> The judgment of the awful day, when all
> The race of man, divided, shall receive,
> The righteous—joy ; the wicked—endless pain.
> Recalling this,—I pray'd in accents low,
> ' Open warm fountains of my heart ; whilst I
> Smite on my guilty breast, and, with my face

---

[1] In Petrie's edition these verses have been collated and corrected by the aid
of a copy of the tenth century, in the Cottonian MS. Domit. A. i. fol. 51.

Low in the dust, recite deserved woes,
Pour out, I pray you, floods of bitter tears,
And with sad voice confess your sins to Christ.
Keep not one fault conceal'd within your breast;
Let all your foulest crimes be brought to light
In free confession of the heart and tongue.
This the soul's only safe and certain hope,
That, grieving, you lay bare your wounds with tears
Before the great Physician, who can heal
The wounded, loose the bound, and will not crush
The afflicted soul, nor quench the smoking flax.
Let the repentant thief a pattern be
Of true confession, and its blest result;
Who, crucified for his unholy deeds,
Yet in the hour of death cried out in prayer,
And, by that one expression of his faith,
Was blest that day with Christ in Paradise.
Why then defer, O Soul, so long to lay
Thyself all open to that healing hand?
Or why, O tongue, be silent, while yet time
Remains for pardon, and the Almighty's ear
Is ever open to thy faintest cry?
The day approaches when the Judge of all
Shall come, his rightful reckoning to demand.
Prevent with tears his wrath. Why yet remain
In crime's pollution, full of stains, O flesh?
Why not wash out, with floods of tears, thy sins,
And beg the healing balm, while yet the grace
Of tears is granted? To repent is joy,
To weep is health. For God, the Eternal Judge,
Is merciful to those who judge themselves,
Nor visits twice for sins by penance purged.
Despise not then the accepted day of grace;
For torments dire await the impenitent,
When from his throne on high the awful Judge
Shall come, strict reckoning to demand from all.
Wonders and signs his coming shall announce;
The earth shall tremble, hills and mountains fall;
Sea and waves roaring, minds perplex'd with fear,
The sky obscured, the stars shall fall from heaven,
The sun be darken'd in the burning east,
The pallid moon shall not afford her light,
But death-announcing signs appear in heaven.
The angelic powers, in glorious array
Assembled, shall surround the heavenly King,
Sitting exalted on his holy seat.
In gather'd crowds before Him we shall stand,
Each to receive according to his deeds.
Before that great tribunal, think what dread
Shall fill all hearts with feelings of dismay;
When countless angels, at the King's command,
Shall bring before Him all who ever lived,
All who live now, and all who shall live after.
All secrets of all hearts shall be made known;
What heart, or tongue, or hand in darkness wrought,
What now you, blushing, dread shall be reveal'd,
Shall then be open laid before all worlds,
Avenging flames shall fill the vault of heaven,
Hasting to take fierce vengeance upon crime,
And sparing, in their fury, none but those
Who thither come from all pollution cleansed.
Nations and tribes shall smite their guilty breasts;
Peasant and prince shall tremble, side by side,
And poor and rich, in equal rank, shall dread
Flames and the undying worm, the sinner's doom.
None in the presence of that Judge can plead
His own deserts; but every heart shall fail,

While utter dread o'erwhelms the sinner's soul.
What wilt thou do, O flesh, in that dread hour,
Which once you joy'd to use in sinful lusts,
When sin is made the means of punishment?
Dost thou not fear the fiery condemnation
Assign'd of old to Satan's wicked host?
Whose pains no heart of man can e'er conceive,
Far less his tongue find language to express :
The depth of hell fill'd with eternal flames,
And chilling cold mix'd with the burning heat,
Whose dreadful alternations never end.
There in the murky night of pitchy blackness,
No sound is heard around but wailings dire,
The face of tortured wretches only seen,
And nought is felt but icy cold or flames,
While vapours of corruption taint the air.
The groaning mouth is choked with flaming fire;
The worm for ever gnaws the tortured flesh,
And bitter pangs of care torment the heart ;
Because the flesh, indulged for a brief space,
Earn'd an eternity of penal chains,
Where not one spark of light is ever seen,
Nor peace, nor pity, nor a hope of rest
Dawns on the wretched, every solace fled ;
No help, no thought of joy can ever come ;
But grief and groaning, tumult, fear and dread,
Loathing and bitterness, and wrath, and pain,
Await the souls shut in the burning pit.
Ended are all the noxious joys of life ;
Wine, feasting, laughter, saucy jokes and mirth,
Dull sleep, soft indolence, and heavy sloth ;
All the unlawful pleasures of the flesh,
Enjoy'd in dissipation's giddy whirl,
Shall drown the wretches in eternal flames.
O blest, O ever blest, who shall escape
That dire destruction, and with saints rejoice
Through endless ages ! He with Christ shall reign
In heavenly kingdoms, where no night shall dim
The sun's bright lustre; there no grief or sighs
Shall ever come, no age and no decay,
Nor hunger, thirst, fatigue, nor any toil.
Banish'd for ever sickness, fevers, plagues,
And chills and heats, griefs and tormenting cares,
Thunder and lightning, wintry storms and snow,
Distress and want, misfortune, pain and death ;
There reign for ever righteousness and peace,
Abounding goodness, never-ending joys,
Gladness and virtue, light and life eternal,
Glory and honour, rest and concord sweet.
For God Himself, for ever present, gives
To all his blessings, cherishes and fills,
And honours all, preserves and glorifies,
Adorns with love and favour all his saints,
Seats them exalted on celestial thrones,
Rewards their love with endless gifts of grace,
Them with angelic troops in order ranks,
With patriarchs and prophets, and the souls
Of apostolic rulers, heart-rejoicing,
A noble army over sin triumphant ;
United also with the white-robed band
Of virgin souls which evermore surround
The blessed Virgin, Mother of our God,
And in their Father's kingdom shine resplendent;
Where holy sons, and fathers of the Church,
In peace eternal, form the heavenly court.
What then can be esteemed too hard toil
For man to suffer here, that he may win

Such grace hereafter, as with them to praise
For ever and for ever, Christ the Lord.
  May Christ in peace and safety keep thy soul,
Brother beloved, and grant thee endless bliss.
At thy request, I wrote this song of grief;
Do thou fulfil thy promise, and commend
Thy poet in effectual prayer to Christ.
Live bless'd by God; and when thou bid'st farewell
To holy brethren, then, O Acca, father,
Remember me, disconsolate and sad,
In kindly prayer before the throne of Christ."

Having culled these flowers from the garden of this holy doctor
of the Angles, let us take the commencement of this work from
his history; beginning from his last sentence, and so recording the
years of our Lord, and carefully arranging the periods of the kings;
describing also, as briefly as possible, the life and miracles of other
believers: for so, in the end of his history, says the blessed and
truthful Beda, as is written in the commencement of this book.[1]

    *   *   *   *   *   *   *   *   *

We have accurately extracted what we have said from the
account of Beda, the holy priest, and the writer of the history of
this nation.   To conclude then, he, at the age of seven, was sent
by his relations to be educated by the very reverend abbot Benedict, and then by Ceolfrid; whose lives afterwards, when he had
come to years, he so ably narrated.   Passing the whole of his life
in residence at the same monastery (namely, Jarrow), he gave all
his attention to the study of Scripture; and along with the observance of the regular discipline, and the daily services of chanting
in the church, he, thrice happy, always took pleasure in learning, or
teaching, or writing.   If any one wishes to know his performances
more fully and perfectly, let him read the twenty-fifth chapter[2] of
the History of the Angles, from which he may abundantly perceive
the depth and sagacity of his learning.   By the help of Christ's
goodness, we shall pursue our work with care and skill, making
this our petition :—

"Come, Holy Spirit, to whose will
  The utterance of each word belongs;
Give to my tongue its gift, since still
  From Thee proceeds the gift of tongues."

A.D. 732. Archbishop Berthwald died,[3] as we before said.   In
the same year, Tatwine was consecrated ninth archbishop of the
church of Canterbury, in the fifteenth year of the reign of Ethilbald, king of the Mercians.   In this year also, king Ceoluulf, being
taken prisoner, received the tonsure, and was sent back into his
kingdom.   He was imbued with an extraordinary love of the Scriptures, as truthful Beda testifies in the beginning of his preface.   In
the same year, bishop Acca was driven from his see; and Cyne-
berht, bishop of the church of Lindisfarne, died.   In this year also,

---

[1] Simeon has here introduced a quotation from Beda, which it is unnecessary for
us here to repeat, as it may be found in that author's Ecclesiastical History,
§§ 449, 450, and part of 451.
[2] Of the Fifth Book.
[3] In 731; see Beda, Hist. Eccl. § 449.

Alric and Esc, with many others, were slain on Thursday the tenth
of the kalends of September [23d August].

A.D. 733. Archbishop Tatwine, having received the pall from
the apostolic authority, consecrated Alwig and Sigfrid bishops. On
the nineteenth of the kalends of September [14th August], about
the third hour of the day, there occurred an eclipse of the sun; so
that nearly the whole of its disc appeared covered as with a very
black and frightful shield.

A.D. 734. About cockcrow, on the second[1] of the kalends of
February [31st Jan.], the moon was stained of a blood-red colour
for about an hour; a blackness succeeding that, it resumed its own
light.[2]   In the same year, Tatwine, ninth archbishop of the city
of Canterbury, died in Kent, on the third of the kalends of August
[30th July].   The first bishop of that city was Augustin, the renowned instructor of the whole kingdom, and illustrious founder of
Christianity, or of the Christian faith and religion.   He, raised to
the joys of the kingdom on high, left the sceptre of his important
rule to Laurentius. He, deservedly called to be a citizen of heaven,
entrusted the charge of the catholic church to bishop Mellitus.
Mellitus next, after his laborious contests, like a veteran soldier,
received the heavenly prize. After him, fourth in order, succeeded
Justus; who, trusting in the Lord God, ascended victorious, as be-
seemed his name, to the height of virtue. Honorius (like one replete
with honour) followed him; who, faithfully exercising the trust committed to his charge, reached the height of heaven according to his
deserts.   Deusdedit, sixth in succession, ascended the episcopal
throne; and following the footsteps of the fathers, obtained an
inheritance in the court of heaven. After him, rose up the very
learned Theodore; who rendered the seventh place illustrious.
Berthwald followed in the eighth place; to whom, as we before said,
succeeded bishop Tatwine.   In the same year, on the sixth of the
ides of September [8th Sept.], Friothubert was consecrated bishop
of the church of Hexham.

A.D. 735. Nothelm was consecrated archbishop; and Egberht,
the first bishop of York after Paulinus, having received the pall
from the apostolic see, was confirmed to the archiepiscopate
of the nation of the Northumbrians. Beda, doctor, died at
Jarrow.

A.D. 736. Nothelm, having received his pall from the Roman
pontiff, consecrated three bishops; to wit, Cuthbert,[3] Heordwald,
and Ethelfrid. .

A.D. 737. Bishop Aldwine,[4] also called Wor, died; and in his
place Hwicca and Tocca[5] were consecrated bishops of the Mercians

---

[1] More correctly, on the ninth of the kalends of February.
[2] The Chronicle of Melrose, which has much in common with Simeon, states
that at this point Beda completed his history; and that what follows is a compilation from various sources.
[3] Cuthbert was bishop of Hereford; it is probable that Herewald was bishop of
Shirburn, and Ethelfrith was of Elmham; see the Appendix to Florence, pp. 375,
377, 378, under the respective sees.
[4] Bishop of Lichfield, Id. p. 380.
[5] The great see of Mercia was now subdivided, Hwicca (or as he is called

and Middle Angles. In the same year, Celuulf resigned the kingdom of the Northumbrians, and became a monk in the island of
Lindisfarne; and Eadberht, his uncle's son, succeeded in his
stead.

A.D. 738. Swebriht, king of the East Saxons, died.

A.D. 739.[1] Ethelheard, king of the West Saxons, died; and in
his place, Cuthred, his brother, was made king. In this year also,
archbishop Nothelm, after an episcopate of four years, departed in
peace; and Aldulf, bishop of the church of Rochester, breathed
his last.

A.D. 740. Ethelwald, bishop of the church of Lindisfarne,
departed to the Lord, and Kynewlf succeeded him in the see.

In the same year, bishop Acca, of revered memory, was raised
to the land of the living.[2] This blessed man was most vigorous
in action, and had in honour before God and man. He was deeply
skilled also in the rules of ecclesiastical discipline; and, to the end
of his life, aimed at the highest rewards of pious devotion: for-
asmuch as from his childhood he was brought up and educated
among the clergy of the most holy and beloved of God, Bosa,
bishop of York. Going from thence, with a view to further pro-
gress, to bishop Wilfred, he spent his whole time in attendance on
him until his death. With him journeying to Rome, he there
learnt many useful institutes of holy church, which he could not
acquire in his own country, and delivered them to those under him.
This holy man was taken from this world on the thirteenth of
the kalends of November [20th Octob.]; his spirit was carried
by angels to the reward of supreme happiness; his body was buried
on the outside of the wall, at the east end of the church of Hexham,
over which he had ruled in episcopal dignity for twenty-four years.
Two stone crosses, adorned with exquisite carving, were placed, the
one at his head, the other at his feet. On one, that at his head,
was an inscription stating that he was there buried. From this
place, three hundred years after his burial, he was translated, in
consequence of a divine revelation made to a certain priest, and
was placed within a shrine in the church, with becoming honour:
there he is to this day held in great veneration. As a testimony
to all of the merit of his sanctity, the chasuble, tunic and sudarium,
which were placed in the tomb with his sacred body, preserve to
this day, not only their form, but their original strength. There
was found upon his breast a wooden tablet, in the form of an altar,
made of two pieces of wood joined with silver nails; on which is
this inscription, "Alme Trinitati. agie. sophie. Sanctæ Mariæ."
It is not known whether relics were placed in it, or why it was

in the Appendix to Florence, p. 389, Huita) remaining at Lichfield; the other,
occupied by Tocca, or Totta, after some migrations, ultimately was established
at Lincoln.

[1] See the Chronicle of Melrose, A.D. 740.

[2] The Chronicle of Melrose here adds, that he was succeeded by Frithebert; so
also the Appendix to Florence. The passage which follows, betrays the Hexham
origin of this part of the work of Simeon. It should be compared with the treatise
entitled, "De Sanctis Ecclesiæ Hagustaldensis, et eorum Miraculis," printed by
Mabillon (Act. Bened. III. i. 204, ed. Venet.), of which a translation will be given in
its due place in this series.

buried with him; but it cannot be supposed to have been enclosed
with his sacred body, in such respect and veneration, without some
reasonable devotional object.   The brethren of the church of
Hexham are wont frequently to show the aforesaid vestments to
the people, by whom they are kissed with every mark of reverence.
Very many miracles are also commonly reported of St. Acca; to give
an account of all of which would occupy too much of our time.
Yet it will be well briefly to record some of these; how, for
instance, on many occasions, he wonderfully and fearfully restrained
his adversaries, when attempting to invade the peace of the church
in which he rests, or striving indeed entirely to overthrow the
church itself; and how he very frequently opposed those who
wished to carry off by stealth relics from his body.

There was in the aforesaid church of Hexham, a certain brother
named Aldred, now resting in Christ, (a man most truthful, and
remarkable for uprightness of character; he was well learned,
moreover, in holy Scripture,) who was wont to relate to his
brethren of the same church this miracle of St. Acca wrought upon
himself.   While he was yet a youth, and brought up in the house
of his brother, a certain priest, who presided over the oft-named
church of Hexham (before that, by the gifts of the second Thomas,
archbishop of York, it was given up to the canons regular, who
to this day serve God there); it was the wish of his said brother to
separate the honoured bones of St. Acca, as yet mingled with the
dust of his body, and to place them by themselves in a casket
which he had prepared for that purpose.   Bringing out, therefore,
the revered relics, he deposited them on the altar of St. Michael,
situated in the south aisle of the church; and there he collected
the bones from the dust, and enclosed them, wrapped in a clean
napkin, in the casket; and whilst he carried it to its proper place
in the choir, he left the aisle, with the relics which remained, under
the charge of his brother before named.   While tarrying there
alone, the thought entered his mind, that any, even a very noble
church, would consider itself endowed with a precious gift, if it
had but one of the bones of so glorious a confessor.   He determined, therefore, to go to the altar and examine, if perchance he
might find, among the dust, any of the small bones, which taking
into his possession, he might bestow upon some church, to the
honour of God and St. Acca.   But not daring to do this irreverently,
he first, prostrating himself on the ground, devoutly chanted the
seven penitential Psalms, beseeching God not to visit him with
his displeasure for such a theft, inasmuch as he designed doing it
with no sacrilegious intention, but out of pious devotion and
veneration.   Rising after this supplication, he attempted to effect
his object.   When he approached the door of the inner aisle, in
which were the sacred relics, lo! he suddenly encountered a heat,
as of fire issuing from the mouth of a burning furnace, which
compelled him to retreat in dismay.   Supposing that this had
occurred because he desired to obtain so great a thing with less
than due devotion, again throwing himself on the ground, he
poured forth to the Lord prayers much fuller and more earnest

than before, that he might be enabled worthily to obtain what he
so devoutly desired.   Rising, therefore, after a short interval, he
approached with fear and great reverence the door of the aisle ;
but was struck back by a much fiercer heat than before, issuing
from it.   Understanding from this, that it was not the will of God
that he should carry off by stealth any of the relics of St. Acca, he
did not venture to attempt it a third time.

But we must not pass by in silence another miracle concerning
the same confessor, beloved of God, which many living to this day
can testify to have been wrought by his relics.   There came to the
aforesaid church of Hexham a certain canon regular and priest,
named Edric, who was sent there the first of the canons, by the
venerable archbishop Thomas ; he found when he came there, a
heap of earth laid up beside the great altar, which was within the
chancel of the church; and this he began to dig, with the intention
of removing it.   When he had dug away a part of it, he found
a wooden casket of no great size; on opening which, he discovered
two leaden seals with letters engraved on them signifying what was
within.   On one of them it was written that the relics of St. Acca
were enclosed.   Therefore, speedily breaking that, he found a dust
like ashes, and some bones mixed with the dust, which he took
out and replaced in a more handsome casket.   There was then in
that town a certain poor miserable nun, whom the aforesaid brother
loved for her simplicity and the innocence of her life.   She had
been for a long time blind, so that she had to be led by another to
church, or wherever she required to go.   One day, the thought
suddenly suggested itself to the aforesaid brother, that he would
wash in holy water one of those bones which he had lately found,
and give the woman some of that lotion, that she might wash her
eyes in it, if perchance it might please God (the merits of his
holy confessor Acca pleading for her) to restore sight to her eyes
by this sacred washing.   He acted upon this idea, suggested, as
was afterwards evident, by divine inspiration.   Washing one of the
bones in holy water, he gave some to the woman, directing her to
bathe her eyes in it.   She did so, and in about the space of two
hours, through the merits and intercessions of St. Acca, she
recovered her sight.

There was likewise in the same town a certain poor man, whose
throat had swelled, in consequence of an inward disease, to such a
degree, that he could neither speak nor eat.   When the same
brother had poured a little of the same water into his mouth, the
skin on the lower part of the swelling, after the space of an hour,
suddenly burst, and so he was cured by the discharge of the
tumour.

Nor would it be right to pass over in silence the way in which
Malcolm, king of the Scots, was restrained from the invasion and
violation of the peace of the church of Hexham by St. Acca, and
the other saints who repose in it,—their merits acting as safeguards
to it.   For although it is very well known by common report, yet,
lest in the lapse of time it should altogether pass from the memory
of men, it should be committed to writing for the information of

posterity. Malcolm,[1] then, king of the Scots, a man truly of most
ferocious and brutal disposition, was wont by frequent incursions
to make sad havoc in the province of Northumbria; and to convey
from thence very many men and women captive to Scotland.
When, upon a certain occasion, he had entered the boundaries of
that province with a more numerous army than usual, intending to
plunder it, the inhabitants, hearing of his approach, almost all fled,
with what property they could carry, to the church of Hexham,
that they might be under the protection of the saints who there
reposed. When Malcolm discovered this, he determined to march
thither, and despoil all who had taken refuge there, and entirely to
destroy the church itself. The priest of the same church, hearing
of this, went out to meet him, and admonished him not to commit
such a crime against the saints of God, the patrons of that church;
but he, despising his warning, thrust him from him with insult.
The priest, hastily returning to the church, exhorted all who had
taken refuge there together, earnestly to beseech the glorious saints
of God, under whose protection they had placed themselves, that
they would deign, with their wonted kindness, to defend them from
so fierce a host of Scots, more savage than wild beasts. And so they
did. On the following night, when the same priest had fallen asleep
from sadness, there appeared to him a man of venerable countenance
and demeanour, who, as if not knowing the cause, asked him why
he was so sad. When he replied that he was in dread of the
cruelty of the approaching enemy, " Fear not," said he, " for before
dawn I will cast my net into the river, by which the passage of the
Scots shall be altogether prevented." Saying this, he disappeared.
When morning came, the river, which is called the Tyne, without
any inundation of rain or violent storm, was found to have swollen
to such an extent, that, without the help of boats, it could not be
crossed. Moreover, on the same night and on the following day,
so great a mist suddenly came on, that the greater part of the army
of king Malcolm, scattered in the darkness, fell away from each
other; so that numbers fled with great haste to the north, many to
the east, and some also to the south,—plainly overthrown by divine
miracle, through the intercession of the saints of the church of
Hexham. But king Malcolm, coming with the small portion of
his army which had remained with him, saw that all possibility
of passage was denied him. He encamped, therefore, on the bank
of the river, intending to wait until the water had subsided so as
to enable him to cross. But after waiting three days, and seeing
the water increase daily more and more without any supply of rain,
startled at so evident a miracle, he retreated with great haste; and
thus all who had fled from his cruelty to the aforesaid church of
Hexham were delivered by the merits of the saints reposing in it.

But now let us resume the lost thread of our history. In that
year[2] in which bishop St. Acca departed to heaven, Arwine the son

---

[1] As his reign extended from the year 1054 to 1093, the incident mentioned
in the text must have occurred between those dates; probably in one of the
invasions which are mentioned by the Saxon Chronicle as having occurred in
A.D. 1079 or 1091.   [2] These incidents are to be referred to A.D. 741.

of Eadulf was slain, on Saturday, the tenth of the kalends of
January [23d December]. The history or chronicle of this country
records, that in the same year Cuthberht, the eleventh archbishop,
received the primacy of the church of Canterbury: but after
Aldulf, Dun assumed the bishopric of the church of Rochester.

A.D. 741. The monastery of the city of York was burnt, on
Sunday, the eleventh of the kalends of May [23d April].

A.D. 744. A battle was fought between the Picts and the
Britons.

A.D. 745. There appeared ·in the air flashes of fire, such as
mortals of that period had never seen before; and they were seen
almost all night, to wit, on the first of January. In the same year,
also, as some say, lord Wilfrid, the second of that name, bishop of
the city of York, departed to the Lord, on the third of the.kalends
of May [29th April]. We indeed say, that before Beda had.com-
pleted his history, that first Wilfrid was removed from this world
to the excellency of the eternal vision. In these same days, the
bishop of the city of London, Ingwald by name, was translated
from the Egypt of this world. At the same period, the bishop of
the Wiccians died.[1] In the same year died also abbot Herebald.[2]
The holy anchorite, Guthlac, flourished at this time.

A.D. 749. Elfwald, king of the East Angles, died; and Hun-
beanna; and Alberht divided the kingdom between them.

A.D. 750. King Eadberht led ·bishop Kyniwlf[3] captive to the
city of Bebba [Bamborough], and made him abide in the church
of St. Peter in Lindisfarne. Also Offa, the son of Aldfrid, an
innocent man, took refuge by compulsion at the relics of St. Cuthbert the bishop; almost dead with hunger, he was dragged unarmed
from the church. In the same year, bishop Alwih[4] was translated
to the enjoyment of another life, and Aldulf, his deacon, was
ordained bishop. Cuthred, king of the West Saxons, rose against
Ethilbald, king of the Mercians.

A.D. 752. There occurred an eclipse of the moon on the day
before the kalends of August [31st July]. Since mention has been
made of this event, it will be well to state, for the benefit of the
uninformed, what an eclipse is; it is a failing or deficiency of the
moon. An eclipse of the moon occurs as often as the moon falls
under the shadow of the earth; for it is said to have no light of
its own, but is supposed to be illuminated by the sun. An eclipse
of the moon will not occur except when the moon is full, that is
to say, on the fifteenth day. An eclipse of the sun happens only
at the commencement of a moon. "It is certain," says Pliny,[5]
" that an eclipse of the sun takes place only on the last, that is the
thirtieth, or the first day of the moon, which is called their conjunction;" but in every year, eclipses of either luminary take place,
under the shadow of the earth, on certain determined days and
hours. But yet, when they occur in the heaven, they are. not

[1] Wilfrid, bishop of Worcester. See Appendix to Florence, p. 379; Godwin, de
Præsul. p. 449.   [2] This passage is an interlineation in the MS.
[3] Bishop of Lindisfarne.
[4] Bishop of the Liudisfari. See the Appendix to Florence, p. 382.
[5] See ii. 13.

always visible, sometimes on account of clouds, more frequently
the circularity of the earth itself interposing.   An eclipse of the
sun occurs, whenever the moon on the thirtieth day comes on the
same line with the sun, and obscures it by interposing its own
body : for the sun appears to us eclipsed, when the moon's orb is
before it.[1]

A.D. 754. Boniface, also called Winfrid, archbishop of the Franks,
received the crown of martyrdom, with fifty-three others.

A.D. 755. Cuthred, king of the West Saxons, died ; of whose
kingdom Sigberht received the sceptre.

A.D. 756. King Eadberht, in the eighteenth year of his reign, and
Unust, king of the Picts, led an army to the city Alcwith ;[2] and
they received the Britons there into alliance on the first day of
August.   But on the tenth day of the same month, nearly the
whole army perished, which he led from Ouoma[3] to Newanbirig ;
that is, to the New Town.   In the same year, Balther the hermit[4] followed the path of the holy fathers in departing to Him
who renewed him after the image of his own Son.   On the eighth
of the kalends of December [24th Novem.], the moon[5] fifteen
days old, that is, at the full moon, was suffused with a blood-red
colour; and then the darkness gradually diminishing, it returned to
its former lustre.   For, very remarkably, a bright star following the
moon itself, and passing across it, excelled it in brilliancy, as much
as it was inferior before the moon's obscuration.

A.D. 757. Ethilbald, king of the Mercians, was treacherously
slain by his guardians.   In the same year, the Mercians were
involved in a civil war.   Bearnred being put to flight, king Offa
was conqueror.

A.D. 758. Eadberht, king of the Northumbrians,[6] of his own
accord, gave up the kingdom bestowed upon him by God, to his
son named Osulf ; who during one single year held, parted from,
and lost, the kingdom : for he was wickedly put to death by his
family, on the ninth of the kalends of August [24th July], near
Mechil Wongtune.[7]

A.D. 759. Ethelwald, who was also called Moll, began to reign
on the nones of August [5th Aug.].   At the commencement of
whose third year [A.D. 761], a severe battle was fought on the
eighth of the ides of August [6th Aug.], beside Eldunum,[8]
near Melrose.   In which, after three days, Oswin was slain, on

---

[1] In the margin of the MS. here occurs this note : " Eata died in Craic, at
York." See under the year 767.

[2] The Alcluit of Beda, Hist. Eccl. § 8 ; now Dumbarton, on the Clyde.

[3] The printed edition of Hoveden here reads " Deouama;" but the MSS. have
(apparently more correctly) " de Ouama." The Chronicle of Melrose does not
contain the sentence.

[4] Namely, of Tiningham, in Berwickshire.

[5] This eclipse occurred on the ninth of the kalends of December, or 23d
November, 755.

[6] This word, added between the lines, does not occur in Hoveden's text, but
is to be found in the Chronicle of Melrose, which compare with Simeon.

[7] Read " Methel-wong-tune ;" the town on (or near) the Meadow of Conference.
Its situation is unknown.

[8] Now Eldon : the words " secus Melros " (near Melrose), occur in the MS.
between the lines, and are unknown to Hoveden and the Chronicle of Melrose.

Sunday [9th Aug.]. King Ethelwald, or Moll, obtained the victory in the battle. In this year also, Unust, king of the Picts, died.

A.D. 762. The aforesaid king Ethelwald took Etheldryth as his queen, at Catterick,[1] on the kalends of November [1st Nov.].

A.D. 764. Deep snow hardened into ice, unlike anything that had ever been known to all previous ages, covered the earth from the beginning of winter till nearly the middle of spring ; by the severity of which the trees and shrubs for the most part perished, and many marine animals were found dead. Also, in the same year, died Ceolwlf, formerly king,[2] at this time a servant of our Lord Jesus Christ, and a monk. To this king the truthful historian, Beda, addressed an epistle, beginning thus : " To the most illustrious king Ceolwlf, Beda, the servant of Christ and priest. At your desire, O king, I most willingly send the History of the nation of the Angles which I lately published ; as formerly to be read, so now to be copied and perused more fully at your leisure." In the same year many cities, monasteries, and vills, in various parts, and moreover kingdoms, were suddenly laid waste by fire; for example, Stretburg,[3] the city of Winchester, Homwic, the city of London, the city of York, Doncaster, and many other places suffered under that calamity ; and the Scripture was fulfilled, "There shall be commotions on the earth." In the same year died Frehelm, priest and abbot ; and the bishop of the nation of the Mercians, Totca[4] by name, died ; and in his place Eadberht was consecrated bishop. At this time also, Frithwald, bishop of Candida Casa [Whitherne], departed this life, and Phectwine was appointed bishop in his stead.

A.D. 765. Flashes of fire were seen in the air, such as formerly appeared on the night of the first of January,[5] as we mentioned above. In the same year, on the third of the kalends of November [30th Octob.], Ethelwald lost the kingdom of the Northumbrians at Winchan-heale ;[6] to whom succeeded in the kingdom Alcrid, a descendant, as some say, of king Ida.[7] In this year died Hemeli, bishop of the Mercians, in whose room Cuthfrid was ordained bishop at Lichfield. At the same time, Bregwine, archbishop of the city of Canterbury, was removed from this life, to whose place of rule Lamberht[8] succeeded. Aldulf also, bishop in Lindsey, in the same year, left this life for another ; after whom Ceolwlf was elected and consecrated.

A.D. 766. Ecgberht, archbishop of the city of York, rested in the peace of Christ on the thirteenth of the kalends of December

---

[1] The words "in Caterecta" occur in the MS. between the lines ; they are found in Hoveden, but not in the Chronicle of Melrose.

[2] Namely, of Northumbria. See A.D. 737.

[3] The situation is unknown. Instead of "Stretburg, Wenta," as in the printed copies of Hoveden, the MS. makes one word, "Stretbugrwenta." The Chronicle of Melrose does not contain the sentence.

[4] Tocta, or Totta. See the Appendix to Florence, p. 381.

[5] See A.D. 745.   [6] Conjectured to be Finchale, near Durham.

[7] Descended from Ida through a concubine. See Saxon Chronicle, A.D. 765, and the Epistles of Boniface.

[8] Ianberht; see Appendix to Florence, p. 373.

[19th November], in the thirty-fourth year of his episcopate ; and Frithuberht, bishop of the church of Hexham, departed in the same year from this mortal life to an eternity of true light, on the tenth of the kalends of January [23d December], in the thirty-second year of his episcopate.

A.D. 767. Alberht was consecrated bishop of the city of York, and Alchmund of the church of Hexham, on the eighth of the kalends of May[1] [24th April]. At the same time, Aluberht was consecrated bishop for the Eald Saxons,[2] and Ceolwlf was consecrated bishop in Lindissi. Also, in the same year, Etha the hermit died happily in Cric, which is a place ten miles distant from the city of York.

A.D. 768. Eadberht [formerly king, but afterwards cleric],[3] in the tenth year of the loss of his kingdom, in happiness resigned his soul to heaven, in the ministry and service of Almighty God, at York,[4] on the thirteenth of the kalends of September [20th August]. In the same year Pipin, king of the Franks, died ; and Hadwine[5] was consecrated bishop at Machni. And king Alcred at the same time took Osgearn[6] as his queen.

A.D. 769. Ceteracte[7] was burnt by the tyrant Earnred ; and by the judgment of God, he himself miserably perished by fire in the same year.

A.D. 771. Abbot Sibald died ; and Egric and Lector[8] passed from the course of this transitory life to the fellowship of the elect, where he takes up an endless song of triumph. At this time Offa, king of the Mercians, subdued by arms the people of the Hestingi. In the same year also, Karlmon, the most illustrious king of the Franks, died, cut off by sudden illness. Further, his brother Karl, who previously held half his father's dominion, now became possessed of the monarchy of the whole kingdom, and the rule of the Frankish tribes in unconquered strength.

A.D. 772. Duke Pictel, and abbot Swithulf, died in the Lord. Also, Carl, king of the Franks, gathering a powerful army, and assembling the warriors of his empire, made an attack upon the nation of the Saxons, and, having lost many of his princes and nobles, retired to his own territory.

A.D. 773. Hadwin, bishop of the church of Meath,[9] departed, and Leuthfriht was appointed bishop in his stead. In this year also Wlfhaeth, abbot of Beverley, longing to see the day of the Lord, whose follower he was, it was granted him. At the same time Alberht, bishop of the church of York, received the ministry of the pall sent to him by pope Adrian.

---

[1] More probably in A.D. 768, in which year this date fell upon Easter Sunday.

[2] " . . . . ad Ealdsexos," MS. Hoveden reads, "ad Eastsexos;" no assistance is obtained from the Chronicle of Melrose. The individual here meant was probably Aluberht, bishop of the South Saxons. See Appendix to Florence, p. 618.

[3] The passage here printed within brackets is introduced between the lines in the MS., and is not recognised by Hoveden. See the Chronicle of Melrose.

[4] The words, "at York" are also between the lines in the MS., and do not occur in Hoveden. Concerning this king, see A.D. 758.   [5] See A.D. 773.

[6] Called Osgeiva in the Chronicle of Melrose.   [7] Catterick, in Yorkshire.

[8] See Chronicle of Melrose; probably an error for " Egric lector."

[9] " Migensis ecclesiæ."

A.D. 774. Duke Eadwlf was withdrawn from the wreck of this
life; and, at the same period, king Alcred, by the design and consent
of all his connexions, being deprived of the society of the royal
family and princes, changed the dignity of empire for exile. He
went with a few companions of his flight, first to the city of Bebba
[Bamborough], afterwards to the king of the Picts, Cynoht by
name. The city of Bebba is exceedingly well fortified, but by no
means large, containing about the space of two or three fields,
having one hollowed entrance ascending in a wonderful manner by
steps. It has, on the summit of the hill, a church of very beautiful
architecture, in which is a fair and costly shrine. In this, wrapped
in a pall, lies the uncorrupted right hand of St. Oswald, king, as Beda[1]
the historian of this nation relates. There is on the west and
highest point of this citadel, a well, excavated with extraordinary
labour, sweet to drink, and very pure to the sight. Moreover,
Ethelred, the son of Ethelwald, in the place of this person, received
the kingdom; who, crowned with so great honour, held it scarcely
five years, as the subsequent narrative of the writer tells. At the
same time Karl, the most warlike king of the Franks, after a long
siege, took Ticina [Pavia], the chief city of the Lombards; and with
it captured the king himself, Desiderius, and the empire of the
whole of Italy.

A.D. 775. Cynoth, king of the Picts, was taken from the whirl
of this polluted life; and duke Eadwlf, taken by cunning treachery,
was in a short space of time killed, buried, and forgotten. Also,
abbot Ebbi paid the debt of nature, going at his departure to Him
who died to give eternal life. Lastly, Karl, as we before said, the
most warlike king of the Franks, supported and adorned with the
whole courage, power, and array of his army, being surrounded
with the legions which he had levied, attacked the nation of the
Saxons, whose territory he laid waste in most severe battles, great
and indescribable, raging with fire and sword like one distracted in
mind. He finally added to his own great empire the two cities
Sigeburht and Aresburht, and the province of Bohweri, formerly
subdued by the Franks.

A.D. 777. Pichtwine,[2] bishop of Candida Casa, departed from
this life on the thirteenth of the kalends of October [19th Sept.],
to the enjoyment of everlasting salvation, having presided over that
church fourteen years. Ethelbyrht succeeded him.

In the fourth year of king Ethelred, that is, the year 778, three
dukes, namely, Aldwlf, Cynwlf, and Ecga, at the command of the
same king, were treacherously put to death by the princes Ethelbald and Heardberht, on the third of the kalends of October [29th
Sept.]. What happened in the year 779 the following narrative will
declare.

A.D. 779. Ethelred, expelled from his royal throne, and driven
into exile, was forced to undergo sad changes, and experience
much wretchedness. Elfwald, the son of Oswlf, on the expulsion

[1] See Hist. Eccl. § 166.
[2] The Chronicle of Melrose, here differing from Hoveden and Simeon, ascribes
this to the year 776.

of Ethelred, obtained the kingdom of the Northumbrians, and held
it ten years.   He indeed was a pious and upright king, as will
appear in the sequel.

A.D. 780. Dukes Osbald and Athelheard, having gathered an
army, burnt Bearn, a nobleman of king Elfwald, in Seletune,[1] on
the ninth of the kalends of January[2] [24th Dec.].   In the same
year, archbishop Alberht[3] departed from the light of this world to
the light of eternity, Eanbald having been ordained to the same see
while he was yet living.   In the same year also, bishop Cynewlf,[4]
relinquishing secular cares, upon the choice of the whole community, committed the government of the church to Higbald.   In the
same year also, bishop Eanbald received the pall sent to him from
the apostolic see; and, having obtained it, he was solemnly confirmed in his episcopate.

A.D. 781. Hibald was consecrated bishop.[5]   Alchmund, bishop of
the church of Hexham, a man of exemplary piety and great virtues,
after having nobly ruled the aforesaid church thirteen years, in the
third year of the reign of Elfwald, the very glorious king of the
Northumbrians, ended this life on the seventh of the ides of
September [7th Sept.], and was, for the reward of his good deeds,
made partaker of eternal life.   He was buried near his predecessor
of revered memory, the bishop St. Acca.   From which spot he was
translated, more than two hundred and fifty years after, by divine
revelation in this manner :—

There was at that time in the territory of the church of Hexham
a certain Dregmo,[6] one who greatly feared God, and diligently
devoted himself, as far as his means allowed, to the exercise of
works of charity, leading a life differing in all respects from the
manners of his countrymen.   For he was a man of remarkable
simplicity and innocence, and of profound devotion and reverence
towards the saints of God; on which account all his neighbours
held him in great honour, and called him a true worshipper of God.
As he was reposing one night in his bed, there appeared to him a
man adorned with a pontifical mitre, and holding in his hand a
pastoral staff.   Striking him with it, he said to him, "Arise, go and
tell Elfred, the son of Westneor, priest of the church of Durham,
that, assembling the population of the territory of Hexham, he
must translate my body from the place where I am interred, and
deposit it in a more honourable position within the church; for
it is right that they should receive veneration from all on earth,
whom the King of kings deigns to clothe with the robe of glory and
immortality in heaven."   When he inquired, "Lord, who art thou?"
he replied, "I am Alchmund, bishop of the church of Hexham,

---

[1] Possibly Silton, in Yorkshire.
[2] In the Saxon Chronicle this outrage is said to have occurred on 25th Dec.
[3] Namely, of York.   [4] Bishop of Lindisfarne.
[5] The entry respecting Hibald (Higbald, bishop of Lindisfarne, see Flor. Wig.
A. D. 779) occurs in the margin of the MS., and is not found in Hoveden, or the
Chronicle of Melrose.
[6] Probably not a proper name, but a Scandinavian designation of a class of
tenants; thus, Ralph, bishop of Durham, addresses a writ to his "thanes and
drenges" of Islandshire and Norhamshire. See Hickes, Thesaur. i. 149, 150, and
Ettmüller, Lexicon Anglo-Saxon. p. 572.

who, by the grace of God, presided over that see the fourth in succession after the blessed Wilfrid.   My body was placed near my
predecessor of revered memory, the sainted bishop Acca.   At its
translation do you also assist with the priest."   Thus speaking, he
disappeared.   When morning came, the man hastened to the
priest before named, and recited to him in order what he had seen ;
and repeated the mandate which he was ordered to convey to him.
The priest greatly rejoicing, called together a very large multitude
of people, made the matter known to them, and fixed a time for
the translation of the venerable relics.   On the appointed day,
therefore, the aforesaid priest, going to the tomb, commanded it to
be cleared from the earth.   Which being done, (the man to whom
the revelation had been made also assisting,) crowds of people
standing on every side, he collected the sacred bones from the
mound, and placed them, wrapped in linen and enclosed in a
shrine, upon a bier ; and since, in consequence of the great solem-
nity of the day, the hour of offering the holy sacrifice to the Lord
was gone by, they placed it that night in the aisle of St. Peter, at
the east side of the church of Hexham ; intending on the following
day to remove it into the church with psalms and hymns, and the
celebration of masses.   But on that night, while the priest before
mentioned kept watch with his clerks around the sacred relics, the
others having fallen into a deep sleep, he went and opened the
shrine, and taking by stealth one of the small bones, (to wit, a part
of one of the fingers,) he laid it by him, desiring to bestow it on
the church of St. Cuthbert at Durham, to the honour of God and
St. Alchmund.

   At the return of day, a very great multitude of people assembled
to witness the removal of the holy corpse.   When it drew near the
third hour, at the command of the priest, taking hold of the bier,
they endeavoured to lift it ; but were unable to remove it in the
least degree.   Those who first made the attempt being dismissed,
as considered unworthy to raise on their shoulders the relics of so
great a father, others made the trial, who, like the former, spent
their labour in vain.   After this others, and others again, applying
themselves, no force was of the least avail to move it.   All who
were present were troubled in mind, and stood gazing on each
other in wonder and amazement at this prodigy.   Then the priest
who had committed the act, not suspecting that he himself was the
cause, exhorted all to beseech God that He would deign to reveal
to them for what fault this had been brought upon them.   And so
it came to pass, while those who passed the night in the church
were praying to God on this account, Saint Alchmund again
appeared to the same man as before, who chanced then to be within
the church, overpowered by slumber, which had suddenly over-
taken him, and, with a somewhat severe countenance, addressed
him thus : " What is this that you have endeavoured to do ?   Do
you suppose that you can carry me, mutilated in my members, into
the church in which I served God and his apostle Saint Andrew,
with my whole body and spirit ?   Arise, therefore, and proclaim
before all the people that the portion which has been rashly :

abstracted from my body must speedily be restored; otherwise you will be utterly unable to remove me from my present position." Having said this, he showed him his hand, wanting the middle joint of one finger. When the day broke, this man, standing in the midst of the people, announced to all what had been revealed to him that night, declaring in vehement language, that whosoever had done this deserved punishment. Then the priest, perceiving that he was discovered, started up in the midst, and made known to all for what cause, and with what intention, he had committed this act; and, restoring to St. Alchmund what he had taken from him with a pious and devotional purpose, he, by fit reparation, there obtained pardon; and the clerics who were present, going up, raised the body without any difficulty, and transferred it to the church, on the fourth of the nones of August [2d Aug.]; where to this day it is reverenced by the faithful with becoming honour, to the praise and glory of our Lord Jesus Christ. The holy Tilberht was called in his place to the episcopate,[1] and was consecrated and raised to the throne of the episcopal see, in the place which is called Uulfeswelle, that is, the Wolf's Well. This took place on the sixth of the nones of October [2d Oct.].[2]

A.D. 783, (which is the fifth year of king Elfwald,)[3] died Werburhg, formerly queen of the Mercians, then abbess, always, as it is meet to believe, to live with Christ. At this time, also, bishop Kimuulf, of whom we have before spoken,[4] left earthly affairs to pass blissfully to the heavenly country, in the fortieth year of his pontificate.

A.D. 786, (which is the eighth year of king Elfwald,) Botuune,[5] the venerable abbot of Ripon, in the sight of his brethren standing by, left the prison-house of this laborious life, to receive the reward of the year of jubilee. At his decease, Alberht was elected, and consecrated abbot in his stead. In the same year, Aldulf was consecrated bishop, by archbishop Eanbald and bishops Tilberht and Hygbald,[6] in the monastery which is called Et Corabrige,[7] and, enriched with many gifts and donations, was honourably sent back to his own church. In these days, Ricthryth, formerly queen, then abbess, obtained the desired rewards of another life, carrying oil in her lamp,[8] in the holy sight of the Lord.

At that time[9] Kinnulf, king of the West Saxons, was barbarously put to death by the perfidious tyrant Kynheard; and that cruel murderer was slain without remorse by duke Osred,[10] in revenge of his lord: and Brihtric took the kingdom of the West Saxons.

At this period[11] legates from the apostolic see were sent to

---

[1] That is, he succeeded Alchmund in the see of Hexham.
[2] This date is apparently inaccurate.
[3] Hoveden here styles him "the just king."
[4] See A.D. 740 and 780.
[5] Read, with Hoveden and Chronicle of Melrose, Bothwine or Botuine.
[6] Namely, Aldulf of Lichfield, Eaubald of York, Tilbert of Lindisfarne, and Hygbald of Hexham.   [7] Corbridge, near Hexham.   [8] See St. Matt. xxv. 4.
[9] The Saxon Chronicle and Florence ascribe this occurrence to the year 784.
[10] Read "Osric." See Ethelward, ii. 18; Saxon Chronicle, A.D. 775; Florence, 784.
[11] In A.D. 785. See Saxon Chronicle. Hoveden follows Simeon in the errors here noted.

Britain by the lord pope Adrian, among whom the venerable bishop Georgius[1] held the primacy; who renewing amongst us the ancient friendship, and the catholic faith which St. Gregory taught by blessed Augustine, were honourably received by the kings and bishops, princes and primates of this country, and returned home in peace, with great gifts, as was proper.

A.D. 787. A synod met at Pincahala,[2] on the fourth of the nones of September [2 Sept.]. At which time Alberht, abbot of Ripon, breathed out his spirit from among the stormy blasts of this life to the best joys of eternal felicity. Soon after his death, Sigred was ordained in his stead.

A.D. 788. King Elfwald, a conspiracy being formed by his patrician, Sicga by name, was miserably slain on the ninth of the kalends of October [23d Sept.], at a place called Scythlescester, near the Wall. The body of this excellent king was brought to Hehstealdesige [Hexham] with a great company of monks, and with the chanting of clergy, and was honourably buried in the church of St. Andrew the apostle, which the most worthy father, archbishop Wilfred, had built to the praise and honour of the aforesaid apostle.[3] The work of that monastery is superior to the other edifices in the nation of the Angles, although they are numerous, and in most places indescribable; but this place excels them all in its length and breadth and beauty. In this monastery the walls are decorated with various colours, and historical events are depicted, according to the directions of the said bishop Wilfred. Moreover, lord Acca, who governed that place after him, adorned it with splendid ornaments. The king being buried, as we said before, his nephew, Osred, the son of Alcred, reigned in his place one year. On the spot where the just king Elfwald was slain, light sent down from heaven is said to have been seen by many. There a church was built by the faithful of that locality, and consecrated to the honour of God, and of saints Cuthbert the bishop, and Oswald the king and martyr.

A.D. 790. Ethelred was freed from banishment,[4] and again, by Christ's favour, seated on the throne of the kingdom. But king Osred, overreached by the treachery of his princes, having been taken prisoner and deprived of his kingdom, assumed the tonsure in the city of York, and afterwards, driven by necessity, went into exile. In his second year (A.D. 791), duke Eardulf was taken prisoner, and conveyed to Ripon, and there ordered by the aforesaid king to be put to death without the gate of the monastery. The brethren carried his body to the church with Gregorian chanting, and placed it out of doors in a tent; after midnignt he was found alive in the church. In the same year, Baduulf was consecrated bishop at Candida Casa [Whitherne] in the place called Hearrahaleh,[5] which may be interpreted, "the place of lords."

---

[1] See Pagi, A.D. 787, § 18.   [2] Supposed to be Finchale, near Durham.
[3] See the description by Heddius in his Life of Wilfrid; this passage does not occur in Hoveden.
[4] See A.D. 779.
[5] "Hearrahalh," Hoved. MS.; the printed copy reads "Hearrahaldh." The Chronicle of Melrose does not contain this clause.

Bishop Ethelberht in the previous year (A.D. 789) relinquishing his own see on the death of the holy bishop Tilberht, he, the first-mentioned bishop, took the episcopate of the church of Hexham under his own rule.

A.D. 791. The sons of king Elfwald, having been carried from the city of York by force, and drawn from the principal church by deceitful promises, were miserably slain by king Ethelred in Wonwaldremere; their names were Oelf and Oelfwine.[1] Also, in that year, Lamberht,[2] archbishop of the church of Canterbury, passed from the darkness of this light to the bliss of the true light. Ethelherd, abbot " Hludensis monasterii,"[3] was chosen and consecrated bishop of the same see.

A.D. 792. Charles, king of the Franks, sent to Britain a synodal book[4] forwarded to him from Constantinople; in which book, it is deeply to be lamented, were found many things improper and contrary to the true faith; chiefly, that it was agreed by the unanimous assertion of almost all the oriental doctors, not fewer, or rather more, than three hundred bishops, and by them confirmed, that men should adore images; a thing altogether abhorred by the Church of God. Against which Albinus wrote an epistle, strongly supported by the authority of holy Scripture, and took it, with the same book, to the king of the Franks, with the countenance of our bishops and princes. Lastly, in this year, Osred, induced by the oaths and pledge of certain nobles, came secretly from his exile in Eufania [Man], and there his soldiers deserting him, he was captured by the aforesaid king Ethelred, and put to death by his order, at the place called Aynburg,[5] on the eighteenth of the kalends of October [14th Sept.]. His body was brought to the mouth of the river Tyne, and buried in the church of the noble monastery there. In the same year, king Ethelred took as his queen Elfled, daughter of Offa, king of the Mercians, at Catterick, on the third of the kalends of October [29th Sept.].

A.D. 793, (which is the fourth year of king Ethelred,) fearful prodigies terrified the wretched nation of the Angles; inasmuch as horrible lightnings, and dragons in the air, and flashes of fire, were often seen glancing and flying to and fro; which signs indicated the great famine, and the terrible and unutterable slaughter of multitudes which ensued. In this year also, duke Sicga, who murdered king Elfwald,[6] died by his own hand; his body was

---

[1] Aelf and Aelfwine, MS. Hoved.   [2] See A.D. 765.

[3] Where this monastery was situated is uncertain; William of Malmesbury tells us, that he was first abbot of the monastery of Malmesbury, then bishop of Winchester, and lastly, archbishop of Canterbury. See Godwin, de Præsul, p. 46.

[4] It is not intended here, to enter upon an inquiry into the authenticity or history of the Caroline books; a question which has been discussed with much warmth. It is enough to direct the reader, who may seek for further information upon this head, and on image worship generally, to the following works: "Augusta Concilii Nicæni II. Censura, hoc est, Caroli Magni de Impio Imaginum Cultu, libri quatuor; edidit cum præfatione et dissertatione critica C. A. Henmannus," 8vo. Hanov. 1731. Dorschens (J. G.) "Collatio ad Concilium Francofurdiense, sub Carolo Magno Imperatore Habitum," 4to. Argent. 1649. Mabillon, Acta SS. Bened. sec. iv. para i. præf. § 13. Forbes, Instr. Hist. Theology, vii. 11. Basnage, Hist. de l'Eglise, p. 556, seq.

[5] The situation is unknown. The printed copy of Hoveden reads " Dingburch;" the MSS. have " Dynburg," or "Chynburg."   [6] See A.D. 788.

carried to the isle of Lindisfarne, on the ninth of the kalends of
May [23d April].[1]   Lindisfarne is a large island in circumference,
that is to say, extending eight miles or more.   On it is a noble
monastery, in which was laid the illustrious prelate Cuthbert, with
other bishops, his most worthy successors ; to whom may fitly be
applied the verse, "The bodies of the saints are buried in peace."[2]
The river which runs into the sea is called the Lindis, and is two
feet broad when it is "Ledon," that is, at low tide, and when it
can be seen ; but when it is "Malina," that is, high tide, then the
Lindis cannot be perceived.   The tide of the ocean follows the
moon, as if, by its attraction, it were drawn up at the flow, and
ebbed when its force was withdrawn.[3] * * *

For as the moon every day rises and sets four points later than
it did the day before, so each tide of the sea, be it day or night,
morning or evening, flows and retires later by the same space of
time.   A point is the fifth part of an hour, for five points make
an hour.   Of this argument of the sea and moon a certain poet,
Bishop Aldhelm, says :

> "The laws which regulate the sea
>   I too my guides have found,
> Revolving with the answering skies
>   The monthly seasons round ;
>
> As from my light-diffusing form
>   The glory doth decay,
> So from its full and swelling tide
>   The waters fall away."

But the island of Farne, in which the most blessed Cuthbert led
his solitary life, is not so large as Lindisfarne, but is so situated in
the sea that it is exposed by day and night to great violence of the
waves.   Having passingly stated these things, let us return to the
order of our narrative.

In the same year, of a truth, the pagans from the Northern
region came with a naval armament to Britain, like stinging hornets,
and overran the country in all directions, like fierce wolves, plundering, tearing, and killing not only sheep and oxen, but priests
and Levites, and choirs of monks and nuns.   They came, as we
before said, to the church of Lindisfarne, and laid all waste with
dreadful havoc, trod with unhallowed feet the holy places, dug up
the altars, and carried off all the treasures of the holy church.
Some of the brethren they killed; some they carried off in chains ;
many they cast out, naked and loaded with insults; some they
drowned in the sea.   It was well said of them as follows :

> "With deadly ills, the penalty of guilt,
> Blind fortune oft the innocent afflicts :
> While with a haughty mien perverse men sit
> Enthroned in power, and tread with impious foot,
> By an unrighteous chance, on hallow'd necks ;
> Bright virtue in thick darkness lies conceal'd,
> And on the just is laid the charge of sin."

---

[1] A marginal note in the MS. copy of Hoveden here states, upon the authority
of Gildas, that Lindisfarne was called Medcant by the Britons.
[2] Ecclus. xliv. 14.
[3] A passage from Beda, De Natura Rerum, cap. xxxix. (Opp. ii. 39, ed. fol. Basil,
1563), is here quoted, but a reference is sufficient.

I shall truly relate what befel them in the following year, after they
departed, rejoicing both in their plunder and their evil deeds.

A.D. 794. The aforesaid pagans, ravaging the harbour of king
Ecgfrid, plundered the monastery at the mouth of the river Don.[1]
But St. Cuthbert did not allow them to depart unpunished; for
their chief was there put to a cruel death by the Angles, and a
short time afterwards a violent storm shattered, destroyed, and
broke up their vessels, and the sea swallowed up very many of
them; some, however, were cast ashore, and speedily slain without
mercy: and these things befel them justly, since they heavily
injured those who had not injured them. At that time Colcu,[2]
priest and lector, departed from this life to the Lord, where he
received for his earthly labours glory and happiness. At this
period Ethelheard, formerly duke, but then cleric, died on the
kalends of August [1st Aug.], in the city of York. The venerable
pope Adrian was, in the same year, exalted to see God, on the
seventh of the kalends of January [26th Dec.], having occupied
the see twenty-six years, ten months, and twelve days. He was
buried in the church of St. Peter, the prince of the apostles; and
over his tomb a marble slab, fixed to the wall, records his good
deeds in golden letters, and written in verse. This marble, king
Charles, when he was invested with the royal diadem, caused to be
placed there, on account of his love, and as a remembrance of the
aforesaid father.

A.D. 795. The same mighty king, Charles, reduced with a strong
hand the nation of the Huns, despoiling them by arms; put their chief
to flight, and overcame or destroyed his army, carrying off from
thence fifteen wagons full of gold and silver and rich silk vestments;
each wagon being drawn by four oxen. All which things the same
king ordered to be divided among Christ's churches and poor, on
account of the victory granted him by the Lord; he, together with
all his warriors, giving God thanks.

A.D. 796, (which is the seventh year of king Ethelred,) Alric,
formerly duke, then cleric, died in the city of York. And a little
after, that is, on the fifth of the kalends of April [28th March],
an eclipse of the moon took place between cockcrow and dawn.
In the same year, king Ethelred was slain at Cobre, on the fourteenth
of the kalends of May [18th April], in the seventh year of his
reign; Osbald the patrician was appointed to the kingdom by some
chiefs of that nation, and twenty-seven days after, forsaken by the
whole company of the royal family and princes, having been put to
flight and expelled from the kingdom, he, with a few followers,
retired to the island of Lindisfarne, and thence went by ship, with
some of his brethren, to the king of the Picts. Eardulf, of whom
we have before spoken,[3] the son of Eardulf,[4] recalled from exile,
was raised to the crown, and was consecrated on the seventh of the

---

[1] We should here read, "at the mouth of the river Wear." This error, which
occurs also in Hoveden and the Chronicle of Melrose, has originated in a mis-
apprehension of one of the texts of the Saxon Chronicle, A.D. 794.
[2] See the Correspondence of Alcuin, Ep. iii., Opp. i. 6, ed. Froben.; Mabill.
Annal. Ord. S. Bened. xxvi. § 10.   [3] See A.D. 790.
[4] In Hoveden and the Chronicle of Melrose he is called Earnulf.

kalends of June [26th May], in York, in the church of St. Peter, at the altar of the blessed apostle Paul, where that nation first received the grace of baptism. Not long after, that is, on the seventh of the kalends of August [26th July], Offa, the most potent king of the Mercians, died, after a reign of thirty-nine years; to him succeeded in the kingdom his son Ecgferth, who, in the same year, was cut off by an untimely death. Moreover, Coenuulf, the father of St. Kenelm, martyr, then with great honour received the crown of the kingdom of the Mercians, and held it, with surpassing ability, by the vigorous energy of his government. Also in this year, Ceoluulf [bishop] of Lindisse, laid down this temporal life, looking for the consolation of a future world. And a little after, that is, on the fourth of the ides of August [10th August], archbishop Eanbald died in the monastery called Etlete,[1] and his body, accompanied by a great multitude, being conveyed to the city of York, was honourably interred in the church of the blessed apostle Peter; and another Eanbald, a priest of the same church, was at once elected to the episcopate; bishops Ethelbert, Hygbald, and Badwlf meeting at his consecration, at a monastery called Sochasburg, on Sunday the eighteenth of the kalends of September.[2]

A.D. 797. This latter Eanbald, having received the pall from the apostolic see, was solemnly confirmed in the episcopate of the nation of the Northumbrians, on the fourth of the ides of September [8th Sept.], on which day is celebrated the Feast of the Nativity of St. Mary, of whom the poet says,

> "Graced with unclouded glory bright, the day shall ever shine,
> When Mary, virgin, saw the light, blest child of David's line."

In the same year died Ethelbert, bishop of Hexham, on the seventeenth of the kalends of November [16th Oct.], at the place called Barton; his body was brought to Hestaldesige [Hexham], and reverently buried by the brethren of that monastery. In his place Headred was elected to the episcopate, and, in the course of a few days, that is, on the third of the kalends of November[3] [30th Oct.], was ordained in the spiritual dignity by archbishop Eanbald and bishop Hygbald,[4] at the place called Wduforda.

A.D. 798. Duke Wada, entering into a conspiracy formed by the murderers of king Etheldred,[5] fought a battle against king Eardwlf, in a place called by the Angles Billingahoth,[6] near Walalege; and many on both sides being slain, duke Wada, with his men, was put to flight, and king Eardwlf royally gained the victory over his enemies. In the same year, London was destroyed by an accidental fire, with a great multitude of people. At this time, Kenwlf,[7] king of the Mercians, entering the province of the

---

[1] Where situated is unknown; "Aet Læte," MS. Hoved. "Edete," ed.
[2] We should read, nineteenth kalends of September [14th Aug.], which fell upon a Sunday in this year.
[3] This date is suspicious.   [4] Hygbald was bishop of Lindisfarne.
[5] Read "Ethelred." See A.D. 796.
[6] Billingahou, Hoved. edit.; Billingahoh, Hoved. MS.: probably Billingham, co. Durham.   [7] Compare the Saxon Chronicle, A.D. 796.

Kentish men with the whole force of his army, mightily devastated it in a lamentable pillage, almost to its utter destruction. Eadbert, king of the men of Kent, was at the same time taken prisoner, whose eyes the king of the Mercians ordered to be put out, and his hands to be cut off without pity, on account of the arrogance and deceit of his people. Then, having obtained the help of the Lord, he added the government of that kingdom to his own kingdom, taking the crown on his head and sceptre in his hand. In the same year also (which is the third of the aforesaid king Cenwlf), at a synod assembled at the place called Pincanhalth [Finchale?] under the presidency of archbishop Eanbald, with very many other princes and ecclesiastics, they consulted on many things affecting the interest of God's holy church, and of the nation of Northumbrians, and of all the provinces, and concerning the observance of the paschal feast, and of decisions, divine and secular, which were made in the days of righteous kings, and good dukes, and holy bishops, and other wise men, monks and clerics, of whose wisdom, and justice, and divine virtues, the state of the kingdom of the Northumbrians was at that time sweetly and unspeakably redolent. They took care, by wise counsel, to make arrangements for the honour of God and the necessities of his servants, and to augment the service of God, that for these things they might receive the good recompense of eternal reward. The lord bishop Eanbald commanded the faith of the five councils to be recited, of which it is thus said in the History of the Angles :[1]

" We receive the five holy and universal councils of the saints and fathers beloved of God, as the text of the present book contains. We truly glorify, and adore, and worship, our Lord Jesus Christ, as they glorified Him, adding or taking away nothing ; and with heart and mouth we anathematize them whom the aforesaid fathers anathematized ; glorifying God the Father Almighty, without beginning, and his only-begotten Son, begotten of the Father before the worlds, and the Holy Spirit, proceeding in an unspeakable manner from the Father and the Son, as those whom we named before, the holy apostles and prophets, preached, and we believe, and therefore have we spoken. We declare that we constantly believe these aforesaid fathers, piously and orthodoxly, according to their divinely inspired doctrine ; and we confess, according to the holy fathers, properly and truly, Father, Son, and Holy Spirit, the Trinity consubstantial in Unity, and the Unity in Trinity ; that is, one God in three real Persons, consubstantial, of equal glory and honour." Having asserted and confirmed these things, they returned home, praising God for all his benefits.

We read elsewhere this account of the unity of that faith by which, as other righteous men trusted, we hope to be saved :

"Since in the Father the Word is, the Father in the Word,
From Father and from Word proceeds One Spirit, God and Lord ·
So without doubt one only God, in blessed Persons Three.
Must, with unhesitating faith, ever confessed be."

---

[1] Beda, Eccl. Hist. § 305.

And further :

> "The Word, the Father's only Son, all things creates, and still
> Rules all things, yet in nothing acts without the Father's will ;
> One will, one motive, and one mind, in Persons both are found,
> Of equal goodness, in one love by the same Spirit bound."

And after this :

> "God's power is of and in Himself; His property is this,
> To be to endless ages still unchanged what now He is.
> True light from true light shines ; and who acknowledges the Son
> Begotten of the Father, knows the unbegotten One."

> "The Godhead of the Three in One ; their very Being One ;
> The Spirit from the Father flows the same as from the Son ;
> No work of theirs can be disjoin'd ; their power must equal be,
> Since but one principle pervades the blessed One in Three."

Having detailed so much concerning the orthodox faith, let us return to the narrative of our history.

A.D. 799. Very many ships were wrecked by a violent storm in the British sea, and shattered or dashed to pieces and sunk, with a great number of men. In the same year died Brorda, prince of the Mercians, also called Hildegils. The abbot called More Atilthegno,[1] was put to a grievous death by his steward. Duke Moll, also, was soon afterwards slain by the urgent command of king Eardwlf. Also, at the same time, Osbald, once duke and patrician, and for a time king, after that abbot, breathed his last ; his body was buried in the church of the city of York. Duke Aldred, the murderer of king Etheldred,[2] was slain by duke Thortmund, in revenge of his lord, the same king. Some other events in the same year must be recorded. The Romans also were divided amongst themselves, and had great dissensions, in which they seized and bound the most holy pope Leo,[3] whose tongue, forcibly drawn between his jaws, and cruelly stretched in his throat, was by them cut off. The eyes of the said pope, also, they utterly put out, which deed was made a cruel spectacle to all beholders. Then, leaving him, without any humanity, half dead, they hastily returned home. But the great Creator of the world, from above beholding all things, and whom only, because He beholds all things, we can call the true Sun, did not so disregard his faithful servant. The Almighty Lord, therefore, after a short space of time, so healed him by his saving remedy, that within a while he could see clearly, and speak ; altogether removing the blindness from his eyes, and granting him a tongue, whole as before ; so that he was perfectly able to preach, and creditably fulfil all his duties.

> "While yet dark clouds of ignorance remain,
> The wondrous works of God shall never cease."

This miracle was quickly spread through the four quarters of the world, that, to the glory and honour of Christ's name, it should by

---

[1] The authorities differ respecting the name of this individual; "More Altilthegno," Hoved. ed.; "More a Thiltegno," "More Athiltegno," Hoved. MS. ; "Mora a Tilthegno," Chron. Mailr. We should probably read, "The abbot called More was put to a grievous death by his steward, Tilthegn."

[2] Read "Ethelred." See A.D. 798.   [3] Namely pope Leo III.

all be everywhere proclaimed and glorified that God is wonderful in
his saints.[1]

A.D. 800. Headred, bishop of the church of Hexham, came to
his last end in the third year of his episcopal government, in whose
room Eanbryth was elected and consecrated bishop, in the place
called Cettingaham.   In the same year, Alchmund, son of king
Alcred, as some say, was seized by the guardians of king Eardwlf,
and by his order put to death with the companions of his flight.
Also, in this year, on the day before the Nativity of our Lord, the
ninth of the kalends of January [24th Dec.], a great wind arising
from the south-west or west, by its indescribable violence destroyed
and threw to the ground cities, many houses, and numerous vills,
in divers places ; innumerable trees, also, were torn up by the roots
and thrown to the earth.   In this year an inundation of the sea
burst beyond its bounds, not fulfilling what the psalm[2] says, "Thou
hast set them their bounds which they shall not pass."   A great
destruction of cattle occurred in divers places. Also, a little before,
in this year, Charles,[3] king of the Franks, of renowned valour,
entered the walls of the city of Rome with a great multitude of his
army, and remained there for some months ; and having worshipped in frequent visits at the holy places, he enriched and
adorned them with royal munificence.   Especially the church of
the blessed apostle Peter, and also of St. Paul, he adorned with
royal gifts, gold and silver and precious stones.   He also gave
magnificent presents to the venerable pope Leo,. and dispersed his
adversaries; some he destroyed or condemned to banishment, some
he killed, who wickedly raised a conspiracy against him.   These,
and many other things which pertained to the honour and correction of the churches of Christ and of Christian people, being
settled, on the day of the Nativity of our Lord Jesus Christ
[25th Dec.], this mighty emperor, with dukes and· magistrates and
soldiers, went to the church of the most holy prince of the apostles,
where he was robed with the royal purple by the lord pope Leo, a
crown of gold was placed on his head, and a sceptre in his hand.
This dignity he deserved on that day to receive from every people,
that he should be called, as he was, emperor of the whole world.
At that time, also, came ambassadors from the Greeks, sent to
him with large gifts from Constantinople, begging him to accept
their kingdom and empire.   In like manner, ambassadors were
sent from Jerusalem by the Christian people dwelling there ; who,
coming to Rome, brought to the king, among other gifts, a silver
standard, and offered to him the keys of the holy places of our
Lord's resurrection, and of others, earnestly beseeching him to be
their helper and defender.   They desired that he would preserve,
rule, and defend the holy monasteries devoted to the Christian
religion, and would rise in warlike valour and royal majesty against
the insurgent nations.   The most gracious monarch assented to the
blessed entreaties of those who flocked to him, and said that he
was ready to overcome their enemies, not only by land, but also

---

[1] This passage about Leo does not occur either in Hoveden or the Chronicle of
Melrose.   [2] Ps. civ. 9.   [3] See Pagi ad an. 800, §§ 8, 9.

by sea, if necessity so required.   He understood that states would
be happy if either persons desirous of wisdom were in power, or if
it came to pass that their rulers applied their minds to wisdom.
Coming[1] to the city of Ravenna, he went thence to Aix-la-Chapelle,
to treat with his nobles about all these matters.

A.D. 801.   Edwine, also called Eda, formerly a duke of the
Northumbrians, then, by the grace of the Saviour of the world,
an abbot strong in the service of God, like a worn-out soldier,
came to the end of his life, in the sight of the brethren, on the
eighteenth of the kalends of February [15th Jan.].   He was
honourably interred in the church, in his monastery called Et
Gegenforda.[2]   At this time, Eardulf, king of the Northumbrians,
led an army against Kenwlf, king of the Mercians, because he had
given an asylum to his enemies.   He also, collecting an army,
obtained very many auxiliaries from other provinces, having made
a long expedition among them.   At length, with the advice of the
bishops and chiefs of the Angles on either side, they made peace,
through the kindness of the king of the Angles.[3]   An agreement of
sure peace was made between them, which both kings confirmed
by an oath on the gospel of Christ, calling God as a witness and
surety, that as long as they retained this life, and bore the crown
of government, a firm peace and true friendship should exist
between them, unshaken and inviolate.   It thus came to be fulfilled in them, as it is said,—

> " When ceaseth the south wind of showers to give warning,
> More kindly the bright stars their lustre display;
> When darkness hath fled from the face of the morning,
> Her rose-colour'd coursers drive onward fair day."

" The bright stars their lustre display;" that is, the chiefs were
enlivened with joy when the kings so kindly made peace between
themselves.   " The south wind" is a warm wind which usually
portends showers.   " The rose-coloured coursers," that is, the
whole kingdom was filled with exultation when times of serenity
returned to the men of that age, through the bounteous favour of
the Lord, who calms the stormy tempests, and who

> "In equal measure weighs the elements;
> Tempers the heat with cold; the solid earth
> In balance with the waters holds; for else
> Would fire unmingled rage, or o'er the earth,
> Sunk by its ponderous weight, the waters roll."·

In the same year, Hathuberht, bishop of the city of London, took
his departure from this temporal life.   And, soon after, a great part
of that city was destroyed by accidental fire.

In the year eight hundred and two from our Lord's incarnation,
died Brichtric, king of the West Saxons,[4] who, for seventeen years,
had gloriously reigned over that nation; after whom, Ecgberht, of

---

[1] See Annal. Lauresp. 801, ap. Pertz. Monum. Germ. i. 38, Einhardi Annal. 801,
p. 189.
[2] At Gainford, in Yorkshire. See Camd. Brit. col. 940.
[3] The MS. of Hoveden here reads, " the king of the Angels."
[4] The word "Saxons," here omitted in the MS. of Simeon, and the Chronicle of
Melrose, is supplied from Hoveden.   According to the Saxon Chronicle, he died
A.D. 800.

the royal family of that nation, took and held the government and kingdom. Brichtric, king of the West Saxons, had taken in marriage Eadburga, daughter of Offa, king of the Mercians, who ordered the great wall to be built between Britain and Mercia, that is, from sea to sea. And when the daughter of the king was raised to so many honours, she became inflated with marvellous pride, and began to live in her father's tyrannical manner, and to ban all men; so that she was utterly detested by all, not only dukes and magistrates, but also by the whole populace. She never ceased to bring accusations to the king against all ecclesiastics; and this cursed woman gained such power over her husband by her wiles, that those whom she accused he was ready to condemn to death or banishment; and if she could not obtain her wish from the king, she did not hesitate to destroy them secretly by poison. There was at that time a certain wealthy young man, much esteemed and beloved by the king before named, whom, after having attempted, but without success, to bring him under the king's displeasure, this wicked woman put to death by poison; of which poison the king, having unwittingly partaken, died. She, nevertheless, had not intended to administer the poison to the king, but to the youth; whom the chief anticipating, both these persons drank of the cup of death, and perished by the fatal draught. At the death of the king, the infamous poisoner, struck with terror, took flight beyond sea, with countless treasures, going to Charles, the most illustrious king of the Franks. When she presented herself before his throne, and laid before the king costly gifts, he thus addressed her: " Choose, Eadburg, whom you will have, me, or my son, who is with me on the throne." She, without any consideration, foolishly answered, " If the choice is given me, I would rather take your son than you, because he looks younger." To which king Charles is said to have thus replied: " If you had chosen me you might have had my son; but since you have chosen him, you shall have neither the one nor the other." He was so regardless of what was right, that he bestowed on her an excellent monastery; in which, having laid aside the secular habit, and with most hypocritical pretence assumed the nun's attire, she passed a very few years; for, as this detestable and lamentable woman had lived wickedly and foolishly in her own land, so it was discovered that she was living in a foreign land in a much more wicked, miserable, and senseless way.

> " The summer's heat, as one hath sung,
>   Bedecks with golden corn the fields;
>   Autumn with fruit her boughs hath hung;
>   And falling showers the winter yields."

But neither the beauty of summer, nor the cold of winter, availed to restrain the mind of this worst of queens from lust; for after a short period, while she was occupied as some thought in holy things, she was debauched by a certain man of low birth of her own nation.

> "While yet dark clouds of ignorance remain,
>   Strange wonders shall not cease;"

as is said of the woman taken in adultery.

There is, therefore, nothing which you can wonder at, for there is nothing hid which shall not be known. After this, by the command of the great emperor Charles, she was expelled from her monastery, to her great grief and vexation of mind; and in poverty and misery she passed her life in a discreditable manner to the end. At last, accompanied by one wretched slave, begging her daily bread, from one house, city or village, to another, she died miserably in Pavia.

The noble king Brichtric being dead, king Ecgberht took the rule and government of the Western kingdom after his decease; who, sprung from the royal line of that nation, placed on his head the crown of the whole kingdom, ruling with a powerful sceptre. For he was a most energetic and able man, and subjected many kingdoms to his rule. He reigned thirty-six years. And to Ecgberht succeeded his most potent son, Ethelwlf; to whom succeeded his son Ethelbald; after him his brother Ethelbyrht; after whom his brother Ethelred; and after him their brother Elfred. Ethelwlf, in fact, had by his noble wife four sons, namely, Ethelbald, Ethelbert, Ethelred and Alfred, who each in turn succeeded to the kingdom.

A.D. 803. Bishop Hibald died, and Egbert succeeded him.[1]

A.D. 830. Celnod was consecrated bishop, and abbot Felgild died, and Egred was made bishop.

A.D. 846. Eanbert received the episcopate.[2]

In the year of our Lord's incarnation eight hundred and forty-nine, there sprung up a light out of darkness; there was born, in the royal vill, called by the Angles Wantage, Elfred,[3] king of the Angles, whose pedigree is unfolded in this order. King Elfred was the son of king Ethelwlf, who was the son of Egberht, who was the son of Alhmund, who was the son of Affa,[4] who was the son of Eoppa, who was the son of Ingild; Ingild and Ine were brothers. Ine was the most famous king throughout the limits of the whole nation of the Angles; he royally governed the kingdom of the western regions; and after many years spent in his kingdom, he went to Rome, resigning his present country and kingdom, that he might obtain an eternal one with Christ, who granted him this empire of divine majesty. These were the sons of Coenred, who was the son of Ceolwald, who was the son of Guda, who was the son of Cuderwine,[5] who was the son of Ceawlm,[5] who was the son of Cinric, who was the son of Creoda, who was the son of Cerdic, who was the son of Elesa, who was the son of Gewis, from whom the Britons name all that nation Gewis. He was the son of Brand, who was the son of Belde, who was the son of Woden, who was the son of Frithuwald, who was the son of Frealaf, who was the son of Fridrenwulf,[6] who was the son of Geta, whom the heathens

[1] A considerable gap here occurs in Simeon, namely, from 803—830, concerning which see the Preface. Hibald and Egred were bishops of Lindisfarne, and Ceolnoth was archbishop of Canterbury.
[2] This entry occurs on the lower margin of the MS. Eanbert was bishop of Lindisfarne. See Florence of Worcester, A.D. 845.
[3] From this point to the year 887, compare Asser's Life of Alfred.
[4] See the Saxon Chronicle, A.D. 718.   [5] Read "Cuthwine," and "Ceawlin."
[6] Read "Fritheuulf."

of old worshipped as a god. Of him the famous poet Sedulius makes mention in his Paschal Ode, commencing thus:

> "Since heathen poets in high-sounding phrase
> Their own delusions bellow out,
> And all their art of song employ to praise
> Their vain god Geta, with bombastic shout."

This Geta was the son of Cetwa, who was the son of Beaw, who was the son of Seldwa, who was the son of Heremod, who was the son of Itermod, who was the son of Hatra, who was the son of Wala, who was the son of Bedwig, who was the son of Sem, who was the son of Noe, who was the son of Lamech, who was the son of Matusalem, who was the son of Enoch, who was the son of Malaleel, who was the son of Canaan, who was the son of Enos, who was the son of Seth, who was the son of Adam, the first man. The mother of king Elfred was called Osburg. She was an exceedingly religious woman, and noble in disposition, which nobility she adorned with discretion of mind. The father also was called Oslac, he was the devoted and most trusty cupbearer of king Ethelwlf. He sprung from the Goths and Jutes, of the race of Stuph and Wihtgar, two brothers. Having premised these things, let us now, to the best of our ability, pursue the work which we have undertaken.

A.D. 851, (the third year of the birth of Elfred,) earl Ceorl fought against the Danes, and the Christians obtained the victory over their enemies. The Danes also wintered in the island called Scepige [Sheppey], that is, the Isle of Sheep. In the same year, a great army of pagans came, with three hundred and fifty ships, to the mouth of the river Thames. They pillaged Canterbury, that is, the city of the men of Kent, and put to flight Berhtulf, king of the Mercians, with all his army, who had gone out to battle against them. After this, the Danes became more bold, and assembled their whole army in Suthrige [Surrey]. Hearing of this, Ethelwlf, the warlike king of the Saxons, together with his son Ethelbald, also assembled a numerous army in the place called Aclea [Ockley], that is, the Plain of the Oak.[1] And when the flower of the English nation appeared, resplendent in clashing armour, there ensued a long battle between the English and Danes; the former fighting bravely, when they saw their king conduct himself so fiercely in war; and thus they proved superior to their enemies in the contest. And when they had manfully contended for a very long time, and the fight was courageously and stoutly maintained on both sides, the greatest part of the pagan multitude was entirely overthrown and routed, so that never, in any country, in any one day, either before or since, had so many met their death. On that very day the Christians gloriously obtained the victory, and remained masters of the field of slaughter; rendering thanks to God in hymns and confessions.

A.D. 852. King Ethelslan and earl Alchere met a great army of

---

[1] Hoveden here adds that he fought with the pagans, and routed them with great slaughter.

the pagans in Kent, at the place called Sandwich, which they there, by God's help, almost destroyed, and took nine of their ships ; the rest, struck with panic, took refuge in flight.

A. D. 853, (the fifth year of the birth of Elfred), Burhred king· of the Mercians, by ambassadors, besought Ethelwlf king of the West Saxons to grant him his aid, in order that he might bring under his dominion the Midland Britons who dwell between Mercia and the Western sea, and who were frequently rebelling against him. And king Ethelwlf, accepting his embassy, put his army in motion, furnished him with subsidies, and fearlessly went out with king Burhred to battle. He presently began to ravage that country, seized, reduced and subdued it to king Burhred ; who, rendering him thanks, dismissed him to return with gladness to his own affairs.

In the same year, king Ethelwlf sent his son Elfred to Rome, attended by a large band of noble soldiers. At this time, the blessed pope Leo[1] presided over the apostolic see, who consecrated the aforesaid child as king, by anointing; and receiving him as his own son by adoption, confirmed him, and then sent him to his country and his father, with the benediction of St. Peter the apostle. At this period, earls Alchere and Wada,[2] together with the men of Kent and Surrey, had a hard fight with the host of the pagans, in the isle which is called in the Saxon tongue Tened, in the British language Ruim. At first the Christians had the victory ; but the battle continuing a long time, many on each side perished, and a countless multitude were drowned and slain in the river. Both the aforesaid leaders fell there, fighting in defence of the liberty of their nation.

In this year, after the Feast of Christ's holy Resurrection,[3] king Ethelwlf, of glorious power, gave his daughter to Burhred, king of the Mercians, with great pomp, as is customary with kings, in the town called Chippenham ; where, the marriage being performed, she received the rank and title of queen.

A. D. 854. Archbishop Wlfere[4] received the pall, and Eardulf received the episcopate of Lindisfarne.[5]

A. D. 855, (the seventh of the birth of the aforesaid king), an army of pagans took up their quarters for the whole winter in the isle of Sheppey. At this time king Ethelwlf tithed the whole realm of his kingdom, for the salvation of his own soul and those of his forefathers. In that year he went with great honour to the threshold of the chief of the apostles, taking with him his son Elfred, inasmuch as he loved him more than the rest. He was honourably received by the apostolic man, and remained there a whole year diligently occupied in prayers and almsgiving. On his return to his own country, he was violently disliked by his son Ethelbald, and Ealhastan bishop of Sherborn, and many others. The most gracious king Ethelwlf, then, lived two years after he undertook his journey to

---

[1] The fourth pope of that name.
[2] According to Asser, his name was Huda.
[3] Easter day occurred this year upon 2d April.   [4] Archbishop of York.
[5] See Simeon's History of the Church of Durham, chap. xx., and Hoveden.

the Roman see. Among his other good deeds of the present life and attention to regal duty, he took forethought concerning his departure; and in order that his sons might not quarrel after his decease, he wrote an epistle, of eloquent composition, in which he arranged whatever pertained to him by right. He ordered, for himself and all his successors, that throughout the whole inheritance of his land, among ten manors, one poor person, either a native or stranger, should always be assisted or maintained with food, drink, and clothing. For the salvation of his soul, he also ordered three hundred mancuses[1] to be sent to Rome; one hundred to the church of St. Peter, specially to buy oil; and one hundred for the honour of St. Paul; one hundred to the universal apostolic pope. Thereupon, at the death of the glorious king Ethelwlf, his son Ethelbald, contrary to the prohibition of Jesus Christ and the teaching of Christians, contrary also to the custom of all heathens, going up to the bed of his father, took in marriage (to his great disgrace) Judith, daughter of Charles king of the Franks; and after the death of his most noble father, he ruled for two years and a half, without restraint, the kingdom of the West Saxons.

A.D. 860, (the twelfth of the birth of the illustrious Etheling Elfred), Ethelbald died, and was buried in Sherborne. He being taken from the world, his brother Ethelbyrht added these provinces to his kingdom; that is to say, Kent and Surrey, also Sussex, with all their towns and territories, as was right. In his reign a large army of pagans coming by sea, attacked and pillaged the city of Winchester. But as the said army was returning with great booty to their vessels, Osric, the most noble duke of the men of Hampshire, came up with his people, and the illustrious earl Ethelwlf with the men of Berkshire, met them courageously, with an immense army; and joining battle, the pagans were everywhere slain by the English, assisted by the angelic spirits. And when these terrible enemies could no longer stand by reason of their wounds, a very great multitude perished cruelly, some hiding themselves in coverts of thick brambles, and some taking flight like women. The English, by the favour of fortune, remained masters of the field of slaughter. And so king Ethelbyrht for five years governed peacefully, mildly, and with honour, the kingdom committed to him, and went the way of all flesh, to the great grief of his nobles, bishops, and all the people. Leaving the monarchy of the earthly kingdom, he became partaker of another. He was buried beside his brother in Sherborne, where he awaits the consolation of a future resurrection.

A.D. 864. The pagans wintered in the island called Thanet, which is surrounded on all sides by an estuary of the sea. They entered into a firm league with the Kentish men, and the Kentish men promised to pay them money for the preservation of the treaty. The Danes remained quiet for a few days; yet in the meanwhile, stealing like foxes out of their camp secretly by night, in violation of the treaty, and despising the promise of money,

---

[1] A marginal note in the MS. here states, that "a mancus consists of thirty pence."

O infamy! they devastated the whole east border of the Kentish
nation. They knew that they would get more money by thievish
plunder than by peace; and so indeed it came to pass.

In the following year, that is, in eight hundred and sixty-
six, (the eighteenth of Elfred's birth,) Ethelred, brother of
Ethelbyrht, king of the West Saxons, took the helm of the
kingdom. In the same year, a great fleet of pagans from the
Danube entered the territories of Britain, and so wintered in
the kingdom of the East Angles, which is called in the Saxon
tongue Eastengle; and there this numerous army was formed
into cavalry, riding and rushing about hither and thither, seizing enormous plunder, and sparing neither men nor women,
widows nor virgins. In these days Elfred the Atheling began, by
means of assiduous study, to be imbued with divine doctrines, who
was, from his very cradle, loved with extraordinary affection beyond
his brethren, by his father and mother. As he grew in stature to
youthful age, he appeared more graceful in form than his other
brothers; he was remarkable for the brightness of his countenance,
and sparkled with eloquent discourse. As the hart pants for the
waterbrooks, so he longed that the depths of his heart, and the
recesses of his mind, should be penetrated and imbued with sound
learning. But, sad to say, by the neglect of his parents and tutors,
he remained ignorant of his letters until the twelfth year of his age.
This glorious youth and future king endeavoured also day and night
to learn the Saxon poems. When, therefore, one day his most
excellent mother was showing him and his brothers a certain Saxon
book of poetry, she said to them, "Which ever of you, my dearest
sons, can first learn this volume, I will give it to him." But he,
moved with a divine impulse, and delighted with the beauty of the
capital letter, replied to his mother, "Will you indeed give it?"
She, smiling, rejoicing and assenting said, "I will assuredly give
it." He quickly took the book from the hand of his mother, went
to the master, showed the book, and read, his preceptor instructing
him. In the course of no long time, he came before his beloved
mother, and recited the book from memory. She gave great
thanks to the Saviour's goodness, acknowledging that the grace of
God was in the mind of the youth. After that, inflamed with the
desire of divine love, he devoutly learnt very many psalms, and
the daily course, that is, the celebration of the hours; which,
having collected into one volume, he carried inseparably in his
bosom night and day. O happy race of men! O wise king! You
carry that which carries you; you carry the keys of wisdom: thou
lovest wisdom and shalt be wise, doing judgment and justice in the
earth. O ye clerics, attend, and observe the king carry this book
in his bosom day and night. You neither know, nor desire to know,
the law of God. The same man, when he became king, especially
bewailed his son, that is, his mind, that it had not been instructed
in the liberal arts.[1]

A.D. 867, (the nineteenth of the birth of Elfred,) the aforesaid
host of pagans crossed from the East Angles to the city of York,

[1] There appears to be some confusion in this obscure sentence.

which is situated on the north bank of the river Humber. At the same time, a very great strife was kindled among the Northumbrian people; and no wonder, for he who loves strife shall find it. In those days, the nation of the Northumbrians had violently expelled from the kingdom the rightful king of their nation, Osbryht by name, and had placed at the head of the kingdom a certain tyrant, named Alla. When the pagans came upon the kingdom, that dissension was allayed by divine counsel and the aid of the nobles. King Osbryht and Alla, having united their forces and formed an army, came to the city of York; on their approach, the multitude of the shipmen immediately took to flight. The Christians, perceiving their flight and terror, found that they themselves were the stronger party. They fought on each side with much ferocity, and both kings fell. The rest who escaped made peace with the Danes. In this year Ealhstan, bishop of the church of Sherborne, left the way and life of a temporal world; after having for fifty years honourably ruled his see, he rests in the peace of the church, being honourably interred in this seat of the episcopate.

A.D. 868. In his twentieth year, king Elfred took a wife from Mercia, noble by descent, the daughter of Ethelred, earl of the Gaini, who was called by the Angles "Mucel," on account of his being large in stature and old in wisdom. At that time, the aforesaid host of pagans left the Northumbrians, and made their dreaded approach to Nottingham, which city in the British tongue is called Tignocebanc,[1] which means the House of Caves; in which place these treacherous strangers wintered that year, their arrival being unpleasing enough to all the people. But the mighty king of the Mercians, called Burhred; and all his nobles, hearing of their coming, held counsel with his earls and warriors, and all the people under him, how they might, by their warlike valour, overcome their enemies, or repel them from the kingdom. He sent also messengers with great speed to the man of renowned valour, Elfred, and to Ethelred his brother, begging that they would render him fraternal assistance, by which they might subdue them with victorious might; which they, like undaunted lions, did not hesitate to do. Elfred thus stirred up, gave speedy orders to assemble an army, bearing in mind the saying, "A man though rich never does anything, if, trembling and groaning, he fancies himself poor." A strong man can by no means accomplish what he desires if he is timid, and thinks himself poor, that is, in sad plight, though he may do what he wishes by manfully striving. His brother being inflamed with the same zeal, they came as far as Nottingham, prepared for the enterprise. But the pagans, secured by the fortifications of the citadel, offer battle; form their line; present a numerous army; yet fearful, perceiving by clear signs that the Christian people in tens of hundreds and thousands would resist their adversaries, stimulated by their devoted leaders. At length, by the favour of the Almighty Lord, the blast of the whirl-

---

[1] Or more correctly (according to Petrie), "Tigguocobauc;" concerning which name, see Camd. Brit. col. 577.

wind ceased; the hearts of the wicked were subdued, asking of the Christians peace and a treaty, as if they had besought the favour of Christ in this spirit,

> " The raging floods of strife suppress,
>   Thou Ruler of the earth and sky;
> And the firm earth securely bless
>   With the same peace which reigns on high."

Peace was made between the kings and the pagans; and they, departing from each other, were separated as sheep from the goats.

A.D. 869, (the twenty-first of Elfred's age,) the before-mentioned host again went to the nation of the Northumbrians, and there remained a whole year, raging and storming, killing and destroying a multitude of men and women.

A.D. 870. In the following year, however, while the splendour of the sun illuminated the circuit of the world, and the year of the incarnation of our Lord eight hundred and seventy had arrived, then shone the period when king Elfred completed twenty-one years. An[1] enormous multitude of Danes and, so to speak, troops of legions were assembled, so that many thousands seemed to be present, as if they had increased from one thousand to twenty myriads. They came after this through Mercia to the East Angles, and fearlessly wintered in the city called Thetford; but king Eadmund at that time reigned over all the kingdoms, as the event which occurred at the termination of his most holy life proved. In the same year the aforesaid king, with his men, fought fiercely and manfully against that army. But since the merciful God foreknew that he would come by a martyr's crown to the crown of heavenly glory, he there fell gloriously;[2] the honour of whose passion may well be mentioned in our history, that the sons of men may know and acknowledge how terrible is Christ, the Son of God, in the counsels of men; and with how glorious a triumph He adorns those whom here He afflicts with the honourable mark of suffering, thus fulfilling the saying, " No man is crowned except he strive lawfully." [2 Tim. ii. 5.] The devout king Eadmund took the government of the East Angles, which also he held with the strong right hand of power, always adoring and glorifying God for all his good things which he had enjoyed. In the same year in which this illustrious king and martyr entered, by the martyr's crown, upon the joys of supreme felicity, Ceolnoth, archbishop of the city of Canterbury, went the way of all flesh, and was buried by the clergy in that city.

A.D. 871, (the twenty-second[3] year of the birth of Elfred, the glorious king of the Saxons,) the host of pagans, of hated memory, left the East Angles, and entered the kingdom of the West Saxons, coming to the royal vill called Reading, on the south side of the river Thames, in that district which is called by the inhabitants of that country Berkshire. On the third day of the arrival of these enemies of the Angles, their earls, with a large body of men, made

---

[1] Hoveden here adds, that the Danish army was under Hinguar and Hubba.
[2] Simeon elsewhere states, that bishop Humbert was killed along with him. See also Gaimar, p. 765.   [3] More correctly, in his twenty-third year.

a foray on the border of that river, and plundered an immense number. Some of them moreover endeavoured to make a vallum between the rivers Thames and Kennet; but the design and work of the Danes was overthrown by the aid of the Angles, so as to fulfil in them that saying of the scholar:—

> "Though richly clothed in purple robes,
>   And with bright jewels crown'd,
> The wicked move in lonely might,
>   Hated by all around."

And again:

> "Think not that those in happy honour live,
>   Whose honours servile wretches only give."

While the mischievous plunderers were actively labouring at their work, presently there came Ethelwlf, duke of the district of Berkshire, a man of remarkable energy, accompanied by his troops, and girt with the strength of a triple breastplate. On perceiving the multitude of the barbarians, the prince of the Christian people said to his followers, "Their army is numerous, but is not to be feared. Though when put in array against us it be the stronger, yet Christ, who is our leader, is still stronger than they." The Christians then met the Danes, trusting in the protection of the name of Christ; the aforesaid duke, forming his excellent troops in the place called Englafield, earnestly exhorted them to resist their opponents; and here was fought a very severe battle, in which many on each side fell wounded, and many were slain. There fell one of the princes of the Danes, with a great multitude of his army, the rest escaping by flight. The Christians obtained the palm of victory, and were masters of the field of slaughter.

These things being accomplished, in the course of four days after, the mighty king Ethelred and his brother Elfred, visiting their numerous armies, (such was the power and the valour of these kings,) came to Reading, desiring either to live with honour in the kingdom, or to fall in battle for Christ. And as the valiant king Ethelred, with his beloved brother, had reached the gates of the citadel, slaying and overthrowing their enemies before and behind; on the other side, the pagans, resisting with hostile fury, made slaughter. But, alas! grievous to state, the enemies of the Angles on that day obtained the victory. Also Ethelwlf of Berkshire, who at first chafed like a lion in the battle, there fell with other faithful ones in Christ. Excited by this distress and shame, the people of the Angles implored the assistance of the Angels, that they would vouchsafe to render aid from above. Then indeed again after four days, they march their army against the aforesaid enemies, take up their arms, and station their troops in the place called Etscesdun,[1] which may rightly be rendered, The hill of the ash. And there these illustrious men, most valiant in fight, go forth with all their forces, eager for the battle. The Danes also, with much skill, dividing themselves into two bands, prepared to fight manfully with their troops. They had also two kings and many dukes, and, adopting a wary system, they assigned one half

---

[1] More correctly Escesdun; now Ashendon.

of the army to the two kings, the other half to all the dukes.   The
Angles, observing this, also formed two divisions, and constructed
engines of war and engineering defences.   King Elfred then very
promptly advanced with his troops to the engagement, knowing full
well that the victory would be gained, not by the multitude of men,
but by the mercy and compassion of God.   King Ethelred indeed
was in his tent, engaged in prayer and attentively hearing mass
and attending divine service ;   and these holy mysteries were of
much benefit to the king and Christian people, as will appear
in the sequel.

The Christian people and the Angles, then, most devotedly
determined to engage with confidence in battle against their
enemies; and that king Ethelred, the bravest of princes, should
contend with his tens of thousands against their legions, that is to
say, one king of the Angles against two of the Danes; and king
Elfred, with his dukes and warriors, lieutenants and people, should
try the issue of battle against all the chiefs of the pagans, as had
been determined : which arrangement was exceedingly satisfactory
to both the kings and to the people.   These matters having been
then determinately appointed on both sides, as king Elfred delayed
long in prayer, and the pagans came rapidly into the field, prepared
for a severe contest, Elfred, though then only the second in the
kingdom, could no longer endure the hostile array, without an
attempt either to overcome them in battle, or to perish.   In a
sudden excitement of mind, he rushed upon the dense masses of
the Danes, with the consecrated troops of the Angles ; then came
the king, girt with arms and with prayers, who perceived that the
army of his brother was very skilfully managed, as if the warlike
Judas had gone out to battle.   They contended with manly resolution on both sides, and in that place fell one thousand one hundred
and fifty men.   Those who died for their country and their country's
laws, were carried, as it is meet to believe, to the country of everlasting happiness ; the others were given over to him of whom it
is said, " He is the author of all unrighteousness."   The kings,
verily, not only by words exhorted their people to be firm, but also,
by their military valour, overthrew their enemies by arms.   At
length the Danes, seeing that the lines of their troops were broken,
became troubled, astonished, and alarmed, and then were seized
with a great panic.   For the Danes were struck to the heart with
terror from God, not being able longer to endure the attacks of
the Angles in that meeting.   They, betaking themselves to an
ignoble flight, dropping their swords, owned themselves conquered,
and begged for quarter.   The kings, stretching out their swords,
with difficulty restrained the fighting multitude.   The ignoble
rabble fled in all directions, whom the Anglian people pursued
throughout the day.   On that occasion many thousands were cut
down, the destruction of whom the kings witnessing, ascribed great
glory to God who had that day bestowed on them such a palm of
victory.   There also fell king Bergsecg,[1] and with him three dukes,
duke Sidroc, a veteran warrior, to whom may be applied the saying,

[1] Or Bagsecg.

" Grown old of evil days." There perished also duke Sidroc the younger, and Osbern, a leader of the army, and duke Frana and duke Harald with their troops ; who, going the broad and easy way, descended into the depth of the pit. They knew not the way of instruction, neither understood they the path thereof; it was put far from their face.[1]

This glorious battle being finished, the kings and all the people were filled with unbounded exultation, seeing the flight of the Danes and the firmness of the Angles. After the lapse of fourteen days, the most excellent king Ethelred, disregarding that the year of jubilee[2] is one of forgiveness, aided by the trusty help of his brother, called together the army, collected the spoils, and divided arms and many gifts among his comrades. These princes of the people were well aware that states would be happy, if either those persons who loved wisdom were in power, or if it came to pass that their rulers applied their minds to wisdom. The Angles and Danes again met in battle, and applying their utmost strength, the Danes nearly obtained the victory.

In the same year king Ethelred, full of age and accomplished in goodness, after the achievement of famous wars, entered on the bliss of a future life and endless kingdom, with the King of worlds in the land of the living. The aforesaid king being taken from this world, Elfred was presently chosen by the dukes and bishops of the whole nation, and was besought, not only by them, but by the whole people, that he would rule over them, " to be avenged of the heathen and to rebuke the people."[3] Having obtained the government of the whole nation, he was always eminent in valour, and victor in all wars, fortune favouring and Christ acting for him. The aforesaid host waged war against him with great fierceness, and finding the roughness of the Angles, and perceiving their own weakness, turned their backs in flight. But, alas ! provoked by the audacity of their pursuers, they returned again to the battle, obtaining the prize of victory and remaining masters of the field of death. In this year also, the Saxons made a treaty of peace with the same pagans, on condition that they should depart from them.

A.D. 872, (the twenty-fourth of Elfred's age,) the aforesaid host of pagans came to London and there wintered ; the Mercians made peace with them.[4]

A.D. 873, (the twenty-fourth[5] year of the birth of Elfred, king of the Angles,) the oft-mentioned host, leaving London, marched to the country of the Northumbrians, and there wintered ; the Mercians again made a peace with them.

A.D. 874, (the twenty-fifth[6] of the birth of Elfred, king of the Angles,) the above-named host left the province of Lindsey, went to Mercia, and wintered at Hripadun [Repton]. Also they expelled Burhred king of the Mercians from his kingdom, and compelled him to depart to Rome, in the twenty-second year of his reign.

[1] See Baruch iii. 20, 21.   [2] See Levit. xxv. 14, 17.   [3] See Ps. cxlix. 7.
[4] See Simeon's Hist. of the Church of Durham, chap. xxi.
[5] Read, " the twenty-fifth."   [6] Read, " the twenty-sixth."

After his arrival at Rome he did not live long in this world, but went to Him who is the true life, and was honourably interred in the church of St. Mary, mother of our Lord Jesus Christ, ever Virgin, waiting for his second advent, when He will bounteously grant just rewards to the righteous, and dispense dread punishment to the wicked. The Danes, moreover, after his expulsion brought the kingdom of the Mercians under their own dominion. They entrusted it to a certain soldier of that nation named Ceolwlf, on this condition, that when they wished, they should have it again without guile and without injury.

A.D. 875, (the twenty-sixth[1] year of the birth of king Elfred,) the aforesaid army left Repton, and divided itself into two bodies. One division went with Haldene to the country of the Northumbrians,[2] laid it waste, and wintered near the river called the Tyne; and subdued the whole nation under their dominion; they devastated also the Picts and the Stretduccenses[3] [the Strathclyde Britons]. Bishop Eardulf and abbot Eadred, taking the body of St. Cuthbert from Lindisfarne, wandered about with that treasure for nine years, flying before the face of the barbarians from place to place. The other division of that host went with Guthrum and Oscytel and Amund, kings of the pagans, to the place called Grantabric [Cambridge], and there wintered. King Elfred, prepared for a naval engagement, met six ships upon the sea, bravely engaging with which he took one; the rest fled, seized with alarm.

A.D. 876, (the twenty-seventh[4] of king Elfred's birth,) the aforesaid host, departing by night from Cambridge, entered the castle called Wareham. Of whose sudden approach the king of the Saxons having obtained previous notice, made a league with them, taking hostages, on condition that they should depart from his kingdom. But they, in their wonted manner, caring neither for hostages nor oaths, in violation of the treaty, turned aside one night to Exeter, which is called in British Cairwisc, in Latin Civitas aquarum, The city of waters.

A.D. 877, (the twenty-seventh[5] of Elfred's birth,) that infamous host left Exeter, went to the royal vill of Chippenham, and wintered there. King Elfred at this time suffered great tribulation, and led a harassed life. Encouraged however by St. Cuthbert[6] in a manifest revelation, king Elfred fought against the Danes, and obtained the victory at the time and place which the saint had ordered; and was always afterwards terrible and invincible to his enemies, and held St. Cuthbert in especial honour. How he overcame his enemies a short time after may here be read.

Lastly, in the same year, Inguar[7] and Healifilene, with twenty-three ships, rushing like fierce wolves from the country of Demetia[8]

---

[1] Read, "the twenty-seventh."

[2] See Simeon's History of the Church of Durham, chap. xxi., where further details of this inroad are given.

[3] Read, "Stretcludenses."   [4] Read, "the twenty-eighth."

[5] Read, "the twenty-ninth."

[6] See Simeon's History of the Church of Durham, chap. xxv.

[7] Compare the Saxon Chron. A.D. 878, and Asser, p. 458, by which it appears that we must here read, "the brother of Inguar and Healfdene."

[8] South Wales. See Camd. Brit. col. 473.

in which they had wintered, after perpetrating much slaughter upon the Christians, and burning monasteries, sailed to Devonshire, and there they were slain by the brave ministers of the king, with one thousand two hundred men, before the citadel of Cynwith,[1] since in the same fortress very many servants of the king, as has been said, had shut themselves, for the sake of refuge. King Elfred, trusting in the Lord God, attended by a few troops, entrenched himself in the place called Athelney; dwelling in which with his comrades, he frequently and 'indefatigably harassed the enemy from the fortress. He did this at the time of the Resurrection of our Lord Jesus Christ [23d March]; and seven weeks and one day (that is, fifty full days) after, he came to Ecgbert's stone,[2] which is in the east part of the forest called in the Anglian language Mucelpurlu; in the Latin, Magna Silva, The great wood; and in British, Coitmapur.[3] There, all the inhabitants of Somerset, Wiltshire, and also Hampshire, met the much-loved king; and at the sight of him rejoiced with great exultation of heart, as though receiving him as one raised from the dead. On the third day after, he came with a large army to the place called Edderandun,[4] near which he found immense battalions of pagans in a dense mass prepared for battle. At the first dawn of day, the king and all the flower of his people arrayed themselves in their martial accoutrements, as in the triple breastplate of faith, hope, and the love of God. They, rising from the earth, boldly incited the common people to battle, trusting in the goodness of the Creator, secure and fortified as with a rampart by the presence of the king, whose countenance shone like that of an angel. Both sides then engaged in battle for a great part of the day, and their shouts and clashing of arms were heard to a great distance.

The Great Overlooker, therefore, beholding from his secret place on high the desire of his earthly king, granted him the assistance of the angelic power. He, at length gaining the victory, overthrew his enemies, giving thanks to the most high Saviour with joyfulness of heart. And while the king with his troops was there rejoicing, his enemies who survived were weeping with great lamentation, on account of the severity of hunger and cold, and the fear of so great a king; and they now, who were always opposed to it, beg the favour of peace. They promise hostages and offer oaths. The king giving ear to all these things, moved in his heart with pity, granted all they asked. Their king, Guthrum by name, averred that he wished to become a Christian, and, under the hand of the most religious king, was royally received in the cleansing of baptism. This Guthrum, whom the king of the Saxons took as the son of his adoption, was washed in the baptism of salvation, with thirty other chosen men. After he was baptized, he remained with him twelve nights in great honour, and his spiritual father bestowed on him, and on all who had received the Christian faith, great and untold gifts.

[1] See Asser, p. 458, note [3].   [2] See Asser, p. 459, note [3].
[3] Read, "Coitmawr."
[4] Read, "Ethandun;" and see Asser, p. 459, note [6].

A.D. 879, (the twenty-eighth[1] of the birth of king Elfred,) the aforesaid host of pagans, rising as they had promised from Chippenham, went to Cirencester, which in the British tongue is called Cairceri, and there remained the space of one year. Also in that year came an immense army of pagans from foreign countries to the river Thames, and, uniting with the aforesaid body, they banded together, as is the manner of the wicked. An eclipse occurred the same year, between the ninth hour and the evening.

A.D. 880, (the twenty-ninth[2] of the age of the glorious king Elfred,) the often-mentioned host of pagans, leaving Cirencester, went to the East Angles, and dividing that country, took up their residence there. The pagans who had wintered at Fulham, forsook Britain, and began to visit France with their dire acquaintance, where they remained one year.

A.D. 881, (the thirtieth[3] year of Elfred's age,) the aforesaid army, mounted on horses, made a descent upon the territories of the Franks; and it seems wonderful that these unskilled enemies should dare to attack so brave and warlike a people; but then the fierce Franks, rushing bravely with indomitable strength from their castles, towns, cities and towers, were roused to wrath like lions, at seeing the impious powers of the ungodly break forth, the wicked exulting with joy and gladness, good men prostrated with fear, the innocent weeping, the guilty rejoicing. Taking prudent counsel, the brave Franks engaged in a hard fight with the pagans. At the end of the battle the Franks returned in triumph; the pagans, who had obtained horses, rode in different directions. In these days many monasteries in the same nation were overthrown and desolated. Moreover the brethren of the monastery of St. Benedict,[4] taking with them his relics from the tomb where they had been laid with great splendour, wandered hither and thither.

A.D. 882, (the thirty-first[5] of the age of the glorious king Elfred,) the army of pagans towed their vessels up the river called the Maese, into the territory of the Frankish nation, and wintered there one year. Lastly, in the same year, Elfred, king of the Saxons, the bravest of leaders, prepared for a naval engagement, encountered the pagan vessels on the sea, of which he, victorious no less at sea than on land, by his great bravery, conquered two ships, the whole of their crews perishing. For this victory this prince of princes rendered due thanks to the Author of salvation. We must relate what next took place. After this he severely wounded the captains of two vessels, with all their shipmates, who helplessly laying down their arms, with bended knees and suppliant prayers, gave themselves up to this great king, as long as a spark of life should remain in them.

In the following year, that is, eight hundred and eighty-three, (the thirty-second[6] of the age of the most illustrious king Elfred,)

[1] Read, "the thirty-first."   [2] Read, "the thirty-second."
[3] Read, "the thirty-third."
[4] Concerning this incident, see Mabill. Annal. Ord. S. Bened. lib. xxxviii. § 8.
[5] Read, "the thirty-fourth."   [6] Read, "the thirty-fifth."

that infamous host drew their vessels up the river called Scheldt, and there remained a year.

Guthred, from a slave, was made king; and the episcopal see was restored at Chester-le-street.[1]

A.D. 884, (the thirty-third[2] of the birth of the most illustrious king Elfred,) that most base host separated itself into two divisions. One went into East France, the other coming to Britain went to the place called Rochester, in Kent. Before its gate the pagans erected a fortress, but yet could not take the city, because the citizens bravely defended themselves, until king Elfred, the protector of the whole realm, came upon them with a large army. At the sudden approach of the king, the Danes, seized with alarm, speedily took refuge in their vessels, leaving their fortress and the horses which they had brought with them from France, and also the captives of the same nation whom they had taken from France. At this time in the same year, this mighty king sent his fleet, full of warriors, from Kent to the East Angles. And when they approached the mouth of the river Stoure, suddenly there met them thirteen ships of the pagans ready for battle, who, fiercely engaging on all sides, all the pagans were routed, and all their ships, with the whole of their treasure, taken. But those of the Danes who had contrived to escape, collected vessels confusedly from every quarter, and engaging in a sea-fight with the Angles when they were drowsily asleep, they were beaten; an unarmed multitude, to whom may fitly be applied the saying, " Many shut their eyes when they ought to keep a look-out."

In that same year, a host of pagans from Germany came down upon the country of the Old Saxons, against whom warlike men uniting on every side, that is, the Saxons and the Frislanders, contended manfully and bravely; when in two battles the Christian people, by the favour of the divine goodness, obtained the victory.

At that period pope Marinus,[3] of most sacred memory, went the way of all flesh, yielding up his spirit to Him who gave it. He freed the Saxon school, in the city of Rome, from all tribute, out of loving regard to the most gracious king Elfred; he also sent him many gifts, among which he gave him a part of the most blessed cross on which our Lord Jesus Christ hung for the salvation of the whole human race.

There were born to the king sons and daughters, very distinguished, and of fair beauty, whose names are here emblazoned, Eadward and Ethelward, Ethelfled and Ethelgifu, and Elfthrid. The king's son Eadward, and his sister Ealfthrid, were always brought up in the king's court with great attention by their tutors and nurses; moreover, they studiously learnt psalms, and the Saxon books and poems. Ethelward, his younger brother, placed under the exercises of literary discipline, distinguished himself amongst most of the children of the soldiers, both noble and of

---

[1] This last sentence is an interlineation in the MS. See Simeon's History of the Church of Durham, chap. xxviii.   [2] Read, " the thirty-sixth."
[3] He probably died in the May of this year, eight hundred and eighty-four. See Jaffé, p. 293.

lower rank. Ethelfled, their sister, was united in marriage to Eadred, prince of the Mercians; their sister Ethelgyfu was placed under the rules of the monastic life.

At this period archbishop Plegmund faithfully and gloriously ruled the church of Christ; this revered man shone with the fruits of wisdom, being exalted on the four pillars, to wit, justice, prudence, temperance, and fortitude.

At the same time Warfrid[1] adorned the sceptre of the government of the little city of Worcester by his most devoted disposition of mind. He, by the command, and at the earnest desire of the king, translated Gregory's Book of Dialogues into the Saxon tongue; sometimes very elegantly rendering sense for sense. He had invited also the illustrious priests, Ethelstan and Werwulf, to come to him from Mercia, on account of their being more excellently and fully skilled in the knowledge of the divine law; these he especially loved and honoured, and by their teaching and erudition this pacific king was glorified above all the kings of the earth.

A.D. 886, (the thirty-fifth[2] of the age of the glorious king Elfred,) the infamous host of the Danes again came into the country of the West Franks, and took a position on the river called the Seine. They came to the city of Paris, and there wintered, depriving the citizens of the passage of the bridge. But God granting the aid of his true help, and the citizens bravely defending themselves, they were unable to effect a breach in the fortifications.

At the same time the king of the Angles nobly restored and rendered habitable the great city of London, after many burnings of cities and slaughters of the people, and committed it to the care of Ethelred, the chief duke of the Mercians; and all, Angles and Saxons, who before had been everywhere dispersed with the pagans, or were freed from captivity, came before the king of their own accord, submitting to him as their lord; and he, who was of most gracious disposition, granted to all the patronage of his kindness.

A.D. 887, (the thirty-sixth[3] of the birth of the renowned king Elfred,) the aforesaid host, leaving the city of Paris, went up the Seine; and thence up the mouth of the river called the Marne; and from thence they came to a place called Chezy, a royal vill, in which place they took up their quarters for a whole year. And in the following year they entered the mouth of the river called the Yonne, not without great damage to the country, and there they stayed a year.

[4]At that time, moreover, Elfred, king of the Saxons, instinct with the divine blessing, was enabled both to read and to interpret the sacred writings; and he was afflicted with many tribulations in this world, although he was settled in the royal power. We have also seen and read letters sent to him from Jerusalem, from the patriarch Bel,[5] and divers gifts. How he extended the empire of his realm, and restored the walls of cities, and strengthened the

---

[1] See Asser, p. 465.   [2] Read, "the thirty-eighth."
[3] Read, "the thirty-ninth."
[4] The following sentences are unconnected extracts taken from Asser.
[5] Read, "from the patriarch Abel." See Asser, p. 472, note [3]

fortifications of such castles as had been broken down, and erected
them where there had been none before, who is sufficiently adorned
with polished eloquence as to declare with praising lips? Who can
tell also how he enriched holy places with ornaments and royal
gifts? He was frequently distressed in mind against princes and
rulers, and all the race of the perverse, because they would not
follow him in the studies in which he laboured. But yet he alone
endeavoured to guide the helm of his government, as an excellent
steersman guides his vessel, so as to bring the life of his glorious
soul to the harbour of a peaceful paradise. He was wont to keep
in constant remembrance what the poet sings:

> " Wise is the man who firmly builds
>   His house upon a rock,
> Lasting and strong, which no wild storms
>   Or fiercest winds can shock."

And again:

> " Though winds to fury lash the sea,
>   And earth's strong fabric shake,
> No dread confusion ere can cause
>   The wise man's heart to quake.
> Secured within a rampart strong,
>   He leads a quiet life;
> Serenely calm, he smiling views
>   The elemental strife."

Reflecting upon these things with spiritual searching of heart, this
king of most pious mind was adorned with indescribable acts of
the fruits of virtue. On the sacred festivals what bounties he bestowed on his bishops and dukes and soldiers who can relate?
Then the poor leaped with joy; then the orphans and widows
praised him with exceeding gladness of heart. He well knew that
saying of the wise man, " Then is money precious, when it has
been transferred to others; in the exercise of bounty possession
ceases." Finally, he made it his business, not only to admonish
bishops shining with heavenly lustre, that they should correct the
faults of the people and check the folly of the multitude by reproof;
not only did he admonish the pastors of the people, but also he
taught his princes and most loved ministers, that they should
always apply themselves most wisely to the common advantage of
the whole kingdom.

The same king founded a very fair monastery in the place called
Athelney, near which, on the western side, a well-fortified castle
was constructed by the command and execution of the said king.
In this monastery he assembled from all quarters monks of diverse
orders, and established them there. He founded also another
monastery near the east gate of the city called Shaftesbury, very
suitable for the abode of nuns, in which he placed as abbess his
daughter Ethelgifu, a virgin devoted to God. To both monasteries
he granted such great gifts and possessions as would suffice them
for food and for clothing as long as they should exist.

These things which we have related being fully and firmly accomplished, the oft-named king Elfred, with his wonted acuteness of
disposition, began to turn over in the depth of his mind, and in
turning over to meditate upon, that which is written in holy Scrip-

ture, "Though[1] thou offerest rightly, and dost not divide rightly, thou hast sinned." And that saying of Solomon the wisest of kings was thoroughly laid to heart, "The king's heart is in the hand of the Almighty." [Prov. xxi. 1.] His revenue he divided into three parts, in the following manner. The first portion of his income he annually bestowed upon his warriors; the second, on the workmen, whom he had gathered from many nations; the third, upon the strangers who came to him from all parts; ever bearing in mind that "God loveth a cheerful giver." Though enthroned in regal power, he verily was exercised by many and various thorns of sufferings.[2]

A.D. 888. Prince Beocca carried to Rome the alms of king Elfred. On that journey died Ethelsuith, the sister of the same king, and was buried in Pavia.

A.D. 890. Abbot Beornhelm conveyed to Rome the alms of king Elfred and the West Saxons. In the same year died Guthrum, king of the Northumbrians.[3] King Elfred, as before stated, received him at baptism, and called him Ethelstan. In this year the before-mentioned host went from the Seine to St. Lo, which is situated between Brittany and Gaul, but were put to flight by the Bretons, many being drowned in the river hard-by.

A.D. 891. Heathured received the episcopate.[4]

A.D. 892. Wlfhere, bishop of York, died in the thirty-ninth year of his archiepiscopate.

A.D. 893. The East Saxons and Northumbrians gave hostages and swore fealty to king Elfred against the aforesaid pagans, who had now returned into England.

A.D. 894. The aforesaid army which besieged Exeter, laid waste all about Chichester. But, not long after, they were put to flight by those who were in the city; many were slain, and many were captured out of their vessels. In this year king Guthred[5] died.

A.D. 899. King Elfred died,[6] after having reigned twenty-eight years; his son Edward succeeded him, having been carefully admonished by his father that he should specially honour St. Cuthbert. Likewise bishop Eardulf died in Cunceceastre [Chestre-le-street], whither he had translated the body of St. Cuthbert, with which he had fled from place to place before the host of the pagans, in much toil and want, for nine years. To him succeeded Cutheard[7] in the see.

A.D. 900. Ethelbald was consecrated to the bishopric of the church of York.

A.D. 901. Osbrith was driven from his kingdom.

A.D. 902. Brehtsig[8] was slain.

[1] No such passage occurs in the Vulgate.
[2] At this point Asser ends.
[3] This is an error: he was a king, not of the Northumbrians, but of the Northmen.
[4] This entry occurs in the margin of the MS., but is out of place, as Heathured, bishop of Lindisfarne, succeeded bishop Ecgbert in 819. See Hardy's Le Neve, iii. 278.   [5] See Simeon's History of the Church of Durham, chap. xxix.
[6] The correct date is A.D. 901.
[7] See Simeon's History of the Church of Durham, chap. xxxi.
[8] See the Saxon Chronicle, A.D. 905.

A.D. 906. King Edward, compelled by necessity, confirmed a peace with the East Angles and Northumbrians.

A.D. 910. The Angles and Danes fought at Teontanbole.[1] King Edward took London, and Oxford, and what pertained to it. In this year a large band of pirates assailed with cruel devastation the places about the river Severn; but there very soon nearly the whole perished.

A.D. 912. King Reingwald and earl Oter and Osvul Cracabane broke into and plundered Dunbline.

A.D. 914. King Niel was slain by his brother Sihtric.

A.D. 919. King Inguald[2] stormed York.

A.D. 920. King Sihtric stormed Devonport.

A.D. 923.[3] King Edward died, leaving the government to his son, Ethelstan.

A.D. 925. Wigred was consecrated bishop to the see of St. Cuthbert.

A.D. 927. King Ethelstan drove king Gudfrid from the kingdom of the Britons.[4]

A.D. 933. King Ethelstan ordered his brother Eadwin to be drowned in the sea.

A.D. 934. King Ethelstan, going with a large army to Scotland, came to the tomb of St. Cuthbert, commended himself and his expedition to the protection of the saint, bestowed on him many and divers gifts becoming a king, and lands; delivering to the torments of eternal fire whoever should take away any of these from him. After this he subdued his enemies, laid waste Scotland with his land force as far as Dunfoeder and Wertormore, and with his navy he ravaged as far as Caithness.

A.D. 937. King Ethelstan fought at Wendune[5] and put to flight king Onlaf, with six hundred and fifteen ships; also Constantine king of the Scots and the king of the Cumbrians, with all their host.

A.D. 939.[6] King Ethelstan died; to him succeeded his brother Edmund in the kingdom. In this year king Onlaf first came to York; thence marching south, he besieged Northampton; but effecting nothing there, he made a diversion to Tamworth and plundered all around; when on his return he had reached Leicester, king Edmund met him with an army. There was no hard fight, since the two archbishops, Oda and Wlstan, reconciling the kings to each other, put a stop to the battle. And so peace being made, Watling-street became the boundary of each kingdom, Edmund governing the south, Onlaf the north part.

A.D. 941. Olilaf,[7] having plundered the church of St. Balter,

---

[1] Read, "Teottenhale," and compare the Saxon Chronicle, A.D. 910.
[2] More probably Reignold. See the Saxon Chronicle, A.D. 923.
[3] More correctly, A.D. 924.
[4] A mistake, probably, for the Northumbrians. See Florence of Worcester, A.D. 926.
[5] In his History of the Church of Durham, chap. xxxiii., Simeon tells us that this place was also called Brunanburh.
[6] Hoveden ascribes this event to A.D. 940.
[7] Read, "Onlaf," with Hoveden.

and burnt Tiningham, was afterwards killed; whence the men of
York ravaged the island of Lindisfarne, and slew many. The son
of Sihtric, named Onlaf, reigned over the Northumbrians.

A.D. 943. The Northumbrians drove their king Onlaf from his
kingdom.

A.D. 945. King Edmund, the two kings being expelled, obtained
the kingdom of the Northumbrians.

A.D. 948. King Edmund was slain, and his brother Edred
received the kingdom; he was a lover of justice and piety. Presently compassing Northumbria, he obtained possession of the
whole; but the Northumbrians, after swearing fealty to him, set
up a certain Dane, Eiric, as king over them.

A.D. 950. As king Eadred, having ravaged Northumbria, was
then retiring, the Northumbrians assailing him, cut off the rear of
his army. The king resolved to bring back his army and utterly
destroy the whole province, but the inhabitants casting off the king
whom they had appointed, speedily pacified Eadred with gifts.

A.D. 951. Ouvel,[1] king of the Britons, died.

A.D. 952. Here ended the kings of the Northumbrians; henceforth that province was governed by earls.

A.D. 953. Earl Osulf received the earldom of the Northumbrians.

A.D. 955. King Eadred dying, Eadwin succeeded him, the son
of Edmund who reigned before him.

A.D. 956. The blessed abbot Dunstan was expelled by Eadwin.

A.D. 957. At the death of Eadwin, his brother Eadgar succeeded
to the kingdom; he was a man of great devotion to the worship of
God, and therefore held the kingdom in peace and honour,
seventeen years,—eight kings being subject to him. After him
reigned his son Eadward, who, having been slain by the treachery
of his stepmother, rests at Shaftsbury. To him succeeded his brother
Ethelred, the father of king Edward, whom he had begotten of
Emma.

———————

* HERE follows a recapitulation of what has been said about
king Elfred. Then the succession of the kings in order,
who came, and in what way, to the kingdom of the Angles,
from the History of William of Malmesbury.[2]

*   *   *   *   *   *

ALTHOUGH others feared the truth of this prophecy, yet it
excited the derision of archbishop Stigand, who said, "The old man
being at the point of death raves about nonsense." Yet we have
experienced the truth of the prophecy; since England, indeed, has
become the habitation of foreigners, and been brought under the

———————

[1] This was Howel, surnamed Dha, or the Good. See Annales Cambriæ, ap.
Petrie and Hardy, p. 837.

[2] Simeon here introduces a long extract from William of Malmesbury's History
of the Kings, § 154, containing an account of king Edgar's vision, which it has not
been considered necessary to repeat in this place. He then continues as in the
text given above.

tyranny of strangers.   There is at this day not one Englishman,
either duke, or bishop, or abbot.   Foreigners altogether consume
the riches and prey on the bowels of England, nor is there any
hope of a termination of the misery.

In the year from our Lord's incarnation eight hundred and
forty-eight, Elfred, king of the Anglo-Saxons, was born in that
district called Berkshire; of whom the[1] genealogy is developed in
the following order:—King Elfred was the son of Athelwulf king of
the West Saxons; who was the son of Ecgbert, who was the son
of Ealhmund, who was the son of Eafa, who was the son of Eoppa,
who was the son of Ingles.   Ingles and Ine, that famous king of
the West Saxons, were two brothers.   This Ine went to Rome,
and there ending this present life, he went to reign with Christ
in a heavenly country, as Beda relates in his History of the
Angles.   They were the sons of Coenred, who was the son of
Ceolwald, who was the son of Cutha, who was the son of Cuthwine, who was the son of Ceaulin, who was the son of Cinric, who
was the son of Creoda, who was the son of Cerdic, who was the
son of Elesa, who was the son of Esla, who was the son of Gewis,
from whom the Britons name all that nation Gewis.   He was the
son of Wig, who was the son of Freawine, who was the son of
Freothegar, who was the son of Brand, who was the son of
Bealdeag, who was the son of Woden, who was the son of Frithe-
wald, who was the son of Frealaf, who was the son of Frithevulf,
who was the son of Fingoldvulf, who was the son of Geta.   This
Geta the pagans formerly worshipped as a god; of whom the poet
Sedulius thus makes mention in the commencement of his paschal
hymn:

> " With fictions false and vain
> The heathen poets, in high-sounding phrase,
>   And pompous tragic strain,
> Their art of song employ in foolish Geta's praise," &c.

This Geta was the son of Ceatuua, who was the son of Beau, who
was the son of Sceldwa, who was the son of Hermeod, who was
the son of Itermod, who was the son of Hatra, who was the son
of Wala, who was the son of Beaduing, who was the son of Sem,
who was the son of Noe, who was the son of Lamech, who was
the son of Matussalam, who was the son of Enoch, who was the
son of Malaleel, who was the son of Cainan, who was the son of
Enos, who was the son of Seth, who was the son of Adam.   Also
the mother of Elfred was called Osburh, a very religious woman,
noble, both by disposition and descent.   She was the daughter of
Oslac, the famous cupbearer of king Athelvulf.   This Oslac was a
Goth by nation; for he was sprung from the Goths and Jutes, of
the stock, namely, of Stuf and Withgar, two brothers, and also
earls, who, having received the government of the Isle of Wight,
from their uncle king Cerdic and his son Cinric their cousin, put

---

[1] See Asser, p. 443; the Saxon Chronicle, A.D. 855, and Florence of Worcester,
A.D. 849.   It may be sufficient to state, once for all, that as Simeon is under considerable obligations to Asser at this portion of his work, the narrative of that
latter author should be compared with the narrative now printed.

to death at the place called Withgaraburh[1] [Carisbrook], the few
Britons, inhabitants of that island, whom they could find in it. For
the other inhabitants of that island had either been slain or
banished, or had fled.

A.D. 851. Karl, earl of Devon, encountered the pagans at the
place called Wincanbeorh, and the Christians obtained the victory.
The Danes also united in the isle called Sheppey, that is, The isle
of sheep. In the same year a great host of pagans came, with
three hundred and fifty ships, into the mouth of the river Thames,
and pillaged Canterbury, that is, the city of the Kentish men, and
put to flight, with his whole army, Berthulf, king of the Mercians,
who had come out to battle against them. After this the Danes
becoming bolder, their whole army was collected in Surrey. Information of this reaching Athelvulf, the warlike king of the Saxons,
he also, and with him his son Ethelbald, assembled a large army
at the place called Aclea, that is, The plain of the oak. And
when the flower of the English nation appeared resplendent in
clashing armour, there ensued a long engagement between the
Angles and Danes; the Angles fighting the more bravely as they
saw their king conduct himself so fiercely in war; and thus they
proved superior to their enemies, and after a long and stout contest,
in which both sides fought with courage and animosity, the greater
part of the pagan multitude was utterly routed and cut to pieces,
so that never in any country in one day, either before or since,
had so many met their death. The Christians on that day obtained
a noble victory, and were masters of the field of slaughter, rendering thanks to God in hymns and acknowledgments.

A.D. 852.[2] Berthulf, king of the Mercians, departed this life,
whom Burhred succeeded in the kingdom. In that year king
Ethelstane and earl Alchere met a great army of the pagans in
Kent, at the place called Sandwich, which then, by the help of
God, they almost totally destroyed, and took nine of their ships;
the rest, struck with dread, took to flight.

A.D. 853, (the fifth[3] of the birth of Elfred,) Burhred, king of the
Mercians, by ambassadors besought Athelvulf, king of the West
Saxons, that he would grant him assistance by which he might
bring under his power the Midland Britons, who dwell between
Mercia and the West sea, who were violently opposing him. King
Athelvulf, in receiving his embassy, quickly put his army in motion
and marched into Britain [Wales] with king Burhred, and no sooner
had he entered than, devastating that nation, he reduced it to the
dominion of Burhred. This being accomplished, he returned home.

In the same year Athelvulf sent his aforesaid son Elfred (when
he was five years old) to Rome, honourably attended by a great
number both of nobles and persons of inferior rank. Whom the holy
pope Leo [IV.] consecrating at the request of his father, anointed
as king; and taking him to himself as the son of his adoption,
confirmed him, and sent him back to his father with his blessing.

---

[1] See the Saxon Chronicle, A.D. 534 and 544.
[2] A.D. 853. Saxon Chronicle and Florence of Worcester.
[3] See Asser, p. 445, note [1].

A.D. 854, (the sixth of the birth of king Elfred,) king Osbert reigning over the Northumbrians, Wlfere, having received his pall, was consecrated to the archbishopric of York, and Eardulf received the bishopric of Lindisfarne; to which belonged Lugubalia, that is, Luel, now called Carlisle, and Norham, anciently called Ubbanford. Also all the churches from the river Tweed to the South Tyne, and beyond the wild country to the west, at that time belonged to the aforesaid church; and these manors, Carham, and Culterham, and the two Jedburghs, which bishop Ecgred built on the south side of the Teviot; and Melrose, and Tigbrethingham, and Eoriercorn on the west side; Edinburgh, and Pefferham, and Aldham, and Tiningham, and Coldingham, and Tillmouth, and the aforesaid Norham. Warkworth also, with all its appurtenances, was the property of the said church by the gift of king Ceolwlf. For that king, on his renunciation of the world, bestowed that manor, with himself, on the church of Lindisfarne, in which, becoming a monk, he fought for a heavenly kingdom. His body, afterwards transferred to the church of the aforesaid vill of Norham, was there graced by many miracles, as is reported by the inhabitants of that place. Through the means of this king, when he became a monk, there was given to the monks of the church of Lindisfarne the privilege of drinking wine or ale; before that time they used to drink nothing but milk or water, according to the tradition which they had anciently received from St. Aidan, monk and first bishop of that church, coming with whom from Scotland they there received a place of residence, by the gift of king Oswald, and who, providing for a future life, took pleasure in living with great severity. Furthermore, the celebrated bishop Ecgred, having built a church at the place called Gainford, dedicated it to St. Cuthbert. He built also Billingham in Heorternysse, and two other vills, Ilecliff and Wilegeclife, in the south side of the river Tees, which he gave to St. Cuthbert, for the support of his servants. Also Wudecestre, and Hwittingeham, and Eadulfingaham [Edlingham], and Egwiluingeham [Eglingham], were formerly the property of St. Cuthbert, by the gift of king Ceolwlf.

In this year carl Ealchere, with the Kentish men, and duke Wada, with the men of Surrey, fought a hard battle against the pagans, in the Isle of Thanet. At the first encounter the Christians prevailed; but, after long-continued fighting, many on each side fell by the sword, some were drowned in the sea, and at length both chiefs perished.

In this year, Athelvulf, king of the West Saxons, gave his daughter in marriage to Burhred, king of the Mercians, in the royal vill called Chippenham, with profuse liberality of every kind.

A.D. 855. A large host of pagans took up their quarters for the whole winter in the isle of Sheppey, that is, The isle of sheep. In the same year king Athelvulf freed the tenth part of his kingdom from all royal service and tribute, and dedicated it by a perpetual deed of gift on the cross of Christ, to God, One and Three, for the salvation of his own soul and those of his predecessors; and so he went with great honour to Rome, taking also with him now his son

Elfred, whom he had before sent to Rome, and whom he loved
more than the rest; and there he remained for a whole year : at
the end of which he returned to his own country, bringing with
him Judith, the daughter of Charles, king of the Franks.   King
Athelwulf then lived two years after he went to Rome.   Amongst
other good deeds which he performed, he enjoined three hundred
mancuses of money to be sent yearly to Rome : one hundred in
honour of St. Peter, for the purchase of oil to fill all the lamps of
that church on Easter eve, and likewise at the cock-crow ; one
hundred also in honour of St. Paul the apostle, for the same purpose; and one hundred marks for the universal apostolic pope.

After his death and interment at Winchester,[1] his son Ethelbald
governed the kingdom of the West Saxons after his father for two
years and a half; who, contrary to the prohibition of Jesus Christ
and the teaching of Christians, contrary also to the custom of all
heathens, going up to the bed of his father, with great infamy, took
in marriage Judith, the daughter of Charles, king of the Franks.
At the same time the most holy and beloved of God, Eadmund,
sprung from the race of the Old Saxons, a most sincere professor
of the Christian faith, attained the dignity of the government of the
province of East Anglia.

A.D. 860. King Ethelbald died and was buried in Sherborne,
and his brother Ethelberht, as was right, annexed to his dominion
Kent and Surrey, and also Sussex.   In his days a great host of
pagans, coming by sea, attacked and plundered the city of Winchester.   As they were retreating to their vessels with great booty,
they were opposed by Osric, earl of the men of Hampshire, with
his followers, and earl Ethelwulf, with the men of Berkshire, and
joining battle, the pagans were everywhere routed ; and, being
unable any longer to resist, they betook themselves to womanish
flight, and the Christians were masters of the field of slaughter.

Ethelberht then, after having governed the kingdom for five
years, peacefully, mildly and honourably, went the way of all flesh,
to the great grief of his subjects, and rests honourably interred near
his brother in Sherborne.

A.D. 863. St. Swithun, bishop of Winchester, in this year
departed to the Lord.

A.D. 864. The pagans wintered in the Isle of Thanet, and made
a sure league with the Kentish men, who promised to pay them
a sum of money for the preservation of the treaty.   In the mean
while, however, the pagans, stealing out like foxes secretly by night
from their camp, in violation of the treaty, and despising the promise of money, as knowing that they could obtain a greater sum by
thievish robbery than by peace, devastated the whole east border
of Kent.

A.D. 866. Ethered, brother of king Ethelbert, took the government of the kingdom of the West Saxons.

In the same year a great fleet of pagans, under the command of
king Haldane, Inguar, and Hubba, came to Britain from the

[1] See Asser, p. 448, note [1].

Danube,[1] and wintered in the kingdom of the East Angles, called
in Saxon East Angle ; and there that army became for the most
part cavalry, riding and making excursions hither and thither,
seizing enormous booty, and sparing neither men nor women,
widows nor virgins.

[2] In these days Elfred, that is Clito, or the Atheling, began, by
constant study, to be imbued with divine doctrines, who from his
very cradle was loved by his father and mother with extraordinary
affection beyond all his brothers. 'As he grew in stature to a boy's
age, he appeared more graceful in person than the rest of his
brothers, and was remarkable for the bright expression of his countenance, and the elegance of his speech. As the hart pants for the
waterbrooks, so he longed that the depths of his heart and recesses
of his mind should be penetrated and imbued with sound learning.
But grievous to say, by the neglect of his parents and tutors, he
remained illiterate till the twelfth year of his age. But this illustrious youth and future king endeavoured day and night to learn
the Saxon poems ; he was teachable, well practised in the art of
the chase, and unequalled in skill of every kind. One day, as his
excellent mother was showing him and his brothers a certain Saxon
book of poetry, she said to them, " Whichever of you, my dearest
sons, can soonest learn this volume, I will give it to him." He
then, moved by a divine inspiration, and delighted with the beauty
of the capital letter, replied to his mother, " Will you indeed give
it ? " She, smiling with gladness, assented, saying, " I will ; I will
indeed give it." He presently took the book from the hand of his
mother, went to his tutor, showed him the book, and read under
the preceptor's instruction. After no long interval, he came into
the presence of his beloved mother, and repeated the book from
memory. She gave great thanks to the Saviour's goodness, acknowledging that the grace of God was in the mind of the youth. After
this, inflamed with the desire of divine love, he devoutly learnt
very many Psalms, and the Daily Course, that is, the celebration of
the hours, which, collected into one volume, he carried inseparably
day and night in his bosom. O happy offspring of men ! O saga-
cious king ! you carry that which bears you up ; you carry the keys
of wisdom ; you love wisdom and shall be wise, doing justice and
judgment in the earth. O clerics, attend and behold the king carry
the book in his bosom day and night ; you neither know nor desire
to know the law of God. The[3] same man, when he became king,
especially bewailed for his son, that is his mind, that he had not
been instructed in liberal arts.

A.D. 867. The aforesaid host of pagans marched from the East
Angles to the city of York, which is situated on the north side of
the river Humber, and devastated the whole country as far as
Tynemouth.

At that time, by the instigation of the devil, a great feud had
arisen among the Northumbrians, as is always wont to happen to a
people who will incur God's anger. For the Northumbrians had

[1] See Asser, p. 449, note [6].   [2] Compare Asser, p. 450.   [3] See p. 469, note [1].

at that time expelled from the kingdom their rightful king, Osbryth
by name, and had set at the head of the government a certain
tyrant, not born of the royal lineage, named Ella.   But on the
arrival of the pagans, that dissension was somewhat allayed by
divine counsel and the union of the nobles for the common weal.
Osbryth and Ella, joining their strength and assembling an army,
marched to the town of York.   Immediately on their approach,
the pagans took to flight, and endeavoured to defend themselves
within the walls of the city.   The Christians, perceiving their
flight and dread, resolved to follow them within the fortifications of
the city, and to effect a breach in the wall; and this they also did;
for at that time the city had not strong and secure walls.   When the
Christians had broken down the wall, as they proposed, and a great
part of them had entered the city at the same time as the pagans,
the latter, urged by distress and necessity, made a fierce assault
upon them, beat, scattered and overthrew them within and without.
This took place on the twelfth of the kalends of April [21st March],
being the Friday before Palm Sunday.[1]   There nearly all the
Northumbrians were routed and destroyed, the two kings being
slain; the survivors made peace with the pagans.   [2]After these
events the aforesaid pagans appointed Egbert king under their own
dominion; Egbert reigned for six years after, over the Northumbrians beyond the Tyne.

In the same year, Ealhstan, bishop of the church of Sherborne,
died, and was buried in Sherborne.

A.D. 868. A comet was very plainly seen this year.   The worshipful king Elfred, then holding the rank of second personage in
the realm, wooed and obtained in marriage a wife from Mercia,
noble in descent, to wit the daughter of Athelred, earl of the Gaini,[3]
who was surnamed Mucil.   The mother of this lady was called
Eadburg, of the royal line of the Mercian kings; a woman indeed
much to be honoured, and who remained a most chaste widow till
her death, many years after the death of her husband.

In the same year the aforesaid host of pagans, quitting the
Northumbrians, came into Mercia, and entered Nottingham, which
in British is rendered Tigguocabauc,[4] but in Latin Speluncarum
Domus, The house of caves; and in that place they wintered the
same year.   When they arrived there, immediately Burhred, king
of the Mercians, and all the nobles of that nation, sent messengers
to Ethered, king of the West Saxons, and his brother Elfred, humbly
beseeching them to grant them assistance, in order that they might
wage war against the aforesaid host.   This they easily obtained, for
these brothers, not behind their promise, gathering an army from
every part of their territory, entered Mercia, and marched at once
to Nottingham, with one mind desiring battle.   And when the
pagans, defended by the protection of the castle, refused to give
battle, and the Christians were unable to break down the wall,
peace being made between the Mercians and the pagans, these two

---

[1] This date does not occur in Asser, the Saxon Chronicle, or Florence.
[2] An addition to Asser.   [3] See Asser, p. 451, note [5].
[4] See this volume, p. 470, note [1].

brothers, king Elthered and Elfred, returned home with their troops.

A.D. 869. The aforesaid host of pagans again riding to the Northumbrians, entered the city of York, and there remained a whole year.

A.D. 870. The above-named host of pagans passed through Mercia to the East Angles, and took winter quarters in the place called Thetford. In the same year the most holy Eadmund, king of the East Angles, was martyred, as we read in his Passion,[1] by the most heathen king Inguar, on Sunday[2] the twelfth of the kalends of December [20th Nov.], in the second indiction. With him bishop Humbert[3] also was slain. In this year, likewise, Ceolnoth, archbishop of Canterbury, died; to whom succeeded Ethered.

A.D. 871. The host of pagans of detested memory, leaving the East Angles, and entering the kingdom of the West Saxons, came to the royal vill called Reading, situated on the south bank of the river Thames, in that district called Berkshire. On the third day after their arrival, two of their earls, with a large portion of their army, rode out to plunder, while the rest were constructing a wall between the two rivers, Thames and Kennet, on the right side of that royal vill. Athelwulf, earl of the district of Berkshire, encountered them in the place called in English, Englafield, the Plain of the Angles. There a severe engagement took place, which was long and sharply contested on both sides; at last one of the earls of the pagans was slain, and the greater part of the army routed, the rest escaping by flight; and thus the Christians obtaining the victory, were masters of the field of slaughter.

Four days after these events occurred, king Ethered and his brother Elfred, uniting their strength, assembled an army and marched upon Reading. And when they had come to the very gate of the citadel, slaying and overthrowing all of the pagans whom they encountered outside the fortress, the pagans with no less energy fought like wolves; and sallying from all the gates, they threw their whole force into the battle, and then both parties fought long and fiercely on both sides. But, lamentable to state! the Christians at length turning their backs, the pagans obtained the victory, and remained masters of the field of slaughter. And there, amongst others, fell the aforesaid earl Ethelwulf.

The Christians, stirred by this grief and shame, again, after four days, go out with all their forces and with eager desire to battle against the aforesaid army, at the place called Escendun,[4] which means, The hill of the ash. But the pagans, dividing into two bands of uniform strength, make themselves ready for battle. For they had their two kings and many earls; assigning one half the army to the two kings, the other to all the earls. The Christians, observing this, also divided their army into two bands, and formed

---

[1] A reference, apparently, to the legend by Abbo.

[2] This date, added to Asser, is incorrect; the twentieth of November fell upon Monday, and the year 870 was the third of the indiction.

[3] Bishop of Dunwich, or Elmham. See Hardy's Le Neve, ii. 457.

[4] See Asser, p. 453, note [1].

their defence with no less activity; but Elfred, with his men, came more quickly and promptly to the field of battle. For indeed his brother, king Ethered, was then in his tent engaged in prayer, hearing mass, and vowing that he would not stir before the priest had finished mass, for that he would not leave the service of God for that of man. And so he did. And this trust of the Christian king was of much avail before God, as will be more clearly shown in the result. The Christians then decided that king Ethered, with his forces, should meet the attack of the two pagan kings; and his brother Elfred was informed, that with his troops he must try the fortune of war against all the dukes of the pagans. These arrangements having been made on both sides—since the king delayed very long in prayer, and the pagans, fully prepared, were coming up with great speed to the field of battle,—Elfred, then second in rank, no longer able to endure the hostile array without either retreating from the engagement, or throwing himself into the battle against the enemy's forces before the arrival of his brother, at last, although the king had not come, boldly, like a wild boar, forming the Christian forces against the enemy's army as before settled, relying on the divine counsel and supported by his aid, quickly advanced his banners against the enemy, a defence of shields being constructed in good order. At length, the prayers in which he was engaged being ended, king Ethered arrived, and, having invoked the great Ruler of the world, speedily applied himself to the fight. But here it must be notified to the uninformed, that the field of battle was not equally advantageous for the contending parties: for the pagans had pre-occupied the higher position; the Christians formed their line on the lower ground. There was also in the same place one thorn-tree of no great size, around which the opposing forces met in conflict, with loud cries on both sides,—the one were the workers of wickedness, the other were fighting for life, and friends, and country. After a contest carried on for a considerable time with animosity and much fierceness, the pagans, by the judgment of God, being no longer able to resist the attack of the Christians, the greater part of their men having fallen, betook themselves to a shameful flight. In this place one of the two kings of the pagans, and five earls, fell dead; and many thousands of them in the same place, and moreover, over the whole breadth of the plain of Ashendon, being everywhere scattered and routed, perished.

There died king Bagseg, earl Sidroc the elder, earl Sidroc the younger, earl Osbern, earl Freana, earl Harold; and the whole army of the pagans fled until night, and even till the following day, until those who escaped reached the fortress.

Again, fourteen days after this action, king Ethered, together with his brother Alfred, uniting their forces, marched against the pagans at Basing. An engagement ensued, which lasted a long time, when the pagans obtained the victory.

Again,[1] after the lapse of two months, king Ethered and his brother Elfred, encountering the pagans who had divided them-

[1] Compare Asser, p. 454.

selves into two bodies, were for a long time victorious, forcing their adversaries to retreat. But they rallying again, many fell on both sides, and the pagans gaining the victory, remained masters of the field of slaughter.

In the same year, after Easter [15th April], king Ethered, having for five years, amidst many tribulations, governed the kingdom energetically and honourably with good fame, went the way of all flesh.[1] At his death his brother Elfred began to reign.

A.D. 871. This most skilled of the Saxon poets, and most zealous in the service of God, became also a most discerning inquirer in the administration of justice. To him his queen Elfswitha bore two sons, Eadward and Egelward, and three daughters, Eglefleda, the lady of the Mercians, Ethelgeova, a nun, and Ethelthritha.

One month after the commencement of his reign, he, with a few men, fought bravely against the pagans at the hill called Wilton ; but, sad to say, the enemy obtained the victory. And no wonder ; for the Christians had but a small number in the battle. For they had been worn out by eight battles in one year against the pagans, in which one king of the pagans and nine chiefs, with innumerable troops, were slain.

A.D. 872. Alchun, bishop of the Wiccii, dying, Werefrith,[2] brought up at the holy church of Worcester, a man very learned in holy Scripture, was consecrated bishop on Whitsunday,[3] the seventh of the ides of June [7th June], by Athered, archbishop of Canterbury. He, by the command of king Elfred, translated the books of Dialogues of the blessed pope Gregory, from the Latin into the Saxon tongue.

The Northumbrians expelled their king Egbert, and their archbishop Wlfere. The aforesaid host of pagans went to London and wintered there; the Mercians made peace with them.

A.D. 873. The oft-named army, quitting London, marched first to the country of the Northumbrians, and there wintered at Torksey, in the district called Lindsey ; the Mercians again made peace with them.

Egbert, king of the Northumbrians, dying, Ricsig became his successor, and reigned three years; Wlfere was restored to his archbishopric.

A.D. 874. The above-named host, quitting Lindsey, entered Mercia, and wintered at the place called Repton. Burhtred, king of the Mercians, having been expelled by them in the twenty-second year of his reign, went to Rome, and there died, and was buried in the church of St. Mary, in the school of the Saxons.

A.D. 875. The above-named host, leaving Repton, formed two divisions ; one of which, under Halfdene, marching into the country of the Northumbrians, brought the whole region of the Northumbrians under their dominion, and destroyed all the monasteries.

---

[1] On the twenty-fourth of April.   [2] See Asser, p. 465, note [1].
[3] This date, copied by Simeon from Florence of Worcester (p. 220), fixes the consecration of Werefrith as having occurred in 873, and not in 872, as these writers supposed.

Eardulf, bishop of Lindisfarne, and abbot Eadred, taking the body
of St. Cuthbert from the island of Lindisfarne, wandered about for
seven years.

The other division of the host, under the three kings, Guthrum,
Oskitel, and Amund, wintered at Cambridge.

King Elfred, equipped for naval warfare, encountered six ships
on the sea, bravely engaging with which he took one; the rest,
seized with alarm, fled.

A.D. 876. The pagan king Halfdene divided between himself and
his followers the country of the Northumbrians. Ricsig, king of
the Northumbrians, died, and Egbert the second reigned over
the Northumbrians beyond the river Tyne.

Rollo, first duke of the Normans, also called Rodbert, with
his men, invaded Normandy on the fifteenth of the kalends of
December [17th Nov.].

The aforesaid host of pagans, leaving Cambridge by night, seized
the castle of Wareham. Of whose sudden coming the king of the
Saxons being informed, he made a treaty with them, on condition of
their quitting his kingdom, receiving hostages from them. But
they, in their usual manner, caring for neither oaths nor hostages,
one night, in violation of the treaty, made a march upon Exeter,
which in British is called Cairwisc, in Latin, Civitas Aquæ, The city
of water.

A.D. 877.[1] That infamous host left Exeter, went to the royal
vill of Chippenham, and there wintered. At this period, king
Elfred endured great distresses and led a harassed life. At length,
encouraged by St. Cuthbert in an obvious revelation, he gave
battle to the Danes, and at the very place and time which the
saint had ordered ; he obtained the victory; and ever after that was
to his enemies terrible and invincible, and held St. Cuthbert in
especial honour. How he overcame his enemies soon after is here
recorded.

Further, in the same year, kings Inguar and Haldene, with
twenty-three ships, rushing with the fierceness of wolves from the
Demetic territory, in which they had wintered, after perpetrating
great slaughter of Christians and burning of monasteries, sailed to
Devonshire, and there were slain with twelve hundred men by the
brave ministers of king Elfred before the castle of Cymwith, for
very many of the king's servants had shut themselves up in that
castle for protection. And king Elfred, trusting in the Lord God,
attended by a few troops, made a fortress at the place called
Athelney, occupying which with his soldiers he frequently and
indefatigably harassed the enemy from the fortress. This he did
at the time of the resurrection of our Lord Jesus Christ [7th
April]; and seven weeks and one day (that is, fifty days) after, he
came to Egbert's stone, in the east part of the forest called in the
English language Mucel Wudu, in Latin, Magna Silva, The great
wood, and in British, Coitmapur. There all the inhabitants of
Somerset, Wiltshire, and Hampshire, met their much-loved king ;
and at the sight of him rejoiced with great exultation of heart, as

[1] Compare Asser, A.D. 878, p. 457.

if they had received one raised from the dead.   The third day
after, he came with an immense army to the place called Edderandun,[1] near which he found enormous battalions of pagans,
arrayed for battle in a dense mass.   Both nations engaged in
combat for a great part of the day, their shouts and clashing of
arms being heard to a great distance.   At last king Elfred, by the
help of God, obtained the victory, bravely overthrowing his enemies,
and rendering thanks to the most high Saviour with joyfulness of
heart.   And while there, the king with his people rejoiced; and
those of the enemy who survived wept with great lamentations, on
account of the severity of cold and hunger, and their dread of so
powerful a monarch ; they beg the favour of peace who were always
opposed to it, and offer hostages and oaths.   The king, inwardly
moved with pity, giving ear to their request, granted all they
begged for.

A. D. 878.[2] Guthrum, king of the pagans, with thirty of the
most select men of his army, came to king Elfred, at the place
called Aarl [Aller]; the king, receiving him as the son of his
adoption, caused him to be cleansed in the font of holy baptism,
and enriched him with many gifts ; and after the murder of St.
Eadmund, gave him East Anglia.

A. D. 879. The oft-named host of pagans departing, as they had
promised, from Cirencester, went to the East Angles, and dividing
that country, began to take up their residence in it.   In that year
also, there came an immense army of pagans from foreign regions
into the river Thames, who, forming a junction with the aforesaid
body, became banded together, as is the manner of the wicked.
An eclipse of the sun took place in the same year, between the
ninth hour and the evening.   The aforesaid host of pagans also
went this year into foreign countries, and remained one year at
Ghent.

A. D. 881. The host of pagans invading France engaged in fight
with the natives ; after which battle, seizing horses wherever they
could, they rode here and there, laying all things waste ; this must
appear wonderful, that these unskilled enemies should dare to
make an attack upon so brave and warlike a people.   The bold
Franks, forming a prudent plan, fought a hard battle with the
pagans, and were the conquerors.   At the end of the engagement
the Franks returned in triumph ; the pagans rode in all directions
on the horses which they had obtained.   In those days very many
monasteries in that nation were sacked and desolated ; insomuch
that the brethren of the monastery of St. Benedict, which is called
Floriacum, taking with them his relics from the tomb where they
had been laid with great splendour, wandered hither and thither.

A. D. 882. The aforesaid army was transported into the further
part of France in vessels up the river Maese, and there wintered
one year.

In the same year, king Elfred, engaging in a sea fight with the
ships of the pagans, conquered and took two, the whole of their

---

[1] See Asser, p. 459, note [6].
[2] In Asser (p. 460), this forms a portion of the incidents of the previous year.

crews being slain. After this, also, he severely wounded the captains of two vessels, until throwing down their arms, they gave themselves up to him with suppliant entreaty.

A.D. 883. The aforesaid army of pagans, seizing Condé, ravaged there for a year.

The army which, under the command of king Halfdene, had invaded Northumbria, the tyrant perishing by the judgment of God, remained without a leader; Halfdene himself being destroyed, as above stated, together with Inguar, with twenty-three ships, by the ministers of king Elfred in Devonshire. Having already subdued the natives of the country, he usurped the government, and prepared to inhabit the devastated provinces of Northumbria. Then St. Cuthbert, aiding by a vision, ordered abbot Eadred (who because he lived in Luel was surnamed Lulisc) to tell the bishop and the whole army of Angles and Danes, that by paying a ransom, they should redeem Guthred, the son of Hardicnut, whom the Danes had sold as a slave to a certain widow at Whittingham, and should raise him, then redeemed, to be king; and he reigned over York, but Egbert over the Northumbrians. This took place in the thirteenth year of the reign of king Elfred. Guthred, therefore, being by consent of all from a slave promoted to be king, the episcopal see, which was formerly in the island of Lindisfarne, was restored in Chester,[1] anciently called Cunecester, seven years after its removal from the island of Lindisfarne. This is a place between Durham and Hexham, six miles distant from Durham. There also king Guthred, as well as king Elfred, established, to be for ever preserved, the right of sanctuary which St. Cuthbert had enjoined by the aforesaid abbot; namely, that whosoever took refuge at his body should have sanctuary, to be infringed by no one for thirty-seven days. And if any one in any way violated this privilege, they decreed that he be fined ninety-six pounds, as if he had broken the king's peace. Besides this, in augmentation of the former bishopric, the two kings aforesaid, with the consent of all, added the whole land between the Tyne and the Tees, as a perpetual possession of St. Cuthbert. They delivered over, by a perpetual anathema, to the pains of hell, whosoever should attempt by any device to infringe these statutes. Long before this the bishopric of the church of Hexham had ceased to exist.

A.D. 884. Pope Marinus, out of affection for king Elfred, and at his request, graciously freed the school of the Saxons living in Rome from all tribute and custom, and also sent many presents to the aforesaid king. Among which he gave him a considerable portion of that holy cross on which our Lord Jesus Christ hung for the salvation of mankind. Also, at that time, this most holy prelate went the way of all flesh, resigning his spirit to God who gave it.

The aforesaid army of pagans, going up the river Somme to Amiens, there continued for a year.

---

[1] That is, Chester-le-street.

In the time of this king Alfred there came to England Johannes[1] Scotus, a man of clear intellect and much eloquence, who, leaving his country some time before, had gone over to France to Charles the Bald. By him he was received with great respect, and was admitted to close intimacy. He took part with him in matters both of business and amusement, and was his inseparable companion both at table and in his retirement. He was a man of much pleasantry and ready wit, examples of which are still on record; as, for instance, as he was sitting at dinner one day, at the other side of the table opposite the king, after the cups had gone round and the dishes had been removed, after some other matters, Charles with a gay face, having seen that John had done something which might offend Gallic politeness, chid him in a pleasant manner, and said, " What difference is there between a sot and a Scot?" He cleverly returned the joke upon its author, and replied, " Only this table." What can be more facetious than this reply? The king's question referred to the difference of manners, John's answer referred to the difference of place. Nor was the king offended, because he was delighted with his marvellous learning ; nor would he for the jest be angry at the master, as he commonly called him. On another occasion, when a servant had handed to the king at table a dish which contained two very large fishes and one much smaller, he gave it to that master that he might share it with two clerics seated beside him. They were of gigantic stature, and he very small in person. He then, who was always devising something amusing to excite the mirth of the company, keeping the two large fishes for himself, gave the small one to the other two. When the king charged him with the unfairness of the division—" Nay," said he, " I have done well and fairly; for here is one small one," speaking of himself, " and two large ones," pointing to the fishes; " and there also are two great ones," meaning the clerics, " and one small one," pointing to the fish.

At the request of Charles, he translated the Hierarchia of Dionysius the Areopagite, from Greek into Latin, word for word ; in consequence of which it comes to pass, that the Latin version can˙ hardly be understood, since the Greek style is more fluent than ours. He also composed a book which he entitled, Περὶ φύσεων μερισμοῦ, " Concerning the Division of Nature," very useful for solving the difficulty of certain questions, if only allowance may be made for him in certain points, where, by a rigid following of the Greeks, he has deviated from the track of the Latins. On which account he has been considered heretical by some, and one Florus[2] wrote against him : for there are indeed in his book, Περὶ φύσεων, very many things which, if they be not carefully digested,

---

[1] See Asser, p. 466; William of Malmesbury's History of the Kings, p. 122. The question of the identity of this Johannes Scotus with John the Martyr of Malmesbury, is discussed at some length by M. Arnaud in his " Perpétuité de la Foi touchant l'Eucharistie," iv. 177, ed. 1704.

[2] This treatise of Florus Lugdunensis is printed by Mauguin, in his collection of treatises respecting Predestination and Grace, i. 575, ed. Paris, 1650.

may appear repugnant[1] to the catholic faith.   Pope[2] Nicholas is
known to have shared in this opinion, for in an epistle to Charles
he says, " It has been reported to our apostleship that one of your
friends, John, a Scot by birth, has lately translated into Latin
a work of the blessed Dionysius the Areopagite, which he wrote in
the Greek tongue, concerning the divine ranks or celestial orders,
which, according to custom, ought to be sent to us, and presented
for our judgment, especially as the said John, though declared to
be a man of much learning, is marked by common report as
formerly thinking unsoundly on some points."   On account of
this ill report, he grew tired of France and came to king Elfred,
allured by his munificence; and by his appointment, as is plain
from the king's writings, he settled at Malmesbury.   There, after
many years, he lost his life, in severe and painful torture, pierced
by the iron pens of the youths whom he taught; so that he suffered
a cruel death: for a weak hand, urged by strong wickedness, often
failed, and again as often renewed the attack.   For some time he
lay in an unhonoured tomb in the church of St. Lawrence, which
had been the scene of his heinous murder; but when the divine
favour for many nights shed over him a light of fire, the monks,
thus admonished, translated him into the greater church, and
placed him on the left side of the altar.

A.D. 885.   The aforesaid host formed itself into two divisions,
one of which went to the east of France; the other, going back
into Kent, laid siege to the city of Rochester.   But the citizens
bravely resisted them, until king Elfred, coming upon them with
a strong force, drove those pagans from the siege to their vessels;
and in the summer of the same year they returned to France.   In
this year, a fleet, sent by king Elfred to the defence of the places
about East Anglia, having captured sixteen vessels of pirates at the
mouth of the river Stour, put them all to death; but as they
were returning home, the barbarian host brought to oppose them
an infinite number of ships, with which, after a long engagement,
the Danes became victorious.

In this year Carloman, king of the Alemanni, the West Franks,
by a singular accident in hunting, was killed by a boar rending him
with its tusk.   His brother Louis, also king of the Franks, had died
the preceding year.   They were both sons of Louis, king of the
Franks, who died in the afore-named year in which the eclipse of
the sun occurred.   Also he was the son of Charles the Bald, king
of the Franks, whose daughter Judith, Ethelwlf, king of the West
Saxons, took as his queen.

In this year a large army of pagans from Germany was conveyed
in ships into the country of the Old Saxons; against whom the
Saxons and Frieslanders, uniting their strength, fought two battles
in one year and obtained the victory.   In this year, with the free
consent of all, Charles, king of the Alemanni, took, besides the

---

[1] On the orthodoxy or heterodoxy of Johannes Scotus, see a dissertation by
Oudin, ii. 245.
[2] This letter occurs in Labb. Concil. viii. 516, "De Joanne Scotto, quod in
quibusdam bene non senserit."

kingdom of Brittany, the kingdom of the West Franks, and all the
kingdoms which are between the Tuscan sea and the arm of the
sea which divides the Old Saxons and Gauls.   This Charles was
the son of Louis ; Louis was the brother of Charles, king of the
Franks, the father of the aforesaid Judith; and these two brothers
were the sons of Louis.   And this Louis was the son of the famous
and most wise Charlemagne, who was the son of king Pepin.

A.D. 886.   Pope Marinus[1] died.   [2]The oft-named army which
had before retired to the East Franks, returning again to the West
Franks, went up to Paris by the river Seine, where beleaguering the
city for a year, and the citizens bravely resisting, they could not
make a breach in the fortifications.

King Elfred nobly rebuilt and made habitable the city of London,
after many fires and slaughters of the people, and committed it to
the care of Ethered, earl of the Mercians.   All the Angles and
Saxons, who before had been everywhere scattered, or had been with
the pagans without being captives, came to the king and freely surrendered themselves to his dominion.

A.D. 887.   The aforesaid host, quitting Paris, on which they
could make no impression, took their fleet up the Seine, to the
place called Chezy, where they remained a year; and in the following year, entering the mouth of the river Yonne, they spent a year
there, to the great injury of the country.   In this year Charles,
king of the Franks, died ; six weeks after he had been driven from
the kingdom by Earnulf, his brother's son.   At his death the kingdom was divided into five, but the chief part came to Earnulf, to
whom the four others, of their own accord, swore fealty and yielded
submission, because none of the others could claim to be legitimate
heir of that kingdom by paternal descent, except Earnulf alone ;
for the government rested with him.   And this was the division of
the kingdom :—Earnulf obtained the countries east of the river
Rhine ; Hrodulf, the midland kingdom ; Odo the west ; Beorngar
and Wido had Lombardy, and all the countries on that side of the
mountain.   But these kingdoms, thus divided among themselves,
were shaken by great wars with each other; the kings expelling one
another from the realm.   In this year Ethelhelm, earl of the Wiltshire men, carried to Rome the alms of king Elfred.[3]

A.D. 888.   Among the many other good deeds which king Elfred
performed, he founded two noble monasteries, one of monks, in the
place called Athelney, that is, The isle of nobles, where monks
of different nations being brought together, he appointed as the
first abbot John, priest and monk, of the race of the Old Saxons.
The same king also ordered to be built another monastery, near the
east gate of Shaftesbury, fit for the habitation of nuns, in which he
placed as abbess his own daughter, Ethelgeofa, a virgin dedicated
to God, which two monasteries he munificently enriched with possession of lands and all abundance.

---

[1] See the Saxon Chronicle, A.D. 885. Marinus died A.D. 884, probably in the
month of May. See Jaffé, p. 293.   [2] Saxon Chronicle, A.D. 886.
[3] Here Asser ceasing to use the Saxon Chronicle, the similarity between that
latter authority and Simeon likewise is interrupted.

A.D. 889. Ethered, archbishop of Canterbury, died, and Plegmund succeeded him.

A.D. 891. King Guthrum, to whom king Elfred, as we before[1]
said, receiving from the holy font, gave the name of Healstan,
died this year. He dwelt with his followers in East Anglia; and
first inhabited and possessed that province after the martyrdom of
St. Eadmund the king.

A.D. 892. Wulfere, archbishop of York, died, in the thirty-ninth
year of his episcopate.

A.D. 893. The pagan king Hesten, entering the mouth of the
river Thames with eighty galleys, built himself a fortress in the
royal vill called Mideltun.

A.D. 894. Guthred, king of the Northumbrians, died. The
pagans who dwelt in Northumbria established a peace with king
Elfred by oaths.

A.D. 895. The pagans again towed their vessels up the river
Thames, and thence up the river Lee, and began to build themselves a fort near that river, twenty miles from London.

A.D. 896. In the summer time, a great part of the citizens of
London, and as many as possible from the neighbouring places,
endeavoured to destroy the fort which the pagans had built for
themselves; but they boldly resisting, the Christians were put to
flight, and four of the ministers of king Elfred were killed.

A.D. 897. The host of pagans dwelling in East Anglia and
Northumbria heavily oppressed the country of the West Saxons,
robbing and plundering on the sea coast, chiefly in long and swift
vessels, which they had built many years before. To oppose these,
vessels were built by command of king Elfred, twice as long, higher,
swifter, and less unsteady, by the force of which the said vessels
of the enemy might be overcome; which being launched, the king
ordered that they should take alive those whom they could, and put
to death those whom they could not take. Thus it came to pass, that
in that year twenty ships of Danish pirates were captured, of whom
some were slain, some brought alive to the king and hung on the
gallows.

A.D. 898. Rollo, the first duke of Normandy, with his army,
laid siege to the city of Chartres; but Walteline,[2] bishop of that
city, calling to his aid Richard, duke of Burgundy, and Ebalus, earl
of Poitou, carrying in their hands the tunic of St. Mary, by the
divine favour, put Rollo to flight, and delivered the city.

A.D. 899. Elfred, king of the Anglo-Saxons, son of the most pious
king Athelwulf, after reigning twenty-nine years and six months,
died in the fourth indiction, on the fifth of the kalends of November
[27th Oct.]; and was buried in the new monastery of Winchester.
To him succeeded his son Edward, surnamed the Elder, inferior in
polite learning, but in dignity, in power as well as glory, superior.
For, as will appear afterwards, he extended the boundaries of his
father's kingdom. He built many cities and towns, and rebuilt
some which had been destroyed. The whole of East Saxony, East

---

[1] A.D. 878.
[2] See this incident illustrated in the Gallia Christiana, viii. 1108.

Anglia, Northumbria, and many provinces of Mercia, which the
Danes had possessed for a long time, he wrested from their hands.
The whole of Mercia he obtained and held after the death of his
sister Egelfleda.   He received into submission all the kings of the
Scots, the Cumbrians, the Strathclyde and Western Britons.   Very
many kings and dukes were overcome by him in battle and slain.
Of a most noble woman, Egcuuinna, he had his first-born son
Ethelstan; and of his queen Edgiva he had three sons, Edwin, Ead-
mund and Edred, and a daughter Eadburga, a virgin dedicated to
God; and three daughters besides, of whom one became the wife of
Otto, eighty-ninth emperor of the Romans; another married Charles,
king of the West Franks, whose aunt Judith, the daughter of the
emperor Charles, Ethelwlf, king of the West Saxons, married; and
his third daughter, Sihtric, king of the Northumbrians, took to wife.

In this[1] year died Eardulf, bishop of Lindisfarne, to whom
Tuthred[2] succeeded.   Likewise Osbrit was expelled from his
kingdom.

A.D. 900. Ethelbald was consecrated archbishop of York.

A. D. 903. The most valiant duke Athulf, brother of queen
Ealhswitha, the mother of king Edward, and the venerable abbot Vir-
gilius, of Scotland, died.   Also the holy priest Grimbold, a man of
great sanctity, and one of king Elfred's teachers, ascended to the
joys of the heavenly kingdom.

A. D. 904. The Kentish men fought with a multitude of Danish
pirates, at the place called Holme, and were victorious.

A. D. 905. The religious servant of Christ, queen Elswitha,
mother of king Edward, departed this life ; she founded a monastery of nuns at Winchester.

A. D. 906. The host of pagans of East Anglia and Northumbria,
perceiving that king Eadward was invincible, made peace with him
at the place which is called in the language of the Angles, Ytinga-
ford.   In the same year died Rollo, also called Robert, first duke
of the Normans ; to whom succeeded his son William, called
Longsword.

A. D. 908. The city called in British Kairleir, and in Saxon Lega-
cester [Chester], was rebuilt by order of duke Ethered and
Egelfleda.

A. D. 910. The bones of St. Oswald, king and martyr, were translated from Bardonig into Mercia.   The indomitable king Eadward,
because the Danes had broken the contract which they had made
with him, sent an army of West Saxons and Mercians into Northumbria ; who, when they came there, devastating the country without
ceasing for about forty days, slew many of the Danes, and compelled their kings and dukes to renew with king Eadward the peace
which they had broken.

A.D. 911. A famous battle was fought in the district of Stafford,
at the place called Teotenhale, between the Angles and the Danes,
where the Angles obtained the victory.

A.D. 912. Ethered, a man of renowned virtue, duke and patri-

---

[1] See Florence of Worcester, A.D. 900, p. 233.
[2] Read " Cutheard."

cian, lord and under-king of the Mercians, departed from this life after various good deeds which he had performed. After his decease, his wife, Egelfleda, daughter of king Elfred, held the kingdom of the Mercians, (except London and Oxford, which her brother, king Edward, retained for himself,) very ably for no short time, namely, for eight years.

A.D. 913. On the second nones of May [6th May], Egelfleda, lady of the Mercians, came with an army to the place called Sceargete, and there built a fortified castle; after that she built another, on the west side of the river Severn, at the place called Brige [Bridgenorth].

A.D. 914. In the beginning of the year, Egelfleda, lady of the Mercians, went with the men of Mercia to Tomwirthig [Tamworth], and rebuilt that town. Thence she went to Stafford, and built a castle on the south side of the river Stowe.

A.D. 915. Werferth, bishop of the Hwiccians, a man of great sanctity and learning, dying, Ethelhun succeeded him. Egelfleda, lady of the Mercians, built the town called Eadesbirig, and in the end of autumn another called Warwick.

A.D. 916. The most invincible king Eadward, before the feast of St. Martin [11th Nov.], went to Bedford, and received it with its inhabitants into subjection, and remaining there for thirty days, ordered a town to be built on the south side of the river Ouse.

A.D. 917. Egelfleda, lady of the Mercians, sent an army into the land of the Britons, to storm the citadel at Brycenanmere. Having taken the citadel, they carried off the wife of the king of the Britons with thirty-four men prisoners into Mercia.

A.D. 918. Egelfleda, lady of the Mercians, before the kalends of August [1st Aug.], took Derby by storm, and obtained that province. Four of her favourite ministers fell, bravely fighting in the gate of the city.

A.D. 919. Egelfleda, lady of the Mercians, a woman of extraordinary talent, skill, and exalted justice and virtue, in the eighth year in which she, with a vigorous and upright rule, held the sole government of the Mercians, died on the nineteenth of the kalends of July [13th June]; and left as heir of the kingdom her only daughter Elwinna, her issue by the under-king Ethered. Her body was brought to Gloucester, and honourably interred in the church of St. Peter.

A.D. 920. King Eadward sent an army of Mercians into the country of the Northumbrians to rebuild Mammecester [Manchester], and place in it a strong garrison. After this, he totally deprived his niece Elwinna of the government of the kingdom of the Mercians, and ordered her to be led into West Saxony. In the same year Sihtric, king of the Northumbrians, slew his brother Niel, and stormed Devennport.

A.D. 921. The king of the Scots, with all his nation; and Regnald, king of the Danes, with the Angles and Danes dwelling in Northumbria; also the king of the Strathclyde Britons, with his people; chose king Eadward the elder as their father and lord, and concluded a firm league with him.

A.D. 922. Ethelward the Atheling, brother of king Eadward, dying on the seventeenth of the kalends of November [16th Oct.], was taken to Winchester and buried. Athelhun, bishop of the Hwiccians, died, and was succeeded by Wilferth.

A.D. 924. The unsurpassed king of the Angles, Eadward the Elder, who most gloriously presided over all the nations inhabiting Britain—Angles, Scots, Cumbrians, Danes, as well as Britons—after many illustrious deeds, departed this life in the twenty-fourth year of his reign, in the fifteenth indiction, at the royal vill called Fearndun, and left the reins of government to his son Ethelstan. His body, being brought to Winchester, was buried in royal style in the new monastery. Ethelstan was made king at Kingston, and consecrated with great pomp by the archbishop of Canterbury. In his time, the illustrious youth Dunstan was born, in the territory of Wessex.

A.D. 925. The able and glorious king of the Angles, Ethelstan, gave his sister in marriage, with great honour and dignity, to Sithric, king of the Northumbrians, born of the Danish race. In the same year Wigred[1] was consecrated bishop of Lindisfarne.

A.D. 926. Sithric, king of the Northumbrians, departed this life; whose kingdom king Ethelstan added to his own dominion, driving out his son Guthferth, who had succeeded his father in the kingdom. He likewise conquered in battle, and put to flight, all the kings of the whole of Albion, namely, Huval, king of the West Britons, then Constantine, king of the Scots, and Wuer, king of the Wenti. All these, seeing they could not resist his might, begging from him peace, met him at the place called Eamotun, on the fourth of the ides of July [12th July], and made with him a treaty, which they confirmed with an oath.

A.D. 929. Kinewold succeeded Wilferth, the deceased bishop of the Hwiccians.

A.D. 932. Frithestan, bishop of Winchester, a man of exemplary piety, retired to Winchester, Brinstan, a religious man, being consecrated in his stead.

A.D. 933. Saint Frithestan died. King Ethelstan ordered his brother Edwin[2] to be drowned in the sea.

A.D. 934. Ethelstan, the valiant king of the Angles,—because Constantine, king of the Scots, had broken the league which he had made with him,—set out for Scotland with a strong naval force and no small army of cavalry. But, in the first place, going to the tomb of St. Cuthbert, and honouring him with a royal donation of lands and other property, he ravaged Scotland with his land force as far as Dunfoeder and Wertermore, and with his navy as far as Caithness, and in a great measure depopulated it. In consequence, king Constantine was compelled to give him his son as a hostage, with suitable offerings; and the peace being renewed, the king returned to Wessex. In this year died St. Brynstan.

A.D. 935. Elfege, surnamed the Bald, a religious monk, a relation

---

[1] This date is apparently erroneous. See Hardy's Le Neve, iii. 279.
[2] See William of Malmesbury's account of this transaction, in his History of the Kings, § 139.

of the blessed Dunstan, received the episcopate of the church of Winchester.

A.D. 937. Anlaf the pagan, king of the Irishmen and of many of the islands, stirred up by his father-in-law Constantine, king of the Scots, entered the mouth of the river Humber with a powerful fleet. King Ethelstan and his brother Eadmund Atheling encountered them with an army in the place called Brunanburgh, and in a battle, lasting from morning till evening, they slew five kings and seven dukes, whom their adversaries had brought as auxiliaries, and shed more blood than had been shed up to that time in any war in England ; and having compelled the kings Anlaf and Constantine to fly to their vessels, they returned with much joy ; but the enemy, suffering the greatest distress, on account of the loss of their army, returned to their own country with a few followers.

A.D. 940. Ethelstan, the valiant and glorious king of the Angles, departed this life at Gloucester, in the sixteenth year of his reign, on Wednesday, the sixth of the kalends of November [27th Oct.], and being carried to the city of Malmesbury, was there honourably interred. His brother Eadmund succeeded him in the kingdom, in the eighteenth year of his age.

A.D. 941. The Northumbrians, preferring disloyalty to the fealty which they owed to Eadmund, the magnificent king of the Angles, chose Anlaf, king of the Norsemen, for their king. In the same year Richard the elder took the earldom of Normandy, and held it fifty-two years. He was the son of earl William, whose father was Rollo first duke of the Normans. Bishop Wigred[1] died, and Getred succeeded him.

A.D. 942. Eadmund, the magnificent king of the Angles, wrested entirely out of the hands of the Danes five cities, Lincoln, Nottingham, Derby, Leicester, and Stamford, and reduced the whole of Mercia into his power. He attained his power through the servant of God Dunstan, by whose counsels he was rendered glorious ; by him Dunstan, exalted to various honours, was preferred to the rank of abbot at Glastonbury, where he had been educated.

A.D. 943. His blessed queen Elfgiva having borne a son, Eadgar, to king Eadmund, the magnificent the holy abbot Dunstan heard voices as of some singing on high, and saying, " Peace to the church of the Angles in the time of the boy now born, and of our Dunstan." In this year the same king received Anlaf, whom we before mentioned, from the laver of holy regeneration, and bestowed on him a princely donation ; and a short time after, he stood for Reingnold, king of the Northumbrians, at his confirmation by the bishop, and adopted him as his son.

A.D. 944. Eadmund, the magnificent king of the Angles, expelled two kings—namely, Anlaf the son of Sihtric, and Reignold the son of Guthferth—from Northumbria, and subdued it to his own authority.

A.D. 945. Eadmund, the magnificent king of the Angles, overran the land of the Cumbrians, and gave it to Malculm, king of the

---

[1] This is Wigred, bishop of Lindisfarne ; his successor was Uhtred.

Scots, on this tenure, that he should keep fealty with him by sea and land.

A.D. 946. On the feast of St. Augustine the doctor of the Angles, in the royal vill, called in English Puclechurch, Eadmund, the magnificent king of the Angles, wishing to rescue his cupbearer from being slain by the hands of an infamous robber, Leov, was killed by the same man, after a reign of five years and seven months, in the fourth indiction, on Tuesday, the seventh of the kalends of June [26th May]; and being conveyed to Glastonbury, he was there buried by the blessed abbot Dunstan. His brother Edred succeeded him in the kingdom, and was consecrated king by St. Odo the archbishop, at Kingston.

A.D. 948. Aldred,[1] who was bishop after Uchtred, died, and Ailsi succeeded him.

A.D. 949. Wlstan, archbishop of York, and all the Northumbrian nobles, swore fealty to Edred, the illustrious king of the Angles, at the vill called Taddene's-cliff; but they did not keep it long, for they placed over them as king a certain man of Danish extraction, named Eyric.

A.D. 950. Eadred, the illustrious king of the Angles, devastated Northumbria, on account of the unfaithfulness of the Northumbrians, in which devastation the monastery of Ripon, originally built by St. Wilfred, bishop, was destroyed by fire. As the king was returning home, the army, sallying from the city of York, made a great slaughter in the rear of the king's army at the place called Catesford;[2] in consequence of which the king, highly enraged, determined to return thither and utterly destroy all that country. But on this becoming known, the Northumbrians, struck with alarm, cast off Eyric whom they had set up as king, made satisfaction to the king for their insults by honours, for his losses by donations, and pacified his displeasure by no small sum of money.

A.D. 951. St. Elfeg, surnamed the Bald, Bishop of Winchester, who had graced the blessed Dunstan with the degree of monk and of priest, terminated this life; to whom succeeded Elfsin in the see. Likewise died Owel,[3] king of the Britons.

A.D. 952. Eadred, the renowned king of the Angles, closely imprisoned Wlstan, archbishop of York, at Juthanbyrig [Jedburgh], because he had often been accused[4] before him on sure grounds.

A.D. 954. Wlstan, archbishop of York, freed from imprisonment, was restored to the episcopal dignity at Dorchester.

A.D. 955. Eadred, the illustrious king of the Angles, was taken ill in the tenth year of his reign, and his life despaired of. A hasty message was sent to summon his father-confessor, the blessed abbot Dunstan. As he was hurrying to the palace, and had performed half his journey, a voice from above distinctly pronounced in his hearing, " King Eadred now rests in peace." At this sound the horse on which he was mounted, unable to endure the angelic voice, fell

---

[1] See Florence of Worcester, A.D. 968.
[2] Chesterford, in the Saxon Chronicle and Florence.
[3] This was Howel Dha. See the Annales Cambriæ, A.D. 950, ap. Petrie, p. 837.
[4] See Malmesbury's History of the Kings, § 146.

dead to the earth, without any injury to the rider. The body of the king was carried to Winchester, and there committed by this abbot Dunstan to an honourable interment in the old monastery. His nephew Edwy the Atheling, the son namely of king Eadmund and his pious queen Ealgiva, received the monarchy of the kingdom, and was consecrated king at Kingston by Odo, archbishop of Canterbury.

A.D. 956. The blessed abbot Dunstan, being sentenced to banishment by Edwy, king of the Angles, crossed the sea, and during the time of his exile took up his residence in the monastery called Blandunum.[1] Wlstan, archbishop of York, dying on the seventh of the kalends of January[2] [26th Dec.], was buried at Oundle; to him succeeded the reverend man Oskytell.

A.D. 957. Edwy, king of the Angles, acting unwisely in the conduct of his government, fell into contempt of the Mercians and Northumbrians, who renounced him, and elected as king his brother Eadgar the Atheling; and the rule of the kings was so divided that the river Thames formed the boundary of both their kingdoms. King Eadgar speedily recalled from exile with honour and respect the blessed abbot Dunstan. A short time after this died Ceonwald, bishop of the church of Worcester, a man of great humility, and of the monastic order. In his room the blessed Dunstan was elected to the episcopate, and consecrated by Odo archbishop of Canterbury.

A.D. 958. St. Odo archbishop of Canterbury separated from each other, Edwy king of the West Saxons and Elgiva; either because, as it was said, she was near of kin to him, or because he loved her wantonly under the character of a wife. In the same year this archbishop, a man of truly distinguished talent and renowned virtue, and abounding in the spirit of prophecy, departed from worldly affairs, and was carried by the hands of angels to paradise. To him succeeded Elfsin, bishop of Winchester, and in his place Brihtelm was consecrated to the episcopate of the church of Winchester.

A.D. 959. Elfsin, archbishop of Canterbury, died on his way to Rome to obtain the pall, being blocked up in the Alpine mountains by frost and snow. Edwy, king of the West Saxons, died after a reign of four years, and was buried in the New Monastery at Winchester. By the choice of all the nations of the Angles, his brother Eadgar, king of the Mercians, assumed the government, and united the separated kingdoms in one, in the sixteenth year of his age, five hundred and ten years after the coming of the Angles to Britain, and three hundred and sixty-three after the coming to England of St. Augustine and his companions.

Brihtelm, bishop of the people of Dorsetshire, was elected to the patriarchate of the see of Canterbury; but being unequal to

---

[1] Namely, in the Benedictine Monastery of St. Pierre de Gand, over which at this time, Womar, or Woltmar, presided as abbot. See Gallia Christ. v. 192.

[2] Florence and Hoveden, together with some copies of the Saxon Chronicle, agree with this date; but the MS. date of the last-cited authority refers his death to 16th Dec. 957.

so great a charge, at the command of the king he resigned Canterbury, and returned to the church which he had just left. After this the blessed Dunstan, bishop of the church of Worcester, by Divine favour and the counsel of the wise, was appointed primate and patriarch of the metropolitan city of the Angles. By whom and other prudent men, Eadgar, king of the Angles, being ably directed, everywhere repressed the wicked ; reduced by sharp correction the rebellious ; favoured the just and orderly ; restored and adorned the churches of God which had been destroyed. Casting out offenders from the monasteries of the clergy, he assembled companies of monks and nuns to the praise of the almighty Creator, and more than forty monasteries of them were founded by his direction, all of whom he honoured as brothers and loved as dear sons, himself exhorting the pastors whom he set over them, that they should warn them to live orderly and unblameably, so as in all things to please Christ and his saints.

A.D. 960. St. Dunstan having gone to Rome in the third indiction, received the pall from pope John [XII.], and so returned in peace to his own country. A few months after he sought the royal palace, and by suggestion and humble entreaty besought the king's piety that he would promote to the pontifical dignity of the church of Worcester a religious man, a mild and humble monk, nephew to his predecesor Odo, the blessed Oswald, whom he had most truly proved to abound in the fear of God and in holy fruits of virtue. King Eadgar assented to the request of the holy Dunstan, and the blessed Oswald was by him inthroned in the highest rank of the priesthood.

A.D. 963. The venerable abbot St. Ethelwold, brought up by the blessed Dunstan, received the episcopate of the church of Winchester at the death of Brithelm ; and in the same year he filled the old monastery with monks, the secular clergy being expelled by order of the king. For he who was the king's chief counsellor incited him to this, that he should expel the secular clergy from the monasteries, and order monks and nuns to be placed in them.

A.D. 964. Eadgar, the pacific king of the Angles, took in marriage the daughter of Ordgar, duke of Devonshire, after the death of her husband Elfwold, the illustrious duke of the East Angles, of whom he begot two sons, Eadmund and Egelred.[1] Also before this he had by Egelfled the Fair, daughter of duke Ordmer, Eadward, afterwards king and martyr, and by the holy Wlthirtha, Eagitha, a virgin devoted to God. In the same year the same king located monks in the new monastery [of Winchester], and in Middleton ; and appointed over the former Ethelgar, over the latter, Cymeward, as abbots.

A.D. 967. Eadgar, the peaceful king of the Angles, placed nuns in the monastery of Rumesige, which had been erected by his grandfather, Eadward the elder, the king of the Angles ; and over these nuns he placed Merwinna as their abbess.

A.D. 968. Aldred,[2] bishop of St. Cuthbert's in Cunecacestre

---

[1] Or Ethelred. See Florence, p. 246.
[2] See Simeon's History of the Church of Durham, chap. xxxv.

[Chester-le-street], departed this life.   Elfsius succeeded him in the episcopate.

A.D. 969. Eadgar, the pacific king of the Angles, ordered St. Dunstan, archbishop of Canterbury, and the blessed Oswald, bishop of Worcester, and St. Ethelwold, bishop of Winchester, that, driving out the secular clergy, they should place monks in the greater monasteries throughout Mercia.   Upon which St. Oswald, acting according to his desire, expelled from the monastery the clerics of the church of Worcester who refused to receive the monastic habit; but those who agreed to do so he in that year made monks, as he himself affirms, and set over them in the place of dean, Winsinus, a man of much religion.

A.D. 970. The sacred and venerable remains of bishop Swithun, one hundred and ten years after their burial, were taken up from his tomb in the thirteenth indiction, on Friday, being the ides of July [15th July], by the venerable bishop St. Ethelwold, and Elfstan, abbot of Glastonbury, and Ethelgar, abbot of the New Monastery, and were most honourably deposited in the church of the apostles Peter and Paul.[1]

A.D. 971. Eadmund the Atheling, son of king Eadgar, died, and was honourably interred in the monastery of Romsey.   Not long after, Ordgar, duke of Devonshire, the father-in-law of king Eadgar, died, and was buried in Exeter.

A.D. 972. Eadgar, the pacific king of the Angles, directed the church of the New Monastery, begun by Eadmund his father and completed by himself, to be consecrated with pomp. On the death of Oskytill, archbishop of York, his relative St. Oswald, bishop of Worcester, was elected in his place to the archiepiscopate.

A.D. 973. Eadgar, the Pacific, in the thirtieth year of his age, in the fifth[2] indiction, on Whitsunday, the fifth of the ides of May [11th May], was blessed by the holy prelates, Dunstan and Oswald, and the other bishops of all England, in the city of Acamann [Bath], and was consecrated with great honour and glory, and anointed as king.   A short time after that, he with a large fleet sailed round the north of Britain, and landed at the City of Legions [Chester]. There met him there, as he had commanded, eight sub-kings—to wit, Kynath, king of the Scots; Malcolm, king of the Cumbrians ; Maccus, king of many isles ; and five others, Dufnald, Siferth, Huval, Jacob, and Nichil—and swore that they would be faithful assistants to him both by sea and land.   On a certain day he went with them on board a boat ; and they taking the oars, he took the helm, and skilfully steered it up the course of the river Dee ; and a multitude of dukes and nobles also accompanying him in boats, he sailed from the palace to the monastery of St. John the Baptist, where, having offered his prayers, he returned to the palace with the same pomp.   As he entered it, he is reported to have said to his nobles, that from henceforth each of his successors might boast that he was indeed king of the Angles, since so many

---

[1] Namely, at Winchester: the fifteenth of July is the festival of St. Swithun.
[2] A.D. 973 was the first indiction.

kings being in subjection to him, he could attain the dignity of so great honours.

St. Oswald received the pall from Stephen, the hundred and thirty-fourth pope.

A.D. 974. In this year a great earthquake took place over all England.

A.D. 975. The emperor of the Anglian world, the flower and glory of preceding kings, the pacific king Eadgar, no less memorable to the Angles than Romulus to the Romans, Cyrus to the Persians, Alexander to the Macedonians, Arsaces to the Parthians, or Charlemagne to the Franks, having accomplished all things in royal style, departed this life in the thirty-second year of his age, in the nineteenth of his reign over Mercia and Northumbria— sixteen years of which he had reigned over all Anglia—in the third indiction, on Thursday the eighth of the ides of July [8th July], leaving his son Eadward heir of his kingdom and his qualities. His body was carried to Glastonbury, and buried after the royal fashion. In his lifetime he had collected three thousand six hundred stout ships ; of which, after Easter, he stationed one thousand two hundred on the east, one thousand two hundred on the west, and one thousand two hundred on the north coast of the island ; and was wont to sail with the eastern fleet to the western, and leaving it, with the western to the northern, and leaving it, with the northern again to the eastern—thus every year circumnavigating the whole island. He acted thus boldly for defence against foreigners, and for practice in warlike arts to himself and his people. In winter also, and in spring, it was his practice to make a circuit within the kingdom, everywhere throughout all the provinces of the Angles, and diligently inquire how the statutes of the laws and of his decrees were observed by the nobles, lest the poor should suffer damage by the oppression of the powerful ; desirous in the one case of strength, in the other of justice, consulting in both the welfare of the state and kingdom. Hence the fear of him spread amongst his enemies everywhere, and amongst his subjects love.

At his death the condition of the whole kingdom was disturbed, and after a period of happiness (since in his time peace had been established), tribulation began to come in on every side. For Elfere, prince of the Mercians, and very many nobles of the kingdom, blinded by large bribes, expelled the abbots, with their monks, from the monasteries in which the pacific king Eadgar had placed them, and introduced clerics with their wives. But this outrage was opposed by the reverent men, Ethelwin, beloved of God, duke of the East Angles, and his brother Elfwold, and earl Brihtnoth, a religious man ; who, assembled in synod, declared that they would never suffer the monks to be driven away, who preserved all the religion in the kingdom. Then, assembling an army, they defended with great energy all the monasteries of the East Angles. While this was taking place, there arose among the nobles of the kingdom great dissension about the choice of a king. The choice of some fell on the king's son Eadward ; of

others, on his brother Egelred.   On account of which the archbishops Dunstan and Oswald, with their suffragans, and many
abbots and dukes, met together and elected Eadward, as his father
had decreed, and consecrated him when elected, and anointed
him king.   A comet was seen in the autumnal season.

A. D. 976. A great famine assailed England.

A. D. 977. A very great synod was held at the vill called Cirding,[1]
in East Anglia.   After that, while another was held at the royal
vill of Calne, the elders of all England who were there assembled,
with the exception of St. Dunstan, fell from a certain chamber;
some of whom were killed, others barely escaped at the peril of
their lives.

A. D. 978. Eadward, king of the Angles, by the command of his
stepmother, queen Elfthrid, was wickedly killed by her people at
the place called Corvesgate, and was buried at Wareham with no
royal ceremony.   His brother, the excellent Atheling Egelred,
courteous in manner, fair of countenance, and graceful in appearance,
was consecrated to the dignity of the kingdom in Kingston, by
archbishops Dunstan and Oswald, and ten bishops, in the sixth indiction, on Sunday, the eighteenth of the kalends of May [14th April].
after the Easter festival.   A cloud was seen over the whole of England at midnight, at one time bloody, then fiery; after that, changing
to different rays and various colours, it disappeared about dawn.

A. D. 979. Elfer, duke of the Mercians, with a multitude of
people, came to Wareham, and ordered the blessed body of the
beloved king and martyr, Eadward, to be raised from the tomb;
which when exposed was found free from all decay and corruption.
Being washed and enveloped in new vestments, it was brought to
Shaftesbury and honourably entombed.

A. D. 980. Southampton was ravaged by the Danes, and almost
all its inhabitants either slain or taken prisoners.   Not long after,
the same army devastated the Isle of Thanet.   Also in the same
year the province of the City of Legions [Chester] was ravaged by
Norwegian pirates.

A. D. 981. The monastery of St. Petroc,[2] in Cornwall, was devastated by the pirates, who in the past year had devastated Southampton.   After this, they made frequent forays on the coast of
Devonshire and Cornwall.

A. D. 982. Three ships of pirates assailed the province of Dorset,
and ravaged Portland.   The city of London was consumed by fire.

A. D. 983. Elfer, duke of the Mercians, a relation of Eadgar
king of the Angles, died, and his son Alfric inherited his dukedom.

A. D. 984. St. Ethelwold, bishop of Winchester, departed this
life in the second indiction, on the kalends of August [1st Aug.];
to him succeeded Elfege, abbot of Bath.   He had received the
monkish habit in the monastery called Deorhyrst.

A. D. 986. Egelred, king of the Angles, on account of certain
differences, laid siege to the city of Rochester, and finding difficulty

---

[1] Read "Kyrtling." See Florence, p. 249.
[2] Namely, at Padstow (Petroc-stow). See Camd. Brit. col. 23; Dugd. Monast.
i. 213.

in taking it, he departed in a rage and devastated the land of [the church of] St. Andrew the apostle.   Alfric, duke of the Mercians, son of-duke Alfer, was expelled from England.

A.D. 987. In this year two plagues unknown in past ages to the Anglican nation, namely a fever in men and a malady in cattle, called in their tongue "Scitta," or a looseness of the bowels, prevailed very greatly over all England, and raged in an indescribable manner through all the English territories, affecting men with a great pestilence, and entirely destroying the cattle.

A.D. 988. Wecedport [Watchet] was pillaged by the Danish pirates, who also slew the thane of Devonshire, named Goda, and Strenwold,[1] a very brave soldier, with some others.   But yet more of them being killed, the Angles were masters of the field of slaughter.   The blessed archbishop Dunstan departed this life on Saturday, the fourteenth of the kalends of June [19th May], in the first indiction, and went to the throne of the heavenly city : in his place Ethelgar, bishop of Selsey, received the archbishopric, and held it a year and three months.

A.D. 990. Aldune[2] succeeded Elfsy, bishop of Lindisfarne, deceased.

A.D. 991. Siric succeeded Ethelgar, archbishop of Canterbury. In this year the Danes pillaged Ipswich ; their dukes were Justin and Guthmund, the son of Steytan ; not long after, Brithnod, the valiant duke of the East Saxons, engaged in battle with them, but after an immense number had perished on both sides, the duke himself fell, and the fortune of the Danes prevailed.   Moreover in this year, by the advice of Siric, archbishop of Canterbury, and dukes Ethelward and Alfric, tribute to the amount of ten thousand pounds was first given to the Danes, that they should abstain from the frequent plunderings, burnings and slaughters which they constantly carried on on the sea coast, and should preserve a sound peace with them.   St. Oswald, archbishop, on Tuesday, the sixth of the ides of November [8th Nov.], consecrated the monastery of Ramsey, which he and the beloved of God, Ethelwine, duke of the East Angles, had founded, aided by the divine assistance, and supported by his help.

A.D. 992. St. Oswald, archbishop, on Monday, the second of the kalends of March [29th Feb.], in the fifth indiction, departing this life, ascended to the joys of the heavenly kingdom, and rests at Worcester in the church of St. Mary, which he himself had built from the foundations.   To him succeeded the venerable abbot Aldulf, of Medeshamstede [Peterborough].   Not long[3] after the departure of the blessed Oswald, duke Ethelwin of noble memory, beloved of God, died, and was honourably interred at Ramsey.

A.D. 993. In this year the aforesaid host of Danes stormed Bambrough, and carried off all that they found in it.   Afterwards, directing their course to the mouth of the river Humber, they took

---

[1] Apparently we should read Strenwold goda—Strenwold the good.
[2] See Simeon's History of the Church of Durham, chap. xxxv.
[3] According to the Obituary of the monastery of Ramsey (printed in Dugdale's Monast. i. 239) he died on the eighth of the kalends of May [24th April].

great booty, with much burning of vills and slaughter of men in Lindsey and in Northumbria.   Many of the inhabitants assembling went promptly out against them ; but as the engagement was about to commence, the leaders of their army, to wit, Frana, Frethegist, and Godwin, who were Danes by descent on the father's side, acting treacherously towards their followers, set the first example of flight.

A. D. 994. Anlaf, king of the Norwegians, and Suane, king of the Danes, on the feast of the Nativity of St. Mary [8th Sept.], came up in ninety-four galleys to London, which they speedily attempted to storm and burn ; but by the help of God, and Mary his mother, they were repulsed by the citizens, not without some loss of their army.   Wherefore, exasperated by rage and grief, they retreated from thence on the same day, and first in Essex and Kent, and on the coast, then in Sussex and Hampshire, they burnt the towns, laid waste the lands, and without regard to sex destroyed a great number by fire and sword, and took great plunder.   At last, seizing horses for themselves, and madly roving throughout many of the provinces, they spared neither the female sex nor the innocence of infants, but put all to death with brutal ferocity.   Then king Egelred, by the advice of his nobles, sent ambassadors to them, promising to give them tribute and pay, on condition of their desisting altogether from their cruelty ; they, agreeing to the king's request, returned to their vessels, and so their whole army assembling at Southampton, took up their quarters there.   Payment was made to them from all Wessex, and the tribute from the whole of England amounted to sixteen thousand pounds.

In the meanwhile, by the command of king Egelred, Elfege, bishop of Winchester, and the most noble duke Ethelward went to king Anlaf, and hostages being given, they brought him with honour to the royal vill of Andover, where the king was staying. The king nobly received him, caused him to be confirmed by the bishop, adopted him as his son, and presented him with a royal gift.   He promised king Ethelred that he would not again come to England with his army, and after this returned to his ships, and reaching his country early in the summer, he strictly kept his promises.

Richard, first duke of the Normans, died, whose son Richard succeeded him for one year, and after him his brother Robert.

A. D. 995. Bishop Aldune translated the body of St. Cuthbert from Chester to Durham.[1]

A. D. 996. Elfric was consecrated archbishop of Canterbury.

A. D. 997. The host of Danes which had remained in England, sailing round Wessex, entered the mouth of the river Severn, and ravaged at one time North Wales, then Cornwall, then Watchet, in Devon, and burning many vills made a great slaughter of men. Thence returning round Penwithsteort,[2] and going up the mouth of the river Tamer, which separates Cornwall and Devon, they landed, and without opposition continued their burning and renewed their

---

[1] See Simeon's History of the Church of Durham, chap. xxxix.
[2] The Land's End. See Camd. Brit. col. 10.

slaughter as far as Lidford. Moreover having burnt also the monastery of Ordulf, primate of Devon, called Tavistock, they returned to their vessels loaded with great booty, and wintered in the same place.

A. D. 998. The said host of pagans, landing at the mouth of the river Frome, laid waste the greatest part of Dorsetshire; then it frequented the Isle of Wight, and often returned to Dorsetshire; and whilst it lay in Wight it drew its supplies from the province of Sussex and Hampshire. An army was many a time raised to oppose this destructive tempest, but whenever they were about to engage in fight, the Angles, either victims to treachery or some other ill luck, turned their backs, and left the victory to their enemies.

A. D. 999. The oft-named host of pagans, entering the mouth of the river Thames, sailed up the river Medway to Rochester, and blockaded it for a few days. The Kentish men assembled to repel them, and engaged in a sharp battle with them; but after great loss on both sides, the Danes were masters of the field of slaughter. Riding from hence they destroyed nearly the whole west border of Kent. Knowing this, Egelred, king of the Angles, with the advice of his nobles, prepared both a fleet and an army of infantry; but whilst the vessels were getting ready, the leaders of the army, devising from day to day delays in their undertaking, grievously harassed the people; and at last neither the naval nor the land force effected anything for the general good, except the labour of the people and loss of money and encouragement to the enemy.

A. D. 1000. The aforesaid fleet of Danes went to Normandy this year, and returning the ensuing year to England, did more damage than before. King Ethelred ravaged nearly the whole country of the Cumbrians. He ordered his fleet to sail round North Wales, and meet him at an appointed place; but being hindered by adverse winds, it could not. Nevertheless he laid waste the Isle of Monege [Anglesey].

A. D. 1001. The said host of pagans returning from Normandy to England, entered the mouth of the river Exe, and presently proceeded to storm the city of Exeter; but as they were endeavouring to destroy the wall, they were repulsed by the citizens, who bravely defended the town; greatly exasperated at this, they spread over Devonshire in their wonted manner, burning the towns, plundering the lands, and slaughtering the inhabitants. Wherefore the men of Devonshire and Somerset, uniting at the place called Penho, engaged in fight against them. But the Angles, owing to the fewness of their soldiers, took to flight, overpowered by the numbers of the Danes who remained conquerors, having made great slaughter. There having obtained horses, they perpetrated greater evils than before throughout nearly the whole of Devonshire, and returned to their vessels, having taken enormous booty. They thence directed their course to the Isle of Wight; and now in it, now in Hampshire, now in Dorsetshire, they for a long time pursued their accustomed plunder without resistance, and raged against the people with the sword and against the towns with fire, to such a degree, that neither dared a fleet contend with them by sea, nor an army by land. The king was on this account affected by no slight grief, and the people by distress unutterable.

A. D. 1002. Egelred, king of the Angles, holding counsel with the nobles of his kingdom, considered it advisable to make a payment to the Danes, that they might desist from their injuries, and to appease them by a tribute. For this purpose duke Leofsy was sent to them. When he came, he begged them to receive pay and tribute. They, readily entertaining his proposal, acceded to his request, and fixed the amount of tribute to be paid to them for keeping the peace. Not long after, twenty-four thousand pounds were paid over to them. In the meantime the same duke Leofsy killed a noble man, Easic,[1] the chief steward of the king, for which the king, being highly displeased, banished him from the kingdom. In the same year king Egelred took to wife Emma, called in Saxon Elgiva, daughter of Richard, first duke of Normandy; of whom the same king begot king Eadward, and also Alfred, long after slain by the treachery of earl Godwin.

Aldulf, archbishop of York, assembling his suffragans, abbots, priests, and religious men, in the twenty-fifth year of Ethelred, king of the Angles, in the fifteenth indiction, on Wednesday, the seventeenth of the kalends of May [15th April], disinterred the bones of the archbishop St. Oswald, and reverently placed them in a shrine which he had prepared. And not long after, that is, on the day before the nones of May [6th May], he died, and was buried in the church of St. Mary, at Worcester. To him succeeded abbot Wlstan. Also in the same year, king Egelred ordered the destruction of all the Danes dwelling in England, great and small, and of both sexes, because they endeavoured to deprive him and his nobles of their life and kingdom, and to subdue the whole of England under their own rule.

A.D. 1003. In this year, by the ill design, negligence and treachery of the Norman, earl Hugh, whom queen Emma had set over Devonshire, Suane, king of the Danes, took by storm the city of Exeter, pillaged it, destroyed the wall from the east to the west gate, and retreated to his vessels with much spoil. But after this, while he was plundering the province of Wiltshire, a strong army levied from the provinces of Hampshire and Wiltshire went up, prepared to fight boldly and steadily against their enemies. But when the armies had approached so near that they could see one another, the oft-named duke Alfric, who then occupied the place of general of the Angles, immediately practised his old tricks, and in feigned illness began to vomit, saying, that he was seized with a severe complaint, on account of which he was unable to engage the enemy. When the army saw his backwardness and timidity, they retreated in sadness from their enemies without a blow; as the old proverb says, "When the leader in a battle trembles, all the other warriors become timorous." But Suane, seeing the unsteadi-

---

[1] In the Saxon Chronicle and Florence, A. D. 1002, his name is Eafic.

ness of the Angles, led his army to the city of Wilton, plundered and burnt it: also in like manner destroyed Salisbury, and afterward returned to his ships.

A. D. 1004. Suane, king of the Danes, sailing with his fleet to Norwich, plundered and burnt it. Then Ulfketel, duke of the East Angles, a man of great bravery, as they had come unawares, and he had no time to raise an army against them, having taken counsel with the chiefs of East Anglia, made peace with him. But he, violating the treaty, in the third week after this, stealing with his forces from their ships, attacked Thetford, plundered it, remained in it one night, and burnt it at daybreak. When this was known, duke Ulfketel ordered some of the provincials to break up the enemy's vessels. But they either dared not or would not fulfil his command. He in the meanwhile quietly collecting his army as quickly as possible, went boldly up against the enemy. When they were retreating to their vessels, he met them with an unequal force of soldiers, and fought a severe battle with them. Many were killed on both sides, some of the nobles of East Anglia perished, and the Danes with difficulty escaped. But if the strength of the East Angles had been present, they would never have regained their vessels ; for they themselves testify that never did they experience a harder or more severe contest than that which duke Ulfketel fought with them.

A. D. 1005. In this year a great and severe famine pervaded England ; on account of which Suane, king of the Danes, retired to Denmark, to return after no long time.

A. D. 1006. Alfric, archbishop of Canterbury, died, to whom succeeded Elfege, bishop of Winchester, and in his place Kenulf received the episcopate.

In the month of July an innumerable fleet of Danes coming to England, entered the port of Sandwich, and destroying all things by slaughter and flames, took great booty, at one time in Kent, at another in Sussex. King Egelred, therefore, raised an army from Mercia and Wessex, and bravely resolved to fight with them. But they had no desire to enter into fair fight with him ; but now here, now there, carried on continual ravages, and speedily retired as usual to their vessels, and in this way they harassed the army of the Angles through the whole of the autumn. They then returning home as winter was at hand, the Danes went with enormous plunder to the Isle of Wight and remained there till Christmas ; at which time, as the king was then abiding in the province of Shropshire, they marched through the province of Hampshire to Berkshire, and burnt Reading, Wallingford, Cholsey, and many villages. Advancing thence past Eascesdune [Ashdown], they came to Cwichelmeslawe [Cuckamsleyhill]. Returning from thence by another route near the Kennet, they encountered the inhabitants ready for battle, and at once engaged with them and put them to flight, and then retired to their ships with the booty which they had taken.

A. D. 1007. In this year Egelred, king of the Angles, with the advice of his nobles, sent ambassadors to the Danes with instruc-

tions to inform them that he was willing to give them supplies and
pay tribute, on condition that they should desist from their plunderings and keep a firm peace with him. To this demand they assented,
and from that time supplies were given them from all England, and
tribute to the amount of thirty-six thousand pounds was paid them
for keeping the peace. Also in this year king Ethelred appointed
one Edric,[1] surnamed Streone, duke of the Mercians.

A.D. 1008. Ethelred, king of the Angles, gave strict orders that
vessels should be built throughout all England, one galley to be
provided by each three hundred and ten hides, and from any nine
a coat of mail and a helmet. The ships being ready, he placed
in them chosen soldiers with provisions, and assembled them at the
port of Sandwich, that they might defend the coasts of his kingdom
from foreign invasions. At that time the brother of the perfidious
duke Edric Streone, Brithric, (a deceitful man, ambitious and
proud,) unjustly accused to the king Wlnoth, the thane of Sussex.
He speedily fled, to avoid being captured, and having obtained
twenty ships he carried on continual ravages on the sea-coast. But
when news came to the royal fleet, that whosoever chose might
capture him without difficulty, Brithric, taking eighty galleys, set
out in pursuit of him. But after a prosperous voyage for some
time, a furious storm suddenly arising, struck the vessels, shattered
them, and cast them ashore, and soon after Wlnoth burnt them up.
When this was known, the king with his dukes and nobles returned
home, and the fleet by his order went to London, and thus perished
the very great effort which had been made by the whole population.

A.D. 1009. The Danish earl Turkill came to England with his
fleet. After that, in the month of August, another innumerable
fleet of Danes, under the command of dukes Hemming and Eilaf,
came to the Isle of Thanet, and without delay joined the aforesaid
fleet. Both then entered the harbour of Sandwich, and disembarking from their vessels they went up against Canterbury and
laid siege to it. The citizens of Canterbury, with the men of East
Kent, asking of them agreement by treaty, obtained it, and gave
them three thousand pounds for a firm peace. They returning to
their vessels, directed their course to the Isle of Wight; thence
(as they were wont) they made constant plunder on the coast of
Sussex and Hampshire, and burnt a great many vills. Wherefore
king Egelred levied an army from all England, and placed them
through the provinces bordering on the sea to oppose their incursions. But they did not on that account cease from carrying on
their ravages everywhere, according to the facilities afforded by the
position of places. So on one occasion when they as usual made
a plundering inroad far from the sea, and were retreating loaded
with spoil, the king pre-occupied the road by which they were to
return to their vessels, furnished with many thousand armed men,
and ready (as was his whole army) to conquer or to die. But the
treacherous duke Edric Streone, son-in-law to the king (for he had
married his daughter Egitha), strove in every way, both by craft and
cunning speeches, that they should not engage in battle, but on that

[1] See Florence, p. 257.

occasion should permit their enemies to escape. He urged his point so that he carried it, and like a traitor to the country, he thus rescued the Danes from the hands of the Angles, and allowed them to escape; they slipping past their enemies, reached their vessels with great rejoicing. After these things, the feast of St. Martin [11th Nov.] being past, they went down into Kent and took up winter quarters in the river Thames, and seized their supplies from Essex, and the other provinces lying on both banks of the river. They also made frequent attempts to storm the city of London; but were repulsed by the citizens, not without some loss of their men.

A. D. 1010. The said host of Danes, disembarking in the month of January, went through the forest called Chiltern to Oxford, which they pillaged and burnt, and then in returning obtained plunder on both sides of the river Thames. When it was told them that an army was gathered against them at London, and would give them battle, the part of their forces which marched on the north bank of the river, crossed at the place called Staine; and joining together they retreated, loaded with abundance of spoil, through Surrey to their ships, which they repaired in the season of Lent, while they lay in Kent.

After Easter [9th April], going to East Anglia, they landed near Ipswich, and marched to the place called Ringmere, where they knew that duke Ulfketel lay with an army, and fought a hard battle with him on the third of the nones of May [5th May]. But when the fight became furious, the East Angles turned their backs, a certain Danish minister Turkill, surnamed Mirenheafed, first commencing the flight. But the men of Cambridge stood a long time fighting manfully, yet at length were routed and fled. In that battle fell Ethelstan, the son-in-law of king Ethelred, the noble minister Oswy with his sons, Wlfric the son of Leofwin, Edwy the brother of Elfic,[1] and many other noble thanes, and people innumerable. The Danes, being masters of the field of slaughter, occupied East Anglia, and being mounted, continued for three months to make forays through the whole province, to take plunder, to burn towns, and to slaughter men and cattle. They did the same thing everywhere in the fens. After that, they pillaged and burnt Thetford and Cambridge. Having effected these things, the infantry being transported in the ships, the cavalry going on horseback, they returned to the river Thames, but in the course of a few days they again set out on a predatory excursion, and went by a direct route to the province of Oxford, and devastated first it, then the provinces of Buckingham, Bedford, and Hertford, burning the towns and slaughtering men and cattle, and after that returned to their ships with great booty. After this, about the feast of St. Andrew the Apostle [30th Nov.], they came to Northampton, and in its environs committed to the flames whatever they would; and thence crossing the river Thames they came into Wessex, and having burnt Caningamerse and the greater part of Wiltshire, about Christmas they returned as usual to their ships with great spoil.

[1] See Florence, p. 259.

A.D. 1011. On the north side of the Thames, the provinces of East Anglia, Essex, Middlesex, Hertford, Buckingham, Oxford, Bedford, Cambridge, and half of Huntingdon, and a great part of the county of Northampton; and on the south side of the Thames, Kent, Surrey, Sussex, Hants, Wilts, and Berkshire, having been destroyed with fire and sword by the said host of Danes, Egelred, king of the Angles, and the nobles of his kingdom, sent ambassadors to them desiring peace of them, and promising to pay them tribute if they would desist from devastating. Listening to them (as the event proved) not without fraud and deceit, they agreed to their offers. For though supplies were abundantly prepared for them, and tribute paid to their wish, they did not cease anywhere from making excursions in troops through the provinces; they pillaged the towns, and deprived some of the wretched inhabitants of their property, some of their life.

At last, between the Nativity of St. Mary [8th Sept.] and the feast of St. Michael [29th Sept.], surrounding Canterbury, they besieged it. And on the twentieth day of the siege, through the treachery of Almer the archdeacon, (whom St. Alfege had previously rescued from being put to death,) part of the city was burnt, the army entered, and took the town. Some were killed with the sword, some perished in the flames, many were thrown headlong from the walls, and some died, being suspended by the privy members. Matrons dragged by the hair through the streets of the city, at last were thrown into the flames and perished. Infants torn from the mother's breast were carried on pikes, or crushed to pieces by a wagon driven over them. Meanwhile the archbishop Alfege was taken, bound, imprisoned, and tormented in various ways. Almer, abbot of the monastery of St. Augustine, was permitted to depart. There were taken Godwin, bishop of Rochester, Leofruna, abbess of the monastery of St. Mildryth,[1] Elfred, the king's steward; also monks and clerics, and innumerable people of both sexes. Then Christ Church was plundered and burnt; the band of monks and the entire population, as well men as women and children, was decimated. Nine were put to death, the tenth was kept alive. Of these tenths the number consisted of four monks and eight hundred men.

The people now being slain, the city plundered and all burnt, the archbishop Alfege was dragged out bound, was driven along and severely wounded, was carried to the fleet, and then again thrust into prison, and there tormented for seven months. In the mean while the anger of God being aroused against the murderous people, destroyed two thousand of them by dreadful pains of the intestines. Others of them also being seized in a similar way, they were advised by the faithful to make reparation to the prelate; but they refused. Meanwhile the mortality increased, and destroyed them now by tens, now by twenties, now more.

A.D. 1012. The perfidious duke Edric Streone, and all the nobles of England, of each rank, assembled at London before Easter, and

---

[1] Situated in Thanet. See Dugd. Monast. i. 83.

remained there as long as till the tribute promised to the Danes,
amounting to forty-eight thousand pounds, was paid.   Meanwhile,
on the blessed sabbath of the Lord's rest in the tomb [12th April],
a condition was offered by the Danes to archbishop Alfege, whereby
he might obtain life and liberty on payment of three thousand
pounds.   On his refusal they postponed his death till the Saturday
following.   When it came they were inflamed with great anger
against him, both because they were intoxicated with wine, and
because he had forbidden any one to give anything for his ransom.
Therefore he was brought out of confinement and dragged before
their council.   They presently leaped from their seats, knocked
him down with the back of their axes, and overwhelmed him with
stones, bones, and the heads of oxen.   At last one named Thrum,
whom he had confirmed the day before, moved by a sort of impious
piety, clove his skull with a hatchet.   He slept in the Lord on the
thirteenth of the kalends of May [19th April], and his victorious
spirit departed in triumph to heaven.   On the following day his
body was removed to London, received with reverence by the
citizens, and buried in the church of St. Paul by bishops Eadnoth
of Lincoln [Dorchester], and Alhfun of London.   After this, the
tribute being paid, and peace confirmed by oaths, the Danish fleet
was dispersed far and wide as it had been at first assembled. But
forty-five ships remained with the king, and swore fealty to him,
and promised to defend England against foreigners, provided the
king would supply them with food and clothing.

A. D. 1013. Lifing received the archbishopric of Canterbury.

In the month of July, Suane, king of the Danes, came with a
powerful fleet to the port of Sandwich, and after remaining there
a few days, departed, and sailing round East Anglia, entered the
mouth of the river Humber, from which he entered the river Trent
and sailed to Gainsborough, where also he pitched a camp.   And
without delay earl Uthred and the men of Northumbria and Lindsey
first, then the men of the Five Boroughs, and afterwards all the
people who dwelt on the north side of Watling-street, (that is, the
street which the sons of king Wetla formed through England from
the East to the Western sea,) surrendered to him; and peace being
settled with him, they swore fealty to him by giving hostages.   He
ordered them to find horses and supplies for his army.   These
things being effected, and the fleet with the hostages committed to
his son Cnut, taking with him auxiliaries chosen from them who
had surrendered to him, he made an expedition against the southern
Mercians ; and crossing Watling-street, issued his orders that they
should devastate the land, burn the towns, plunder the churches,
put to death (regardless of pity) all of the male sex who might fall
into their hands, preserve the females for the gratification of their
lust, and perpetrate all the evil they could.   Then, acting and raging
with the ferocity of wild beasts, he came to Oxford, and took pos-.
session of it sooner than he calculated, and receiving hostages,
hurried to Winchester.   On his arrival there, the inhabitants of
Winchester, terrified by the extent of his barbarity, at once made
peace with him and gave up hostages, whom and as many as he

desired. Receiving them, he marched his army towards London.
Many of them perished by drowning in the river Thames, as they
were unable to find either bridge or ford. Reaching London, he
endeavoured by various means to take it, either by stratagem or by
assault; but Egelred, king of the English, with the citizens, and by
the aid of the oft-mentioned Danish earl Turchill, who was at that
time with him in the city, bravely defended the walls of the town,
and drove him back. On this repulse, he went first to Wallingford
and then to Bath; as usual, plundering and destroying everything
in his way: and there he took up his quarters to refresh his army.
Then Ethelmar, earl of Devonshire, came to him, and with him
the Western nobles, and making peace with him gave him hostages.
All these things being accomplished according to his will, returning
to his fleet, he was both called and accounted king by all the people
of the Angles; if indeed the man can rightly be called a king who
in almost all things acted as a tyrant. Also the citizens of London
sent him hostages and made peace with him, for they feared that
his ferocity would blaze up against them to such a degree, that after
having carried off all their property he would order their eyes to
be put out, or their hands and feet to be cut off. King Egelred
seeing this, sent his queen Emma in a ship with treasures to
Normandy to his brother Richard, the second earl of the Normans ;
also his sons Eadward and Elfred with their tutor Elfhun, bishop
of London, and Alsy, abbot of Peterborough. He remained
awhile with the Danish fleet, which lay in the Thames at the place
called Greenwich, and afterwards going down to the Isle of Wight,
he celebrated the Lord's Nativity there. When this was over, he
crossed to Normandy, and was received with respect by earl
Richard, with whom he spent the whole period of his residence,
having taken up his quarters in the city of Rouen, where he was
abundantly supplied with every requisite. Meanwhile, the tyrant
Suane ordered a plentiful supply of provision to be furnished for
his fleet, and a tribute almost unbearable to be paid ; and earl
Turchill gave orders in all respects similar for the fleet which lay at
Greenwich. And besides all this, both of them carried off plunder
whenever they chose, and committed many evil deeds.

A.D. 1014. The tyrant Suane, after the innumerable and savage
ills which he had perpetrated, as well in England as in other
countries, as the crowning point of his damnation, dared to exact
a great tribute from the town where rests the uncorrupted body of
the precious martyr Eadmund, which no one had before dared to
do, from the time when the town had been given to the church of
the said saint. He repeatedly threatened that, if this were not paid
immediately, he would most certainly burn the town with its
inhabitants, totally destroy the church of the martyr, and put the
clergy in various ways to the torture. Moreover, he frequently
had the audacity to speak ill of the martyr himself in sundry ways,
and to assert that he had nothing of the saint about him. But
since he would put no limit to his impiety, the Divine vengeance
did not suffer the blasphemer to live longer. At length, just about
the evening of the day on which, in a general meeting held at

Gainsborough, he had reiterated the same threats, when surrounded by dense crowds of Danes, he alone saw St. Eadmund coming armed from the opposite side. At the sight of him he was terrified, and began to shout with a loud voice, "Rescue, fellow soldiers, rescue! See, St. Eadmund comes to slay me!" As he said this, severely stabbed by the saint with a javelin, he fell from the charger on which he sat, and suffering intense pain, he ended his life by a miserable death at evening twilight, in the third of the nones of February [3d Feb.], and was buried at York.

On his death, the naval 'force of the Danes appointed his son Cnut as their king: but the elders of all England with one consent quickly sent messengers to king Ethelred, saying, that they did and would love no one more than their legitimate lord, if only he would govern them more uprightly or treat them more mildly than he had formerly done. On hearing this, he sent to them his son Eadward with their ambassadors, and graciously saluted the chiefs and inferiors of his nation, promising that he would be to them a mild and devoted sovereign; that in all things he would agree to their wishes and would acquiesce in their counsels; and that whatever had been reproachfully or unbecomingly said or hostilely acted against himself or his friends, he would pardon with a calm mind, provided they all would unanimously and without treachery receive him into the kingdom. To this they all kindly responded; and then a thorough friendship was established on both sides by compact and by words. Besides this, the chiefs unanimously pledged themselves that they would no longer admit a Danish king into England. After these transactions the Angles sent to Normandy, and the king was brought back in the time of Lent, and received with respect by all.

In the meanwhile it was agreed between Cnut and the men of Lindsey, that, horses being provided for his army, they should together make an incursion for plunder. But before they were ready, king Egelred came thither with a powerful army, and having driven out Cnut with his naval force, he devastated and destroyed by fire the whole of Lindsey, and slew all the inhabitants whom he could meet; Cnut, taking refuge in rapid flight, directed his course to the south, and being speedily driven to the port of Sandwich, he set on shore the hostages who had been given from all England to his father, and having cut off their hands, their ears, and their noses, he allowed them to escape, and afterwards he himself departed for Denmark, to return in the following year. In addition to all these evils, king Egelred ordered a tribute of thirty thousand pounds to be paid to the fleet which lay at Greenwich. On the third of the kalends of October [29th Sept.] the sea broke over the shore, and overwhelmed many vills in England, and an innumerable multitude of people.

A.D. 1015. In this year, when a great meeting was held at Oxford, the perfidious duke Edric Streone took by craft into his chamber the illustrious and powerful nobles of the Seven Boroughs, Sigeferth and Morkar, the sons of Earngrim, and there ordered them to be secretly slain. The king took possession of their estates, and ordered Algitha, the widow of Sigeferth, to be taken to the town of Malmesbury. While she was there imprisoned, Eadmund the Atheling came thither, and against his father's will took her for his wife; and between the Assumption [15th Aug.] and the Nativity of St. Mary [8th Sept.], setting out to the Five Boroughs, he invaded the land of Sigeferth and Morcar, and subjugated their people to himself. At the same time Cnut, king of the Danes, came with a great fleet to the port of Sandwich, and presently sailing round Kent entered the mouth of the river Frome, and took great booty in Dorsetshire, Somersetshire, and Wiltshire. When king Ethelred was lying sick at Cossham, his son Eadmund Atheling on the one side, and duke Edric Streone full of deceit and treachery on the other, levied a large army; but when they came together the duke laid snares for the Atheling in every way, and attempted to destroy him by treachery. When this was discovered they speedily separated, and gave way to the enemy. Not long after, he enticed over to him forty ships of the king's fleet, manned with Danish soldiers, and going over to Cnut he entered into his service. The West Saxons did the same, giving hostages, and afterwards furnished horses to the army.

A.D. 1016. Cnut, king of the Danes, and the perfidious duke Edric Streone, with much cavalry, crossing the river Thames at the place called Cricklade, made an attack upon Mercia before our Lord's Epiphany [6th Jan.], and plundered and burnt many vills in the province of Warwick, and put to death all on whom they laid hands. When Eadmund Atheling, surnamed Ironside, heard of this, he raised an army; but, when it was assembled, the Mercians would not cope with the West Saxons and Danes, unless king Egelred and the citizens of London were with them; wherefore the expedition being given up, every one returned to his place. But after the festival,[1] Eadmund Atheling again raised a larger army, which being assembled, he sent messengers to London begging his father to meet him as soon as possible with all the men whom he could muster. He, gathering many fighting men, speedily met him; but when the armies came together it was intimated to the king, that unless he took care some of his auxiliaries would betray him. On this account, the army being disbanded, he presently returned to London, and the Atheling went into Northumbria, whence some thought that he would yet raise a greater army against Cnut; but as Cnut and Edric on one side, so he and Uhtred earl of the Northumbrians on the other, devastated some provinces; for they laid waste first Staffordshire, then the provinces of Shropshire and Leicestershire, because they would not go out to battle against the host of the Danes. Meanwhile Cnut and Edric Streone ravaged first the provinces of Buckinghamshire, Bedfordshire, Huntingdonshire, Northamptonshire, Lincolnshire and Nottinghamshire, and then Northumbria. When this was known to Eadmund Atheling, he left off his pillaging and hastened to his father at London, and earl Uhtred speedily returned home, and, forced by necessity, yielded himself, with all the Northumbrians, to Cnut, and gave him

---

[1] Namely, of the Epiphany.

hostages; and nevertheless by his order and permission was slain by Turcbrand, a Danish nobleman, and with him Turketel, the son of Navena. Having committed this act, Cnut appointed Eiric to be earl in place of Uthred; and afterwards, rapidly turning south by another route, he with his whole army regained their ships before the feast of Easter [1st April].

At that time, on Monday, the ninth of the kalends of May [23d April], in the fourteenth indiction, Egelred, king of the Angles, died at London, after a life of many hardships and great tribulations, which on the day of his kingly consecration, after his coronation, St. Dunstan, in the spirit of prophecy, had predicted would come upon him. "Since," said he, "thou hast aspired to the kingdom by the death of thy innocent brother, whom thy infamous mother slew; hear, therefore, the word of the Lord: 'Thus saith the Lord, The sword shall not depart from thy house, but shall rage against thee all the days of thy life, slaying all of thy seed, until thy kingdom shall be transferred to a foreign kingdom, whose manners and whose tongue the nation over whom thou rulest knoweth not. Nor except by long punishment shall thy sin be done away, and the sin of thy mother, and the sin of the men who took part in her wicked counsel.'" His body was buried with honour in the church of St. Paul the Apostle.

After his death the bishops, abbots, dukes, and some nobles of England, assembled together in mutual agreement, and chose Cnut for their lord and king, and coming to him in Hampshire they renounced and repudiated before him all the race of king Egelred; they made peace with him, and swore fealty to him; he also, on his part, swore to them that both before God and the world he would be a faithful sovereign to them. But the citizens of London, and part of the nobles who were at that time in London, with one consent set up Eadmund Atheling as king. He fearlessly ascending the throne, went without delay into Wessex, and being received by all the people with great rejoicing, speedily brought it under his dominion. On hearing of this, many people of the Angles with great speed, of their own accord, submitted to him; but meanwhile, about Rogation-day [7th May], Cnut, with a great fleet, arrived at London. On their arrival they dug a great ditch on the south side of the Thames, and towed their ships to the west side of the bridge. Then, surrounding the city with a wide and deep trench and a blockade, they precluded all ingress or egress, and frequently attempted to take it by storm; but by the brave resistance of the citizens they were driven to a distance from the walls. Therefore raising the siege at that time, and leaving part of their army to guard the ships, they went hastily into Wessex, allowing king Eadmund Ironside no time to raise an army. Nevertheless he, trusting in God, boldly met them with the army which he had collected in so short a time, and encountering them at the place called Pen, near Gillingham, conquered and put them to flight. After this, midsummer being past, having raised anew a larger army than before, he determined to engage bravely with Cnut. He met him in Hwiccia, at the place called Scearstan.

There he arranged his army according to his position and strength, and bringing all his best men to the front, he placed the rest of his army in reserve ; and calling each man by name, he exhorted them and besought them to remember that they were fighting for their country, their children, their wives, and their homes ; and by an excellent address he stirred up the courage of his soldiers. Then he ordered the trumpets to sound, and the troops to advance steadily. The enemy did the same. When they came where the battle could be commenced, they met under the hostile standards with a great uproar ; they fought with spears and swords, and contended with the greatest fury. In the meantime king Eadmund Ironside pressed bravely on, hand to hand, in the first rank, superintended every movement, fought hard himself, struck frequently at the enemy, and fulfilled at one and the same time the duties of a courageous soldier and a prudent commander. But as the most perfidious duke Edric Streone, and Almar the Beloved, and Algar the son of Meu, who ought to have been aiding him with the natives of Hampshire and Wiltshire, were with an innumerable multitude of people on the side of the Danes, his army was too hard pressed. Yet on the first day of the battle, to wit, Monday, so hard and bloody was the fight that each army was unable from fatigue to contend any longer, and when the sun went down and set, they separated of their own accord. But on the next day, the king would have crushed all the Danes, if it had not been for the wiles of the perfidious duke Edric Streone ; for when the battle was at its height, and he saw that the Angles had the better, having cut off the head of a certain man named Osmear, who in face and hair resembled king Eadmund, and holding it aloft, he shouted out that the Angles fought in vain, saying, " Fly headlong, ye men of Dorsetshire, Devonshire and Wiltshire, since you have lost your leader. See, here I hold in my hands the head of your sovereign lord, Eadmund ; flee with all speed." Which when the Angles heard, they were terrified more by the atrocity of the act than by their belief in the statement of the informer. Whence it happened that some of the more irresolute were very nearly taking flight ; but it being immediately ascertained that the king was alive, they plucked up their courage and fell more fiercely on the Danes, and struck down many of them, fighting with their best strength until dusk. At its approach they spontaneously separated, as on the previous day. But when the night had nearly passed, Cnut ordered his men to march silently out of their camp, and taking route for London retreated to the ships, and not long after again besieged London. But when the day had come, and king Eadmund Ironside discovered that the Danes had fled, he returned to Wessex to raise a larger army. His brother-in-law, the perfidious duke Edric, seeing his power, sought him again as his rightful sovereign ; and peace being conceded to him, he swore that he would continue loyal. An army then being raised for the third time, the king freed the citizens of London from the siege, pursued the Danes to their ships, and after two days, having crossed the Thames at the place called Brentford, he engaged in battle for the third time with the

Danes, and putting them to flight remained conqueror. On that occasion many of the English people were drowned while crossing the river without caution. The king then hastened to raise a more numerous army in Wessex, whereupon the Danes returned to London, surrounded it by a blockade, and assaulted it on every side; but by God's favour they effected nothing at all. Retreating thence, on this account, with their fleet they entered the river called the Arenne, and being landed, they marched into Mercia to plunder, killed all they met, burned as usual the towns, took the spoil, and then returned to their vessels. The infantry were conveyed in their vessels to the river called the Medway, the cavalry menaced the live booty by land.

Meanwhile king Eadmund Ironside for the fourth time raised a strong army from all England, and at the place where he had formerly crossed the river Thames, he entered Kent rapidly, and joined battle with the Danes near Ottaford. But not being able to support his attack, they turned their backs and fled with their horses into Sheppey. He slew all of them whom he could overtake; and had not the perfidious duke Edric Streone by his fraud and stratagems detained him at Eangelesford [Aylesford], he would that day have obtained a complete victory. On his retiring into Wessex, Cnut threw his forces into Essex, and marched again upon Mercia for the sake of plunder, and ordered his army to commit greater excesses than on former occasions. And they with the utmost readiness fulfilled his command; and after having destroyed all who fell into their hands, burnt very many vills and devastated the land, they hastened to return to their ships enriched with great abundance of plunder. King Eadmund Ironside pursuing them with the army which he had drawn from all England, came up with them as they were escaping at the hill called Assandun, that is, The ass's hill. There he quickly formed his line in three divisions. Then going through all the troops he warned and besought them that they would be mindful of their former valour and victory, and would defend themselves and their kingdom from the rapacity of the Danes, for the contest would be with those whom they had before conquered. Meanwhile Cnut gradually brought down his army to a level place; but king Eadmund quickly advanced his line against him as he had previously formed it, and suddenly gave the signal to attack the Danes. But the perfidious duke Edric seeing the ranks of the Danes wavering, and the Angles about to gain the victory, took to flight with the Magesetas [the men of Hereford] and the part of the army which he commanded, as he had before promised Cnut, and betrayed by his stratagem his sovereign, king Edmund, and the army of the English, and gave the victory to the Danes by his treachery. In that battle fell duke Alfric, duke Godwin, Ulfketel duke of the East Angles, duke Ethelward, son of Ethelwine duke of the East Angles, beloved of God, and nearly the whole band of the nobility of the English, who in no battle ever received a heavier blow than in this. Eadnoth also, bishop of Lincoln [Dorchester], and abbot Wulsy, who had met to beseech God in behalf of the soldiery engaged in the battle, were among the slain.

A few days after this, when king Eadmund Ironside still wished
to encounter Cnut, the perfidious duke Edric and some others
would on no account allow that to take place, but advised him to
make peace with Cnut, and divide with him the kingdom. When
at length he agreed, though unwillingly, to their suggestions, messengers passing between them, and hostages being given on each
side, the two kings met together at the place called Deorhirst.
Eadmund encamped with his men on the west side of the river
Severn; Cnut with his men on the east. Then both kings were
conveyed in skiffs to an island called Olanege, situated in the middle
of the river. Their peace, friendship, and fraternity being confirmed by agreement and oaths, the kingdom was divided; after
which they exchanged presents of arms and clothes, and, having
settled the tribute to be paid to the naval force, they parted. Yet
the Danes returned to their ships with the plunder which they had
seized; and the citizens of London, giving a sum of money, made
peace with them, and promised that they might winter with them.

After these things, king Eadmund Ironside died at London about
the feast of St. Andrew the Apostle [30th Nov.], in the fifteenth
indiction, and was buried with his grandfather, king Eadgar the
Pacific, at Glastonbury. After his death, king Cnut ordered all the
bishops and dukes, and also the princes, and all the nobles of the
English nation, to be assembled at London. When they came
before him, he artfully interrogated them, like one who did not
know, who were the witnesses between him and Eadmund, when
they made the agreement of friendship and the division of the
kingdom between them; how he and Eadmund had discoursed
between themselves about his brothers and sons, whether his
brothers and sons should be allowed to reign after their fathers in
the kingdom of the West Saxons, in the event of Eadmund dying
during his lifetime? And they began to say, that they knew
without doubt that king Eadmund would not have entrusted
any portion of his kingdom to his brothers, neither while
he was alive, nor after his death. And they said they knew
this, that king Eadmund wished Cnut to be the helper and protector of his sons until they were of age to govern. But (as God
is witness!) they gave false testimony and lied deceitfully, supposing
that he would be more favourable to them on account of their lie,
and that they would receive from him a large reward. Of these
false witnesses some were not long after put to death by the same
king. Then king Cnut, after the aforesaid inquiry, endeavoured to
obtain from the nobles before mentioned oaths of fealty. And
they swore that they would choose him as king, and would cheerfully obey him, and give supplies to his army; and having received
a pledge from his bared hand, and oaths from the chief men among
the Danes, they altogether cast aside the brothers and sons of
Eadmund, and repudiated them as kings. Yet one of the aforesaid
Athelings was the illustrious and much revered Edwy, the brother
of king Eadmund, whom there with the worst design they condemned to banishment. Now when king Cnut heard the adulation
of these men, and the disregard which they expressed for Edwy,

he went with great satisfaction into his closet, and calling to him the perfidious duke Edric, he inquired of him in what manner he might be able to entrap Edwy, so as to endanger his life. He in reply said that he knew a man named Ethelward who could very easily put him to death, with whom he might himself hold a conference and promise him an ample reward. The king, when he heard his name, summoned this man to him, addressing him with subtlety: "Duke Edric has told me so and so, saying that you have it in your power to entrap Edwy the Atheling to his death. Only acquiesce in our designs, and you shall obtain all the honour and rank of your fathers; bring me his head, and you shall be dearer to me than my own brother." He said that he would seek him out, and put him to death if by any means he could accomplish it. Nevertheless he had no intention to kill him, but merely promised this as a cloak, for he himself was sprung from the noblest race of the English.

A.D. 1017. In this year king Cnut obtained the government of the whole of England, which he held with power for nineteen years. He divided it into four parts; Wessex he retained to himself, East Anglia to earl Turkill, Mercia to duke Edric, Northumbria to earl Iric. He made a treaty with the nobles and all the people, and they with him, and established by oaths a firm friendship among themselves, laying aside and extinguishing all old enmities. Then, by the advice of the perfidious duke Edric, king Cnut outlawed the Atheling Edwy, the brother of king Eadmund, who was called the King of the Churls. But, at a subsequent period, Edwy was reconciled to the king; and Edwy Atheling, entrapped by the treachery of those whom till then he had counted his dearest friends, was in this year put to death, although guiltless, by the order and desire of king Cnut. Edric also gave counsel that he should slay the young Athelings, Eadward and Eadmund, the sons of king Eadmund. But as it would bring great discredit on him should they be put to death in England, he sent them after a little time to the king of the Swedes to be murdered; but he, although there was a league between them, would by no means agree to his request, but sent them to the king of the Hungarians, named Salomon, in order that they might be educated and their lives preserved. In process of time one of them, namely, Eadmund, ended his days there, but Eadward took in marriage Agatha, daughter of the brother of the emperor Henry [II.], of whom he begat Margaret, queen of Scots, and Christina a nun, and Eadgar Atheling.

In the month of July king Canute took in marriage queen Emma, the relict of king Egelred; by whom he begot king Ardecnut and a daughter Gunilda, who married Henry, emperor of the Romans. And on Christmas-day, when he was at London, he ordered the perfidious duke Edric to be slain in the palace, because he feared lest he might be ensnared by his treachery, as his former sovereigns, Egelred and Eadmund, had so frequently been outwitted; and he ordered his body to be thrown over the wall of the city and left unburied. With him were slain (though they were

guiltless) duke Northman,[1] the son of duke Leofwin, the brother of
earl Leofric, and Ethelward, son of duke Agelmar, and Brihtric, son
of Elfege, a thane of Devonshire. The king appointed Leofric
duke in place of his brother Northman, and after that held him in
great esteem.

A.D. 1018. In this year seventy-two thousand pounds were paid
to the host of Danes from all England, and fifteen thousand[2] from
London. Aldun bishop of Durham died. A great battle between
the Scots and Angles was fought at Carrum[3] between Huctred, son
of Waldef, earl of the Northumbrians, and Malcolm, son of
Cyneth, king of Scots, with whom there was in the battle Eugenius
the Bald, king of the Cumbrians.[4] The Angles and Danes came to
an agreement at Oxford about observing the law of king Eadgar.

A.D. 1019. This year Cnut, king of the Angles and Danes, went
to Denmark, and remained there the whole winter.

A.D. 1020. Cnut, king of the Angles, returned to England at the
Festival of Easter [17th April], and held a great council at Cirencester. Eadmund received the bishopric of Durham. Living, archbishop of Canterbury, departed this life, to whom succeeded Agelnoth,
named the Good, the son of the noble Agelmar. In the same year
the church which king Cnut and earl Turkill had built on the hill
called Assandun, was dedicated in their presence with great pomp
and ceremony by Wulstan, archbishop of York, assisted by many
other bishops.

A.D. 1021. Cnut, king of the Angles and Danes, before the
feast of St. Martin [11th Nov.], banished from England the oft-
named earl Turkil, with his wife Egitha. Algar, bishop of the East
Angles, died; to whom succeeded Aldwin.

A.D. 1022. Agelnoth, archbishop of Canterbury, went to Rome,
whom pope Benedict [VIII.] received with great honour, and gave
him the pall.

A.D. 1023. The body of St. Elfege the martyr was translated
from London to Canterbury. Wulstan, archbishop of York, died at
York on Tuesday, the fifth of the kalends of June [28th May], but
his body was brought to Ely and there buried. To him succeeded
Afric the provost of Winchester.

A.D. 1026. Alfric, archbishop of York, went to Rome and
received the pall from pope John [XIX]. Richard, second duke
of the Normans, died; he was succeeded by Richard the third, who
died the same year; to whom succeeded his brother Robert.

A.D. 1027. It being intimated to [Cnut] the king of the Angles
and Danes, that the Norwegians held in very low esteem their king
Olave, on account of his simplicity and gentleness, his kindness
and conscientiousness, he sent to certain of them much gold and
silver, beseeching them with many entreaties that, scorning and
setting aside their king, they would yield subjection to him and
allow him to reign over them. They receiving with great greediness

[1] See Florence, p. 269, note [3].   [2] Florence says, ten thousand five hundred.
[3] See Simeon's History of the Church of Durham, chap. xl.
[4] "Rex Lutinensium" (Luelensium?); the men of Luel, or the district of Carlisle. See Fordun, IV. xxi. (vol. i. p. 200.)

the things which he had transmitted to them, sent a message back to him that they would be ready to receive him whenever he chose to come.

A.D. 1028. Cnut, king of the Angles and Danes, sailed to Norway with fifty great ships, drove out from it king Olave, and subdued it to himself.

A.D. 1029. Cnut, king of the Angles, Danes, and Norwegians, returned to England; and after the feast of St. Martin [11th Nov.], under pretence of an embassy,·he sent into banishment the Danish count Hacun, who had married a noble matron Gunilda, the daughter of his sister and of Wyrcgeorn king of the Winidi; for he feared that he would either be put to death by him or expelled from the kingdom.

A.D. 1030. The aforesaid earl Hacun perished at sea; but some say that he was killed in the isle of Orkney. St. Olave (whom king Cnut had driven out), the king and martyr, was iniquitously put to death in Norway by the Norwegians.

A.D. 1031. Cnut, king of the Angles, Danes, and Norwegians, went with great pomp to Rome, and bestowed upon St. Peter, the chief of the apostles, large gifts in gold and silver, and other precious articles; and obtained from pope John [XIX.] that the school of the Angles should be freed from all tribute and custom; and in going and returning he laid out large alms on the poor, and abolished (by paying a great price) many gates on the road where toll was exacted from strangers; and before the tomb of the apostles he vowed to God that he would amend his life and conversation.

A.D. 1032. This year the church of St. Eadmund, king and martyr, was dedicated, and king Cnut having ejected the priests out of it, placed monks therein. Fire prevailed in many places through England. Elfsige, bishop of Winchester, died; Elfwin, the king's priest, succeeded him.

A.D. 1033. Leofsy, bishop of Worcester, a man of great humility and piety, died in the episcopal vill of Kemesey, on Tuesday, the fourteenth of the kalends of September [19th August], and passed, as it is meet to believe, to the kingdom of heaven. His body was reverently buried in the church of St. Mary, at Worcester. To his see was raised Brithteg, abbot of Pershore, sister's son to Wulstan, archbishop of York.

A.D. 1034. Malcolm, king of Scots, died, and Machethad succeeded him.

A.D. 1035. Cnut, king of the Angles, before his death, appointed his son Suane king over the Norwegians; over the Danes he placed as king Hardecnut, his son and queen Emma's; and he appointed his son Harold, born of Elgiva of Hampshire, king of the Angles; and afterwards in this year, on Wednesday, the second of the ides of November [12th Nov.], he departed this life at Shaftesbury. He was buried with much ceremony in the Old Minster at Winchester. After his funeral, queen Algiva settled there; but Harold, having attained the royal dignity, quickly sent his guards to Winchester, and tyrannically took away from her the greater and better part of the treasures and wealth which king Cnut had left her, and sent her off plundered just as she had begun to reside there. And then with the consent of very many of the nobles of England, he himself began to reign as the rightful heir; but not so powerfully as Cnut, because Hardecnut was regarded as the heir by greater right. Wherefore, a short time after, the kingdom of England was divided by lot, and the north part fell to Harold, the south to Hardecnut. Robert, duke of the Normans, died; to whom succeeded, at a boyish age, his son William the Bastard.

A.D. 1036. The innocent Athelings, Alfred and Eadward, sons of Agelred, formerly king of the English, bringing with them many Norman soldiers, transported in a few ships, came from Normandy (where they had continued a long time with their uncle Richard) to England, on a visit to their mother, who was dwelling at Winchester. At this some of the nobles were indignant and offended, because, though it was unjust, they were much more devoted to Harold than to them; and chiefly, as it was said, earl Godwin. He indeed detained and placed in close confinement Alfred, as he was hastening towards London to a conference with Harold, as he had ordered. Some of his companions he dispersed; some he put in fetters and afterwards blinded; some he tortured by scalping, and by cutting off their hands and feet; many he ordered to be sold; and slew six hundred men at Guildford by various and cruel deaths. But now we may believe that their souls rejoice with the saints in Paradise, whose bodies without crime perished so cruelly on earth. On hearing of this, queen Elgiva with great speed sent back to Normandy her son Eadward, who remained with her. Then by the order of Godwin and some others, the Atheling Alfred was carried heavily chained to the isle of Ely; but, as soon as the ship reached the land, immediately his eyes were there most cruelly torn out, and then he was taken to the monastery and delivered to the custody of the monks. Here, a short time after, he departed from this world, and his body was buried with due honour in the south aisle, at the west end of the church, while his soul enjoys the bliss of paradise.

A.D. 1037. Harold, king of the Mercians and Northumbrians, was chosen by the princes and all the people to reign over the whole of England; but Hardecnut was altogether cast off, as he wasted his time in Denmark, and delayed coming to England as he was asked. In the beginning of winter his mother Algiva, formerly queen of the Angles, was without pity driven out of England, and was carried over to Flanders in a boat hurriedly got ready, and was received with respect by the noble count Baldwin. He, as became such a man, made it his business freely to supply her needs as long as occasion required. A little before, in the same year, died Avicus, dean of Evesham, a man of much piety.

A.D. 1038. Agelnoth, archbishop of Canterbury, departed this life on the fourth of the kalends of November [29th Oct.]; on the octave of his death Agelric, bishop of Sussex, died; for he had besought of God that he might not long continue in this world after the death of his dearly beloved father Agelnoth. Grimketel succeeded him in the episcopate. Edsy, the king's chaplain, succeeded Agelnoth in the archbishopric. Also in the same year, on Wednesday, the thirteenth of the kalends of January [20th Dec.], died Brihteg, bishop of Worcester, to whom succeeded Living.

A.D. 1039. There was a very severe winter this year. Brithmar, bishop of Lichfield, died, to whom succeeded Wulsy. Hardecnut, king of the Danes, sailing to Flanders, came to his mother Elgiva. Harold, king of the Angles, son of king Cnut, died.

A.D. 1040. Harold,[1] king of the Angles, died at London, and was buried in Westminster. After his burial the nobles of almost all England sent ambassadors to Hardecnut at Bruges, where he was staying with his mother; and, thinking that they were acting rightly, asked him to come to England, and take the sceptre of the kingdom. He, having prepared fifty ships and manned them with Danish soldiers, sailed to England before midsummer, and was gladly received by all, and presently raised to the throne of the kingdom; but in the course of his government he never did anything worthy of the royal dignity, for no sooner had he begun to reign than, not unmindful of the injuries which his predecessor Harold (who was reckoned his brother) had inflicted either on himself or on his mother, he sent to London Alfric, archbishop of York, earl Godwin, Styr, the steward of the household, Edric his steward, Trouhd his executioner, and other men of great rank, and ordered the body of Harold to be dug up and thrown into a sewer, and after it had been thrown there he ordered it to be dragged out and cast into the Thames. But after a short time it was taken by a fisherman and brought in haste to the Danes, and by them was buried with respect in the cemetery which they had in London. After this, he ordered that eight marks should be paid over all England to each rower of his fleet, and twelve to each helmsman; a tribute so heavy that scarcely any one could pay it. On which account he became in the highest degree odious to all those who at first so greatly desired his coming. Besides this also, he was inflamed with great anger against earl Godwin, and Living, bishop of Worcester, on account of the death of his brother Alfred; Alfric, archbishop of York, and some others accusing them. Wherefore he deprived Living of the bishopric of Worcester, and gave it to Alfric; but in the following year he took it from Alfric, and graciously restored it to Living, to whom he was reconciled. Godwin, in order to obtain the king's favour, gave him a well-built galley with a gilded bow, furnished with the best stores, and handsomely supplied with suitable arms, and manned with eighty chosen soldiers; each of whom had on his arms two golden bracelets weighing seventeen ounces, a triple coat of mail, on his head a helmet partly gilt, at his side a sword with a gilded hilt, a Danish axe adorned with gold and silver hanging at his left shoulder, in his left hand a shield, the boss and spikes of which were gilt, in his right a spear, which in the language of the Angles is called "ategar." Moreover, he swore to the king that his brother had not been

---

[1] Harold Harefoot having died upon 17th March, 1039, some uncertainty appears to have arisen in the minds of chronologists as to whether that event was to be ascribed to 1039 or 1040; hence the double entry.

blinded by his design or will, but that his sovereign king Harold, with the chiefs and nobles of superior rank of almost all England, had ordered him to do what he did.

A.D. 1041. In this year Hardecnut, king of the English, sent his house-carles through all the provinces of his kingdom, to exact the tribute which he had imposed. Two of whom, namely Feadar and Turstan, were slain by the provincials of Worcester with the citizens (a tumult having broken out), for they had fled for concealment to a chamber of a certain turret of the monastery of Worcester. This occurred on Monday, the fourth of the nones of May [4th May]. Wherefore the king, greatly enraged, in revenge for their death sent thither Thuri, earl of the people of the midland districts, Leofric, earl of the Mercians, Godwin, earl of the West Saxons, Siward, earl of the Northumbrians, Roni, earl of the Magesetas [the people of Herefordshire], and the other earls of all England, and almost all his house-carles, with a great army (Alfric was still the bishop of Worcester), and gave them orders that they should, if possible, slay all the men, plunder and burn the city, and lay waste the whole province. On the eve of the ides of November [12th Nov.] they began to ravage both the city and the province, and continued to do so for four days; but they took or killed few either of the citizens or provincials, because having got notice of their approach, the inhabitants had fled elsewhere. And a number of the citizens had taken refuge on a little island situated in the middle of the river Severn, called Beverege, where, throwing up a defence, they so long and manfully maintained themselves against their enemies, that at last, peace being restored, they were freely permitted to return home. Then on the fifth day, having burned the city, every man returned with much spoil to his own neighbourhood, and the wrath of the king was quickly appeased. Not long after, Eadward, the son of Egelred, former king of the Angles, came to England from Normandy, where he had been many years in exile, and being received with honour by his brother, king Hardecnut, abode in his palace.

A.D. 1042. At a feast at the place called Lambeth, in which Osgod Clapa, a man of great influence, gave his daughter Githa, with great rejoicings, in marriage to Tovy, surnamed Pruda, a very powerful Dane, Hardecnut, king of the English, while he stood drinking sound and merry with the said bride and some other men, suddenly, in the midst of his drinking, fell to the ground heavily, and so remaining speechless, expired on Tuesday, the sixth of the ides of June [8th June], and being carried to Winchester, was buried beside his father, king Cnut. His brother Eadward, mainly by the aid of earl Godwin, and Living, bishop of Worcester, was raised to the throne at London. He was the son of Egelred, who was the son of Eadgar, who was the son of Eadmund, who was the son of Eadward the elder, who was the son of Elfred. Bishop Eadmund[1] died; to whose see Edred succeeded by means of money, and died in the tenth month.

---

[1] Bishop of Durham. See Simeon's History of that church, chap. xliv.

A .D. 1043. Eadward was anointed king at Winchester, on Easter
day, the third of the nones of April [3d April], by archbishop Edsy
of Canterbury and Alfric of York, and the other prelates of almost
all England.   In the same year, fourteen days before the feast of
St. Andrew the Apostle [16th Nov.], the king came unexpectedly
from the city of Gloucester to Winchester, with the earls Leofric,
Godwin, and Siward ; and, as they had advised him, he took from
his mother whatever valuables she had in gold and silver, gems,
precious stones and other property, because, either before he was
king or after, she had given him less than he wanted, and had been
very hard upon him.

On the death of Eadmund, Egelric received the bishopric of
Durham, while Siward administered the earldom of the Northumbrians.

A.D. 1044. Alwold, bishop of London, who before and during
his episcopate had presided as abbot over the monastery of Evesham, being no longer able on account of infirmity to govern his
see, desired to reside at Evesham ; but the brethren of that place
would on no account agree to it.   Wherefore, carrying off most
part of the books and ornaments which he had himself bestowed
on that place, and, as some say, what others had bestowed also, he
retired to the monastery of Ramsey, and bestowed all that he
brought on St. Benedict ; and there he settled ; and in this year, on
Wednesday, the eighth of the kalends of August [25th July], he
died, and was there buried.   At a general council held at that time
at London, Wulmar, a religious monk of Evesham, also called
Mannus,[1] was elected to preside as abbot over his monastery, and
was consecrated on Friday, the fourth of the ides of August
[10th Aug.].   In the same year the noble matron Gunhilda,[2] the
daughter of king Wortgern and king Cnut's sister, and the widow
of earls Hacun and Harold, was banished from England, with her
two sons Hemmung and Turkill.   Sailing to Flanders, she spent
some time at the place called Bruges, and then went to Denmark.

A.D. 1045. Brithwold, bishop of Wells, died, to whom succeeded
Hermann, the king's chaplain, born in Lorraine.   In this year
Eadward, king of the Angles, assembled a very powerful fleet at
the port of Sandwich, against Magnus, king of the Norwegians,
who was preparing to attack England, but war declared against him
by Suane, king of Denmark, put a stop to his expedition.

A.D. 1046. Living, prelate of the Hwiccians [Worcester], Devon,
and Cornwall, died on Sunday, the tenth of the kalends of April
[23d March] ; after whose death the bishopric of Crediton and
Cornwall was immediately given to the king's chancellor Leofric, a
Briton ; and Aldred, who was first a monk of Winchester, and
then abbot of Tavistock, received the bishopric of Worcester.
Osgod Clapa was banished from England.   Magnus, king of the
Norwegians, having put to flight Suane, king of the Danes, the son
of St. Olave king, subdued Denmark to himself.

---

[1] The Nag (?)
[2] She was the daughter of Wyrtgeorn, king of the Wends ; concerning whom
see Lappenb. ii. 215.

A.D. 1047. So heavy a snow fell in the west as to break down the trees. Alwin, bishop of Winchester, died, to whose see Stigand was raised. Suane, king of the Danes, sent his ambassadors to Eadward, king of the Angles, and begged him to send a fleet to him against Magnus, king of the Norwegians. Then earl Godwin advised the king to send at least fifty ships manned with soldiers; but as that did not seem advisable to earl Leofric and all the people, he would not send any. After this, Magnus, king of the Norwegians, strengthened by a large and powerful fleet, fought a battle with Suane; and many thousands being killed on both sides, he drove him from Denmark, and afterwards reigned there, and compelled the Danes to pay him an immoderate tribute; and not long after he died.

A.D. 1048. Suane recovered Denmark, whereupon Harold Harvager (son of Siward, king of the Norwegians, and on the mother's side brother of St. Olave and uncle of king Magnus) returned to Norway, and a short time after sent ambassadors to king Eadward, and asked and obtained peace and alliance with him. A great earthquake occurred on Sunday, the kalends of May [1st May], at Worcester, Wic, Derby, and many other places. A mortality of men and animals pervaded many provinces of England; and aerial fire, commonly called forest fire, burnt vills and many crops in the province of Derby and some other provinces.

A.D. 1049. Leo was the hundred and forty-fifth pope. He is that Leo who made the new hymn about the pope St. Gregory. The emperor Henry raised an innumerable army against Baldwin, earl of Flanders, chiefly because he had stormed and burnt his very beautiful palace at Nimeguen. In that expedition pope Leo was present, and very many nobles and honourable men from various countries. Also Suane, king of the Danes, as the emperor commanded him, was present with his fleet, and swore fealty to the emperor on that occasion. He sent also to Eadward, king of the Angles, and begged him not to allow Baldwin to escape if he fled to the sea. On this account the king went with a great fleet to the ports of Sandwich, and remained there until the emperor had obtained from Baldwin all that he wished.

In the meanwhile, earl Suane, the son of earl Godwin and Gytha, (who had before left England because he could not marry Eggiva, abbess of Leominster, whom he had seduced, and had gone to Denmark, falsely asserting that he would in future continue loyal to the king,) returned with eight ships. Earl Beorn, the son of his uncle the Danish earl Ulf, the son of Spracling, the son of Urse, and brother of Suane king of the Danes, promised him that he would obtain from the king the restoration of his earldom. When therefore peace was restored between the emperor and earl Baldwin, earls Godwin and Beorn sailed with the king's leave to Pevensey with forty-two ships, and retaining a few ships there with him, he [the king] ordered the rest of the fleet to return home. When he was informed that Osgod Clapa lay at Ulpe with twenty-nine ships, he recalled as many as he could of the ships that he had sent off. And Osgod having recovered his wife, whom he had sent to Bruges, returned to Denmark with six ships. The others, making an attack on Essex, were returning with no little booty seized about Eadulf's Cape; but on their return a fierce storm assailed them, sunk them all except two ships, which were taken in foreign parts, and all their crew was slain. While these events took place, earl Suane came to Pevensey, and treacherously asked his cousin, earl Beorn, to go with him to the port of Sandwich, and (as he had promised) effect his reconciliation with the king. He, confiding in his relationship, set out to go with Suane, only taking three companions with him. But he took Beorn to Bosanham [Bosham] where his ships were, and putting him on board a vessel ordered him to be bound with tight thongs, and kept him with him until he came to Dartmouth. Having there slain him, the six ships left him, thrown into a deep pit and covered with earth; of which ships the men of Hastings soon after took two, and putting the crews to death, brought the ships to Sandwich and gave them up to the king. Suane escaping with two ships to Flanders, remained there until Aldred, bishop of Worcester, brought him back and reconciled him with the king.

This year pope Leo, at the request of the very pious abbot Hermar, came to France in company with the emperor and some of the principal men of the city of Rome; and he consecrated[1] with great pomp the minster of St. Remigius, the apostle of the Franks, built at Rheims; and afterwards held in that city for six days a great council of archbishops, bishops and abbots; at which were present Aldwin, abbot of Ramsey, and the abbot of the monastery of St. Augustine, who were sent thither by Eadward, king of the Angles.

A.D. 1050. Macbethad, king of Scots, scattered his silver at Rome; Edsy, archbishop of Canterbury, died; to whom succeeded Rodbert, bishop of London, a Norman by descent. Hermann, bishop of Wiltshire, and Aldred, bishop of Worcester, went to Rome.

A.D. 1051. Elfric, archbishop of York, dying at Southwell, was buried in the minster at Malmesbury; the king's chaplain Kinsy succeeded him. King Eadward freed the Angles from the heavy tax, to wit eighty thousand pounds, thirty-eight years after his father had first ordered it to be paid to the Danish soldiers. In the month of September following, Eustace the elder, earl of Boulogne, who had married king Eadward's sister, Goda, landed with a few ships at ¹Dover, where his soldiers stupidly and rashly seeking quarters for themselves, killed one of the citizens. A fellow-citizen who saw this revenged it by slaying a soldier. The earl and his men hereupon becoming highly enraged, killed with their weapons a number of men and women, and trod boys and infants under their horses' feet. But when they saw the citizens assemble to resist them, they with difficulty escaped, with a loss of seven of their companions, by taking to a cowardly flight; and they fled to king Eadward, who was then staying at Gloucester. Earl Godwin, greatly offended and enraged that such things had happened in his county,[2] gathered

---

[1] Upon 2d Oct. 1049 (see Jaffé, p. 369); the synod commenced upon the day following.   [2] He was earl of Kent, Dugd. Baron. i. 13.

a numberless army from all his earldom, namely from Kent, Sussex, and Wessex; as did his eldest son Suane[1] from his, namely from the counties of Oxford, Gloucester, Hereford, Somerset, and Berkshire; and his other son Harold from his earldom, that is, the provinces of Essex,[2] East Anglia, Huntingdon, and Cambridge. This became known to king Eadward. Sending messengers immediately to Leofric and Siward, earls of the Mercians and Northumbrians, he begged them to hasten to him, as he was in great peril, with all the men they could raise. They came to him at first with a few soldiers; but when they found what was the state of affairs, they sent swift posts through all their earldoms, and levied a large army. Also earl Rodulph,[3] the son of king Eadward's sister, Goda, gathered as many as he could from his county. Meanwhile, Godwin and his sons, after the Nativity of St. Mary [8th Sept.], marched with their force into the province of Gloucester and pitched their camp at Langtree; and sending messengers to the king at Gloucester, they demanded under a threat of battle the surrender of earl Eustace and his comrades, and moreover all the Normans and Boulognese who held possession of the castle at Dover. The king was for a while alarmed at this, and in a great strait, and did not very well know what to do. But when he found that the army of earls Leofric, Siward, and Rodulph was at hand, he stoutly replied that he would on no account give up Eustace and the others whom they demanded. On hearing this, the messengers returned empty handed. As they departed, the army entered Gloucester, so excited and unanimously eager for battle, that, if the king would have allowed, they would have gone out at once to fight with Godwin's army. But since some of the best men of all England were gathered on the one side or the other, it seemed to earl Leofric and some others a great mistake to engage in battle with their fellow-countrymen; but that hostages being given on each side, the king and Godwin should meet on an appointed day to settle matters at London.

This counsel being approved, and messengers passing between them, the hostages were given and received, and the earl returned to Wessex. The king raised a larger army from all Mercia and Northumbria, which he took with him to London: and Godwin and his sons came with a great multitude of West Saxons to Southwark; but as his army fell away from him by degrees, he was afraid to engage in conference with the king, but fled on the following night. Therefore, the next day, the king in council, with the unanimous agreement of the whole army, pronounced sentence of banishment against him and his sons. He with his wife Gytha, and Tosti with his wife Judith, the daughter of Baldwin, earl of Flanders, and his two other sons Suane and Gyrth, went in haste to Thorney, where his ship lay ready. Hurriedly putting on board as much gold and silver and other valuables as it could carry, and

---

[1] Dugd. Baron. i. 18.   [2] Id. i. 16.
[3] Goda, the sister of king Edward, married Drogo of Mantes; and upon his death, Eustace of Boulogne. Anderson's Genealog. p. 740. He was created earl of Hereford by Edward the Confessor. Dugd. Baron. i. 21.

quickly embarking, they directed their course to Baldwin, earl of
Flanders. Then his sons Harold and Leofwin going to Bristol,
embarked in a ship which their brother Suane had got ready for
them, and sailed across to Ireland. The king divorced queen
Eadgitha on account of his displeasure against her father, Godwin ;
and sent her very unceremoniously to Wherwell,[1] with only one
waiting maid, and committed her to the charge of the abbess.
After this the Norman earl William came with a number of Normans to England. The king received him and his companions
honourably, and sent him back to Normandy gifted with many and
great donations.

A.D. 1052. Elgiva Emma, the wife of kings Egelred and Cnut,
died on the second of the nones of March [6th March], at Winchester, and was there buried. In the same year Griffyn, king of
the Welsh, devastated great part of the province of Hereford.
The men of that province and several Normans from the castle
went up against him ; but many of them being slain, he got the
victory, and carried off with him great spoil. This battle took place
on the same day on which, thirteen years before, the Welsh put to
death by treachery Edwin the brother of earl Leofric.

A short time after this, earl Harold and his brother Leofwin
returning from Ireland entered the mouth of the river Severn with
many ships, and landing on the borders of Somersetshire and
Dorsetshire, plundered many vills and lands in those parts. A
great many men, gathered from Devonshire and Somersetshire, went
out against them ; but Harold overcame them, slaying more than
thirty noble thanes, with many others. He then returned to his
vessels with the booty, and then sailed round Penwithsteort [Land's
End]. Then king Eadward sent quickly forty ships well supplied
with provisions and chosen soldiers to the port of Sandwich, with
orders to keep out of sight and watch the approach of earl Godwin.
But yet he, unknown to all, returning with a few ships, landed in
Kent, and secretly sending messengers, enticed to his assistance first
the Kentish men, then the men of Sussex, Essex, Surrey, and all
the shipmen of Hastings, and many others on all parts of the coast.
These all with one mouth promised that they would be ready to
live or die with him. When this news reached the king's fleet,
which was lying at the port of Sandwich, they pursued him ; but
he made his escape by flight, and concealed himself where he could;
so they sailed back to the port of Sandwich, and thence returned
to London. When this was known, earl Godwin sailed back to the
Isle of Wight and hovered about the coast until his sons Harold
and Leofwin joined him with their fleet. But from the time of
this junction they desisted from plunder and pillage, yet took supplies for their army as occasion demanded. After alluring to their
aid all whom they could collect on the coast and other places, and
gathering with them all the shipmen whom they met, they directed
their course towards the port of Sandwich. When they came
there, king Eadward was then staying in London, and he was
informed of their arrival. He, quickly sending messengers to all

---

[1] See Dugd. Monast. i. 156.

who had not revolted from him, ordered them to hasten to his assistance; but they were exceedingly dilatory, and did not come in time. Meanwhile, earl Godwin with his fleet sailing up the Thames against the current, came on Monday, the day of the Exaltation of the Holy Cross [14th Sept.], to Southwark, and there waited for the flowing of the tide. In the meantime he had conferences with some citizens of London whom he had previously enticed by various promises, and managed that almost all were willing to do whatever he wished. Afterwards all things were settled and arranged; at the flow of the tide they quickly weighed anchor, and, no one resisting them on the bridge, they sailed upward along the south bank of the river. The land army also came, and taking a position on the bank of the river, formed a solid and imposing front. He then turned the fleet to the north bank, as if to surround the king's fleet (for the king had a fleet and a numerous land army), but since there were very few there who exhibited any courage, either with the king or with Godwin, except a few Englishmen, they were almost all very averse to fight with their friends and fellow countrymen. Wherefore some of the wiser sort on each side, effecting a reconciliation between the king and the earl, ordered the army to be disbanded. In the morning, then, the king held a council, and fully restored their original rank to Godwin, his wife, and all his sons except Suane. For he, brought to repentance for having murdered his cousin Beorn (as we before related[1]), had gone barefoot from Flanders to Jerusalem, and on his return home, died in Lycia of an illness brought on by excessive cold. The king also took back with honour the earl's daughter, queen Edgitha, and reinstated her in her former dignity. Harmony being thus restored, and peace established, both parties promised all the people just legislation, and outlawed all the Normans who had brought in iniquitous laws, pronounced unjust decisions, and given the king many evil counsels against the English. But they allowed a few to remain in England, namely Robert the deacon, and his son-in-law Richard Fitz-Scrob, and Alvered the king's master of the horse, and Anfrid, surnamed Cocksfoot, and some others who were greater favourites with the king than the rest, and who had been faithful to him and all the people. Moreover, Robert, archbishop of Canterbury, and William, bishop of London, and Ulf, bishop of Lincoln,[2] barely escaping with their Normans, crossed the sea. But William, being soon after recalled on account of his goodness, was restored to his see. Osbern, surnamed Pentecost, and his companion Hugh gave up their castles; and going with the leave of earl Leofric through his earldom to Scotland, were received by Macbeoth, king of the Scots. In the same year, on the night of the feast of St. Thomas the Apostle [21st Dec.], there was so great and strong a wind as to destroy many churches and houses, and to break or tear up by the roots innumerable trees.

A.D. 1053. The brother of Griffin, king of the South Welsh, named Res, was put to death, on account of the frequent robberies which he committed, by order of king Eadward, at the place called

[1] See p. 534.   [2] That is, Dorchester.

Bulendum; and his head was brought to the king at Gloucester, on the eve of our Lord's Epiphany [5th Jan.]. In the same year, at the celebration of the second day of the Easter festival [Easter Monday, 12th April], at Winchester, the final catastrophe happened to earl Godwin, when he was seated (as usual) by the king at table; for, suddenly struck by an acute disease, he fell speechless in his seat. His sons, earl Harold, Tosti, and Gyrth, seeing this, carried him into the king's chamber, hoping that he might shortly recover from his illness. But he became utterly powerless, and died on the fifth day after, being the seventeenth of the kalends of May [15th April], and was buried in the Old Minster. His son Harold received his dukedom, and Harold's earldom was given to Algar, son of earl Leofric.

A.D. 1054. Siward, the valiant duke of the Northumbrians, by king Edward's order, went to Scotland with an army of cavalry and a powerful fleet, and fought a battle with Macbeoth, king of Scots; and having slain many Scottish soldiers and all the Normans whom we mentioned above, he routed Macbeoth, and, as the king directed, appointed Malcolm, son of the king of the Cumbrians, king. Yet in that battle his own son, and many of the Angles and Danes, fell.

On the death of Godwin, abbot of Winchelomb, Aldred, bishop of Worcester, on the feast of St. Kenelm [17th July], appointed as abbot in his place Godric, the son of Godman, the king's chaplain. Afterwards the same bishop was sent by the king on an embassy with great presents to the emperor; by whom, and by Hermann, archbishop of Cologne, he was received with great honour, and stayed there a whole year; and he suggested to the emperor on behalf of the king that he should send an embassy to Hungary and bring back his nephew Eadward, the son namely of Eadmund Ironside, and cause him to come to England.

A.D. 1055. Siward, duke of the Northumbrians, died at York, and was buried in the monastery of Galmanho, which he had built; his dukedom was given to Tosti, duke Harold's brother. Not long after, at a council held at London, king Eadward outlawed (for no crime) earl Algar, son of earl Leofric. He went immediately to Ireland, and having procured eighteen piratical vessels, he returned, and went to Griffin, king of the Welsh, and begged him to give him aid against king Eadward. Griffin immediately levied a large army from the whole of his kingdom, and directed Algar to meet him and his army at an appointed place with his forces. Having united their forces, they entered the province of Hereford, to devastate the English marches. The cowardly duke Rodulph, Eadward's sister's[1] son, raised an army, and met them two miles from the city of Hereford on the ninth of the kalends of November [24th Oct.], and (contrary to their custom) he ordered the English to fight on horseback. But as they were about to join battle, the earl with his French and Normans took to flight at the first; and the English seeing this, followed their leader in his retreat. Almost all the enemy pursued them, and killed of them

[1] See p. 535, note [3].

four or five hundred men, and wounded many.   Having thus
obtained the victory, king Griffin and earl Algar entered Hereford
and killed seven canons who defended the doors of the principal
church, and burnt the monastery which that true servant of Christ,
bishop Ethelstan, had built, with all its ornaments and the relics
of St. Agelbert, king and martyr, and of other saints ; and after
having killed some of the citizens, and taken many prisoners, and
likewise plundered and burnt the city, they retreated enriched with
abundance of booty.   When the king was informed of this, he
ordered an army to be speedily raised from the whole of England ;
over which, when it assembled at Gloucester, he appointed the
valiant duke Harold.   Harold faithfully acting according to orders,
actively pursued Griffin and Algar, and having boldly entered the
territories of the Welsh, he pitched his camp beyond Straddale.
Knowing him to be a warlike and brave man, and being afraid to
engage in battle with him, they retreated into South Wales.   When
he found this, he there disbanded the greater part of his army,
counselling them bravely to resist their enemies if occasion required ;
and returning with the rest of the number to Hereford, he girt it
with a broad and high wall, and strengthened it with gates and
bars.   In the meanwhile, messengers passing between Griffin and
Algar, and Harold, and those who were with them, they met at the
place called Byligesleage, and peace being mutually given and
received, they made a firm alliance among themselves.   This being
settled, earl Algar's fleet was brought to Chester, and waited for
the pay which he had promised them, while he himself went to the
king and received from him his earldom.   At that time died the
religious man Tremerin,[1] the Welsh bishop ; he was for some time
deputy for bishop Ethelstan of Hereford, after the latter had become
unable in person to fulfil the episcopal office ; for he was blind for
thirteen years.   Hermann, bishop of the province of Wiltshire,
offended that the king would not allow him to transfer the episcopal
see from the vill called Ramesbury to the abbey of Malmesbury,
resigned his bishopric, and crossing the sea assumed the monastic
habit at St. Bertin, and there remained in that monastery for three
years.

A.D. 1056. Henry [III.], emperor of the Romans, died, and was
succeeded by his son Henry [IV]. Ethelstan, bishop of Hereford, a
man of great sanctity, died on the fourth of the ides of February [10th
Feb.], at the episcopal vill called Bosanbyrig; his body was conveyed
to Hereford and buried in the church, which he had built from the
foundations.   Leofgar, duke Harold's chaplain, succeeded him ;
who, on the sixteenth of the kalends of July [16th June] in the
same year, was slain with his clerks, and Agelnoth the sheriff, and
many others, by Griffin, king of the Welsh, at the place called
Glastbyrig : he occupied the see eleven weeks and four days.
After his death the see of Hereford was committed to Aldred,
bishop of Worcester, until a bishop should be appointed.   After
this the same bishop, and earls Leofric and Harold, reconciled
Griffin, king of the Welsh, with king Eadward.   Earl Agelwin, a

[1] He was bishop of St. David's.   See Hardy's Le Neve, i. 289, 455.

lover of churches, a reliever of the poor, a defender of widows
and orphans, a helper of the oppressed, a preserver of chastity,
who, before his death, was made a monk by Aldred, bishop of
Worcester, departed on the second of the kalends of September
[31st Aug.], at Deorhyrste, and rests honourably interred in the
monastery at Pershore. Agelric, bishop of Durham, voluntarily
relinquishing his see, retired to his monastery called Burh [Peter-
borough], where he was educated and made a monk, and passed
twelve years there. His brother Agelwine, a monk of the same
monastery, succeeded him in his see.

A.D. 1057. The Atheling Eadward, son of king Eadmund Ironside, as his uncle king Eadward enjoined him, came to England
from Hungary, where long previously he had been sent into exile,
as we have said before. For the king had determined to make him
heir of the kingdom after himself: but he departed this life at
London a short time after his arrival. The praiseworthy earl Leofric,
son of duke Leofwin, a man of illustrious memory, died in a good
old age in his own vill called Bromleage, on the second of the
kalends of September [31st Aug.], and was honourably buried
at Coventry; which monastery (among other good deeds of his
life) he and his wife, the noble countess Godiva, a servant of God
and a devout lover of St. Mary the ever virgin, built from the
foundations out of their own means, and had sufficiently endowed
it with lands, and so enriched it with various ornaments, that in no
monastery in England could there be found so great an abundance
of gold and silver, gems and precious stones, as at that time was
contained therein. They enriched also with costly ornaments the
convents of Leominster and Wenlock, and the monasteries of
St. John Baptist and St. Wereburg the Virgin, at Leicester, and the
church which Eadnoth, bishop of Lincoln, built at the famous
place called in English St. Mary's Stow, or St. Mary's place.
They also enriched the monastery of Worcester with lands, and
that of Evesham with buildings, divers ornaments, and lands. As
long as he lived, the wisdom of this earl was of great benefit to the
kings and all the people of England: his son Algar received his
dukedom. Heca, bishop of the South Saxons, died; in whose place
Agelric, a monk of Christ's church in Canterbury, was elected.

A.D. 1058. Algar, earl of the Mercians, was a second time outlawed by king Eadward; but by the help of Griffin, king of the
Welsh, and the assistance of a Norwegian fleet which had come to
him unexpectedly, he quickly recovered his earldom by force.
Aldred, bishop of Worcester, nobly dedicated in honour of Peter,
the prince of the apostles, the church which he had built from the
foundations in the city of Gloucester; and afterwards, by leave of the
king, he appointed thereto as abbot Wulstan, a monk of Worcester,
whom he himself had ordained. Then, resigning the prelacy of the
church of Wiltshire, which had been committed to his government,
and transferring it to Hermann before mentioned, he crossed the
sea and went through Pannonia, now called Hungary, to Jerusalem,
a thing which none of the archbishops or bishops of England is
known to have done till then.

A. D. 1059. Nicolas, bishop of the city of Florence, was elected pope, and Benedict driven out. Kinsi, archbishop of York, and Egelwin, bishop of Durham, and Tosti, earl of York, conducted king Malcolm to king Eadward.

A. D. 1060. Henry, king of the Franks, died, whose eldest son Philip succeeded him. Duduc, bishop of Wells, died, and Gisa, the king's chaplain, succeeded him; both of whom were natives of Lorraine. Kinsi, archbishop of York, died at York, on the eleventh of the kalends of January [22d Dec.]; his body was taken to the monastery called Burh [Peterborough], and honourably buried. In his place Aldred, bishop of Worcester, was elected on Christmas day; and the bishopric of Hereford, which had been committed to him on account of his activity, was given to Walter of Lorraine, queen Egitha's chaplain.

A.D. 1061. Aldred, archbishop of York, went to Rome with earl Tosti, and received the pall from pope Nicolas. Meanwhile, Malcolm, king of Scots, furiously ravaged the earldom of his sworn brother earl Tosti, and violated the peace of St. Cuthbert in the island of Lindisfarne. In the same year pope Nicolas died, and Alexander succeeded him, being the hundred and forty-ninth pope.

A.D. 1062. The venerable man Wulstan was appointed bishop of the church of Worcester. He, beloved of God, was born of religious parents in the country of the Mercians, in the province of Warwick,—his father's name being Eastan and his mother's Wulfgeova; he was excellently instructed in learning and ecclesiastical duties in the monastery called Burh [Peterborough]. Both his parents were of so religious a disposition, that, long before the end of their life, they professed chastity and separated from each other, and delighted to end their days in the conversation of a holy living. The youth himself, instigated by their example, chiefly by the persuasion of his mother, gave up the world, and he received the monastic habit and order, in the same monastery of Worcester in which his father had before served God, from the venerable Brihteg, bishop of that church, by whom also he was ordained to the rank of deacon and priest; and immediately, at the very outset, embracing a life severe and full of devotion, he at once became distinguished in vigils, fastings, prayers, and every species of virtue. Hence, on account of his moral training, he was at first appointed for some time master and guardian of the children. After that, on account of his skill in ecclesiastical duties, he was made, by direction of the elders, at the same time precentor and treasurer of the church. And as the church was thus committed to him, he obtained thereby the opportunity of serving God more freely; and thus he gave himself altogether up to a life of meditation, continuing in it day and night, in prayer or the reading of the Scriptures; he reduced his body by fasts of two or three days' duration; and so devoted was he to sacred vigils, that as he passed without sleep not only a day and a night, but sometimes (which we could scarcely believe unless we had heard it from his own mouth) four days and nights, he ran the risk of his brain being almost dried up, unless he quickly satisfied nature by a snatch of

slumber. And even when compelled by the power of nature to
sleep, he did not indulge his body by slumber in a bed and blankets,
but merely lay down for a little while on any bench of the church,
supporting his head with the book from which he had been praying
or reading. After some time, on the death of Agelwin, the prior
of the monastery, this reverend man was appointed by bishop
Aldred,[1] prior and father of the congregation. Discharging this
office in the most commendable manner, he by no means gave up
the severity of his former mode of life; nay, he in many ways
increased it, in order to set others an example how to live aright.
Then, in the course of a few years, this Aldred, bishop of the
church of Worcester, being elected to the archbishopric of the
church of York, there was a unanimous agreement both of the
clergy and all the people in his election, king Eadward consenting
that they should elect a bishop of their own choice. It so happened at that time that legates from the apostolic see were also
present in his election; namely Armenfred,[2] bishop of Sion, and
another, who being sent by the lord pope Alexander [XI.] on
ecclesiastical business to Eadward king of the Angles, were, by
order of the king, staying at Worcester for nearly the whole of Lent,
waiting until the king's court should meet on the following Easter,
for the reply to the business of their embassy. They observing
during their stay there his laudable conduct, not only agreed in his
election, but particularly instigated both clergy and laity to it, and
confirmed that election by their own authority. But he most
obstinately refused, declaring himself unworthy, and even affirming
with an oath that he would much more readily yield to be beheaded
than take such a high appointment; when often and repeatedly
besieged on this matter by many religious men and venerable
persons, he could by no means be persuaded to consent, till at
length being sharply reproved for his disobedience and obstinacy by
a recluse man of God, by name Wulsius, who was known to have
led a solitary life for more than forty years, and being also put in
fear by a divine miracle, with great grief of heart he was compelled
to consent; and his election was canonically confirmed, and he
received the bishopric on the day of the beheading of St. John
Baptist [29th Aug.], and being consecrated on the day on which
the nativity of St. Mary is celebrated by the church [8th Sept.],
he shone as bishop of the church of Worcester, illustrious in life
and virtues. He was consecrated bishop by Aldred, archbishop of
York; for Stigand, archbishop of Canterbury, was at that time
interdicted from the episcopal office by the apostolic sovereign,
because he had presumed to take the archbishopric while archbishop Robert was yet living; his canonical profession was made,
however, not to his consecrator Aldred, but to the aforesaid Stigand,
archbishop of Canterbury. Moreover, through the intervention of
Stigand himself, on account of the claims of his successors, the

---

[1] Aldred, bishop of Worcester, was promoted to York, 25th Dec. 1060 (see
above), with permission to retain Worcester; but the pope compelled him to
resign Worcester, which he did in A. D. 1061. Hardy's Le Neve, iii. 49.

[2] Ermenfred, bishop of Sion (a diocese in France in the archbishopric of Taren-
taise), occupied that see from A. D. 1055 to 1079. See Gall. Christ. xii. 740.

archbishop of York, his consecrator, was ordered to make a declaration before the king and nobles of the realm, that he would thenceforward claim no right over him of ecclesiastical or secular subjection, either on account of his having consecrated him or made him a monk before his consecration.   This consecration of his took place when he was above fifty years of age, in the twentieth year of king Eadward, and in the fifteenth indiction.

A.D. 1063. After Christmas, by order of king Eadward, Harold, the brave duke of the West Saxons, taking with him a small company of cavalry, set out to Rudelant in great haste from Gloucester, where the king was then staying, for the purpose of slaying Griffin, king of the Welsh, on account of the frequent ravages which he carried on in the territories of the Angles, and the insults which he had frequently offered to his lord king Eadward. But Griffin having warning of his approach, fled with his men, got on board a vessel, and with difficulty made his escape.   Harold, when he found that he had escaped, gave orders to set fire to his palace, and to burn his ships with their stores, and returned the same day.   But about the Rogation days [25th May] sailing with a naval armament from Bristol, he circumnavigated the greater part of the land of the Welsh.   His brother, earl Tosti, met him by the king's orders with an army of cavalry, and then they began to devastate that region; whereupon the Welsh (also called Britons) were compelled to yield and give hostages; and they promised to pay tribute; and having outlawed their king Griffin, they renounced him.

A.D. 1064. Griffin,[1] king of the Britons, was put to death by his own men on the nones of August [5th Aug.], and his head, and the head of his ship with its adornment, were sent to earl Harold, who speedily presented them to king Eadward.   When this was done, the king gave the land of the Britons to his brothers Blechgent and Rithwallan.   They swore fealty to him and to earl Harold, and promised that they would be at their command by sea and land, and that they would obediently pay all that had been previously paid from that land by former kings.

A.D. 1065. The reverend man, Agelwin, bishop of Durham, disinterred the bones of St. Oswin, formerly king of the Bernicians, in the monastery situated at the mouth of the river Tyne, four hundred and fifteen years after their burial, and placed them with great honour in a shrine.   Harold, the valiant duke of the West Saxons, in the month of July, ordered a great building to be erected in the land of the Britons, at the place called Portaskith, and directed to be collected there great provision of food and drink, in order that his sovereign king Eadward might sometimes live there for the purpose of hunting; but Caradoc, (son of Griffin, king of the South Welsh, whom Griffin, king of the North Welsh, had slain some years before, and had invaded his kingdom,) with all the men he had at his command, came thither on the feast of St. Bartholomew the Apostle [24th Aug.], and slew almost all the workmen, with those who were over them, and carried off all the property which was there collected.   Then after the feast of St. Michael the Arch-

[1] See Annales Cambriæ, ap. Petrie, p. 840.

angel, on Monday, the fifth of the nones of October [3d Oct.], the
Northumbrian thanes Gamilbarn, Dunstan the son of Agelnoth,
Gloineorn the son of Heardulf, with two hundred soldiers, came to
York; and on account of the accursed slaughter of the noble Northumbrian thanes, Gospatric,—whom queen Egitha, for the sake of
her brother Tosti, had treacherously ordered to be slain in the
king's court, on the fourth night of Christmas [28th Dec.],—and
Gamel the son of Orn, and Ulf the son of Dolfin, (whom in the
preceding year earl Tosti had treacherously ordered to be slain in
his chamber at York, under an agreement of peace;) and also on
account of the immensity of the tribute which he unjustly took from
the whole of Northumbria, on the same day,—he first put to death
without the walls of the city, his Danish housecarls, Amund and
Ravensheart, whom they took in flight; and, on the following day,
they slew two hundred men of his officials on the north side of the
river Humber. They also broke into his treasury, and retreated,
after having carried off all of his that was there. Almost all his
county having assembled together, afterwards met at Northampton
Harold, duke of the West Saxons, and others, whom, at Tosti's
request, the king had sent to them to restore peace. Where first,
and afterwards at Oxford, on the feast of the apostles Simon and
Jude [28th Oct.], and when Harold and many others wished to recon-
cile Tosti with them, they all with one consent refused, and outlawed
him, and all who had encouraged him to establish an unjust law;
and after the feast of All Saints [1st Nov.], by the aid of earl Edwin,
they drove Tosti from England. He at once went with his wife to
Baldwin, count of Flanders, and passed the winter at St. Omers;
and by the king's order, Morkar[1] was elected earl over the Northumbrians. After this, king Eadward fell by degrees into bad
health. On Christmas-day he held his court as well as he could at
London, and on Holy Innocent's day [28th Dec.] he caused to be
consecrated with great pomp, the church which he had built from
the foundation, in honour of St. Peter, the prince of the apostles.

A.D. 1066. The glory of the Angles, the pacific king Eadward,
son of king Ethelred, after presiding in royal dignity for twenty-
three years, six months, and twenty-seven days, over the Anglo-
Saxons, died at London in the fourth indiction, on Thursday, the
day before the nones of January [5th Jan.], being the eve of the
Epiphany; and, being interred on the morrow in royal fashion, was
deeply lamented with tears by all who were there present. After
his funeral, the under-king Harold, son of duke Godwin, whom the
king before his decease had chosen as the successor to his kingdom,
was by the princes of all England elected to the royal dignity; and
on the same day was solemnly consecrated king by Aldred, archbishop of York. He was no sooner placed at the helm of government than he began to abolish unjust laws, and to frame just ones;
and to be a supporter of churches and monasteries; he favoured,
and at the same time revered, bishops, abbots, monks and clerics:
he showed himself loving, humble and affable to all good men,
but evil-doers he held in detestation. For he ordered the dukes,

---

[1] He was the younger son of Algar, earl of Chester. See Dugd. Baron. i. 6.

magistrates and sheriffs, and his ministers in general, to seize
thieves, robbers and disturbers of the kingdom, and he himself laboured earnestly for the defence of the country by land and
by sea.

In the same year, on the eighth of the kalends of May [24th April],
a comet was seen not only in England, but, as it is said, over the
whole world, which shone with exceeding splendour for seven days.
Not long after this, earl Tosti returning from Flanders, landed at
the Isle of Wight, and after compelling the islanders to pay tribute
and fine, he departed, and went along the coast to the port of Sandwich, committing ravages. When this was known, king Harold,
who then abode at London, ordered a large fleet and an army of
cavalry to be assembled; and he prepared to go in person to the
port of Sandwich. Tosti being informed of this, withdrew, carrying
with him certain of the shipmen, of whom some went willingly, but
others by constraint, and directed his course to Lindoria,[1] where he
burnt many vills, and put to death a number of men. On hearing
of these doings, Edwin, duke of the Mercians, and Morkar, earl of
the Northumbrians, hastened with an army, and drove him out
of that district. Retreating thence he went to Malcolm, king of
Scots, and abode with him all the summer. King Harold in the
meanwhile went to the port of Sandwich, and there waited for his
fleet; when it had assembled, he went to the Isle of Wight. And
as William, earl of the Normans, the cousin of king Eadward, was
preparing to come with an army to England, he kept watch the
whole summer and autumn for his arrival. Also, with a view to
this, he stationed an army of infantry at convenient places on the
coast. But when the Nativity of St. Mary [8th Sept.] had come,
provisions growing scarce, both the naval and land force returned
home.

After these events, Harold Harvager,[2] king of the Norwegians,
brother of king Olave the saint, came unexpectedly to the mouth
of the river Tyne with a very powerful fleet, to wit, more than fifty
great ships. Earl Tosti, with his fleet, met him there as he had
before agreed, and with a quick voyage they entered the mouth of
the river Humber, and so sailing up the river Ouse they landed at
the place called Richale, and took York after a hard struggle.
When king Harold learnt this, he rapidly marched his troops
towards Northumbria. But before the king arrived, on Wednesday
the vigil of St. Matthew the Apostle [20th Sept.], the brother earls
Edwin and Morkar, with a large army, joined battle with the Norwegians at Fulford, near York, on the northern bank of the river
Ouse, and at the first onset of the fight they overthrew many;
but after a long continuance of the contest, the Angles, unable to
resist the force of the Norwegians, turned their backs not without
some loss of their men, and many more of them were drowned in
the river than fell in the field. The Norwegians were masters of
the field of slaughter, and taking five[3] hundred hostages from York,

[1] That is, Lindsey. See Florence of Worcester, p. 295.
[2] See Florence, p. 295, note 1.
[3] Florence of Worcester, p. 296, says one hundred and fifty.

and leaving there a hundred and fifty hostages of their own men, they retired to their vessels.

But on the fifth day after this, that is, Monday, the seventh of the kalends of October [25th Sept.], Harold, king of the Angles, came to York with many thousand fighting men, provided with weapons of war; and meeting the Norwegians at the place called Stamford-bridge, slew with the edge of the sword king Harold and earl Tosti, with the greater part of their army, obtaining a full victory, although it was very severely contested. But Tosti's son, Olave, and an earl from the isle of Orkney, named Paul, who had been sent with part of the army to guard the ships, he freely permitted to retire to their country with twenty ships and the rest of the army, having first received from them hostages and oaths.

In the meantime, while these events were occurring, and the king imagined that all his enemies were crushed, he was told that William, king Eadward's cousin, and earl of the nation of the Normans, had arrived with an innumerable multitude of horses, slingers, and archers, (for he had hired strong auxiliaries from the whole of France,) and had brought his fleet to the place called Pevensey. Wherefore the king immediately marched his army towards London with great speed, and although he well knew that in the two battles some of the bravest of all England had fallen, and that half of his army had not yet come up, he did not hesitate to meet the enemy as quickly as he could, in Sussex; and he came to an engagement with them nine miles from Hastings, where they had fortified a castle, on Saturday, the eleventh of the kalends of November [22d Oct.], before a third part of his army had joined him. But as the English were drawn up in a narrow place, many withdrew themselves from the ranks, and very few of those who remained with him continued firm at heart. But yet from the third hour of the day till twilight he most powerfully resisted his enemies; and so bravely and stoutly did he defend himself in the fight, that he could hardly be slain by the hostile troops. But after very many on both sides had perished, alas! he himself fell at the time of twilight. His brothers also, Gyrth and Leofwin, were slain, and the most illustrious of almost all England. Earl William returned with his men to Hastings.

King Harold reigned nine months and as many days. Earls Edwin and Morkar, who with their men had withdrawn themselves from the contest, when they heard of his death went to London, and taking their sister, queen Aldgitha, they sent her to the city of Chester. Aldred, archbishop of York, and the same earls, with the citizens of London and the shipmen, wished to appoint as king the Atheling Eadgar, grandson of king Eadmund Ironside; and they promised to take up arms in his behalf. But when many were ready to go out to battle, the earls withdrew their aid from them, and returned home with their army.

Meanwhile, earl William overran Sussex, Kent, Hampshire, Surrey, Middlesex, and Hertford, and continued burning vills and slaying men, until he reached the vill called Berkhamptstead; where there came to him Aldred archbishop of York, Wulstan bishop of

Worcester, Walter bishop of Hereford, the Atheling Eadgar, the earls
Edwin and Morcar, and some of the principal men of London,
with many others, and having given hostages they made submission
and swore fealty to him.   He likewise made a treaty with them; yet,
nevertheless, he allowed his army to burn the vills and pillage.   At
the approach of Christmas he went with his army to London, and
was there elevated to the throne.   And because Stigand, archbishop
of Canterbury, was charged by the apostolic pope with not having
received the pall canonically, on Christmas-day (which that year
fell on Monday) he was solemnly consecrated at Westminster by
Aldred archbishop of York, having first done what that same archbishop required of him—namely, promised by oath before the altar
of St. Peter the Apostle, in presence of the clergy and people, that
he would defend the holy churches of God and their rulers, and
would govern the whole of the people subject to him justly and
with royal care; that he would enact and preserve just laws; and
would strictly prohibit depredations and unjust decisions.

In order that the original cause of William's invasion of England
may be known, the events which happened before that event may
briefly be recapitulated.   A grievous disunion having arisen between king Eadward and earl Godwin, (as has already been said,) the
earl with his friends were banished from England.   When he afterwards requested the king's permission to return to his country, he
would on no account consent, unless Godwin would give hostages
for his personal security.   Wherefore, Godwin's own son, Wulnoth,
and his son Suane's son, Hacun, were given as hostages, and were
consigned in Normandy to the custody of earl William the Bastard,
son of Robert, the son of Richard, his mother's brother.   Some
time after this, when earl Godwin was now dead, his son Harold
begged the king's permission to go to Normandy and liberate his
brother and nephew, who were detained there as hostages, and
to bring them back with him in freedom to this country.   "That,"
said the king to him, "shall not be done through my instru-
mentality; nevertheless, that I may not seem desirous to place
obstacles in your way, I permit you to go where you choose, and
try what you can do.   Yet I foresee that your proceeding will tend
to nothing else than the injury of the whole English kingdom, and
your own disgrace; for I know the earl not to be so senseless as
to give them up to you in any way unless he should perceive that
it would be greatly to his own advantage."   So Harold embarked
in a vessel, which being driven by a violent storm into the river of
Ponthieu, called the Maia, was adjuged by the lord of that country
(according to the custom of the place) to bondage to him.   Harold
then being put in confinement, privately sent one of the populace,
allured by the promise of a reward, to earl William, to relate
what had befallen him.   On hearing this, he speedily sent messengers with directions to the lord of Ponthieu, that Harold with his
men should be sent to him free from all injury as quickly as possible,
if he wished still to preserve the ancient alliance hitherto existing
between them.   But as he was unwilling to release the man, he
received a second mandate from William, that he must needs let

Harold go, otherwise he might make himself very sure that William earl of Normandy would enter Ponthieu in arms, for the purpose of carrying off him and his to the last farthing. Alarmed at these threats, he sent the man with his companions, who was received by William with much respect; and replied to him, when he heard why he left his country, that his affair would prosper well if William put no obstacle in his way. So he kept him with him some days, and was very kind and hospitable towards him, in order that by this means he might engage his heart in his projects. At length he discovered to him what were his intentions. He told him, therefore, that long ago while they were both young, king Eadward, when staying with him in Normandy, had promised on his fidelity, that if ever he became king of England he would transmit the authority of the kingdom to him by hereditary right after himself. He then craftily said, " If you will promise me your assistance in this matter, and that you will make a fort at Dover with a well of water for my use, and that you will give your sister whom I may marry to one of my nobles, and will bind yourself to me at the time that we shall agree upon, and moreover, will take my daughter for your wife,—then you shall at once receive your nephew safe, and your brother also, when I come to reign in England. In which kingdom if I am established by your aid, I promise that you shall obtain all that you can reasonably ask of me." Harold perceived the full extent of his danger, and saw no means of escape unless he submitted in all things to the will of William. He yielded therefore. William then, that all might be made sure, bringing forward the relics of the saints, induced Harold to take an oath upon them, that he would fully perform all that had been settled. This being accomplished, Harold, having received his nephew, returned to his country. When, in answer to the king's inquiries, he told him what had happened, and what he had done; " Did I not tell you," said Edward, "that I knew William; and that very great evils to this kingdom might be the result of that expedition of yours? I foresee that from this deed of yours great calamities will come upon our nation; and I pray the love of heaven to grant that they may not happen in my days." King Eadward died soon after, and, according to the appointment which he had made before his death, Harold succeeded him in the kingdom. William sent to tell him that although he had violated his promise by not observing the other points, yet he would patiently endure this if only he would take his daughter to wife, otherwise he might be undoubtedly convinced that William would vindicate for himself by arms the promised succession to the kingdom. Harold replied, that neither would he do the one nor did he dread the other. Highly indignant at the injustice done by Harold, William was animated on this account with a great hope of victory. Preparing therefore a large fleet, he invaded England with nine hundred ships, and in a severe pitched battle Harold fell in fight, and William the Conqueror obtained the kingdom. Of which battle the Franks who were engaged yet testify, that although partial successes happened to each side, yet so great was the slaughter and flight of the Normans, that the victory which they obtained was truly and without doubt to be ascribed to the judgment of God; who, by punishing the crime of perjury, showed that He was a God who would not look upon iniquity.

A.D. 1067. On the approach of Lent,[1] William returned to Normandy, taking with him Stigand archbishop of Canterbury, Agelnoth abbot of Glastonbury, Eadgar the Atheling, the earls Edwin and Morkar, Walthev son of duke Siward the noble thane, Agelnoth of Canterbury, and many others of the nobles of England; leaving, as regents of the kingdom, his brother Odo bishop of Bayeux, and William Fitz-Osbern, whom he had appointed earl in the province of Hereford; and he ordered the castles everywhere to be fortified. Wulsy bishop of Dorchester (or Lincoln) died at Winchester, but was buried at Dorchester.

At that time lived a certain very powerful thane, Edric, surnamed the Forester, the son of Alfric, brother of Edric Streone. The garrison of Hereford and Richard Fitz-Scrob frequently laid waste his land, because he scornfully refused to give it up to the king. But as often as they assailed him they lost many of their knights and squires. The same man Edric, therefore, calling to his aid the kings of the Welsh, to wit, Blethgent and Ritwad, about the Assumption of St. Mary [15th Aug.], overran Hereford as far as the bridge of the river Lucge, and carried off great spoil. After this, as winter was coming on, William returned from Normandy to England, and imposed an insufferable tax on the English. Then, making a hostile expedition to Devonshire, he besieged and speedily took by storm the city of Exeter, which the citizens and some English thanes held against him; but the countess Githa, the mother of Harold, king of the English, and sister of Suane, king of the Danes, with many of the citizens, escaped by flight, and went to Flanders : the citizens gave pledge and submitted themselves to the king.

A.D. 1068. Two popes were made at Rome; namely the bishop of Parma, who was expelled, and the bishop of Lucca, who remained pope. After Easter [23d March], the countess Matilda came from Normandy to England, and on Whitsunday [11th May], Aldred, archbishop of York, consecrated her queen. After this Marleswen and Gospatric, and some nobles of the Northumbrian race,—to avoid the severity of the king, and dreading that like others they might be put in confinement, taking with them Eadgar Atheling and his mother Agatha, with his two sisters Margaret and Christina, —went by sea to Scotland, and there, by the favour of Malcolm, king of Scots, they passed the winter. King William went with his army to Nottingham, where he fortified the castle, and then marched to York, where he fortified two castles, and placed in them five hundred soldiers, and ordered castles to be fortified at Lincoln and other places. While this occurred, Godwin, Eadmund and Magnus, the sons of king Harold, returning from Ireland, landed in Somerset. Eadnoth, who had been king Harold's master of the horse, met them with an army, and, engaging in battle with them, was

---

[1] Ash-Wednesday fell upon 21st Feb.

slain with many others.   Having gained the victory, they returned
to Ireland, with no little spoil from Devon and Cornwall.

A.D. 1069.   The convent of St. German, at Selby, was founded.
In the third year of his reign, king William sent earl Robert, surnamed Cumin,[1] to the Northumbrians on the north side of the
Tyne.   But they all united in one feeling not to submit to a foreign
lord, and determined either that they would put him to death, or
that they all would fall together by the edge of the sword.   Agelwin,
bishop of Durham, met him at his approach, and forewarned him
to beware of the snares laid for him.   But he, thinking that no
one would be so daring, despised the warning.   Entering Durham
with a large body of soldiers, he allowed his men to act everywhere
in a hostile manner, even slaying some of the yeomen of the
church; but he was received by the bishop with all courtesy and
honour.   But the Northumbrians, marching all night with haste to
Durham, at dawn burst the gates with great force, and slew on
every side the earl's men, who were taken unawares.   The affair
was conducted with great ferocity, the soldiers being killed in the
houses and the streets.   They then proceeded to attack the bishop's
dwelling in which the earl had been received; but not being able
to withstand the javelins of the defenders, they burnt the house
with its inhabitants.   So great was the multitude of the slain, that
almost all parts of the city were flowing with blood; for of seven
hundred men none but one escaped.   This slaughter took place on
Wednesday, the fifth of the kalends of February [28th Jan.].

In this year, before the Nativity of St. Mary [8th Sept.], Harold
and Cnut, sons of Suane, king of the Danes, and their uncle, earl
Osbern, and their bishop, Christian, and earl Turkill, coming with
two hundred and forty ships from Denmark, landed at the mouth
of the river Humber.   There they were met by Eadgar Atheling,
earl Walthev, and Marlesswein, and many others, with a fleet which
they had provided.   Earl Cospatric was there also, with the whole
strength of the Northumbrians, who all assembled with one consent
against the Normans.   At the approach of all these, Aldred, archbishop of York, becoming very timid, fell into great weakness, and
in the tenth year of his episcopate, on Friday, the third of the ides
of September [11th Sept.], ended his life, as he had besought God,
and was buried in the church of St. Peter.   On the eighth day
after this, namely on Saturday, the thirteenth of the kalends of
October [19th Sept.], the Normans who garrisoned the castles,
fearing lest the houses which adjoined the castles might be of use
to the Danes in filling up the moats, commenced setting them on
fire.   The conflagration increasing exceedingly, seized on the whole
of the city, and with it consumed the monastery of St. Peter.   But
this was speedily and severely visited upon them by the divine
vengeance.   For before the whole city was burnt, the Danish fleet
arrived on the Monday, and the Danes assailing the castles on one
side, the Northumbrians on the other, they took them by storm the
same day.   And more than three thousand of the Normans being

---

[1] See Simeon's History of the Church of Durham, chap. L.

slaughtered, and William Malet,[1] who then held the office of sheriff, with his wife and two children, and Gilbert de Gant,[2] and a very few others being preserved alive, the Danes returned to their ships with untold spoils, and the Northumbrians to their abodes. When this was made known to king William, he speedily assembled an army, and hastened to Northumberland in great anger, and did not cease for the whole winter from ravaging the country, slaughtering the men, and performing many other acts of ferocity. In the meanwhile, sending messengers to the Danish earl Osbern, he promised that he would privately give him a considerable sum of money, and would allow his army full liberty of seizing supplies on the coast,—provided this were laid down as a condition, that, when the winter was over, they should depart without coming to hostilities. Osbern hereupon, being greedy of the gold and silver, yielded to his wishes, not without great disgrace to himself.

In consequence of the Normans having plundered England,—in the preceding year [A. D. 1068] Northumbria and some other provinces, but in the present and following year [A. D. 1069, 1070] almost the whole realm, yet principally Northumbria and the adjacent provinces,—so great a famine prevailed that men, compelled by hunger, devoured human flesh, that of horses, dogs, and cats, and whatever custom abhors; others sold themselves to perpetual slavery, so that they might in any way preserve their wretched existence; others, while about to go into exile from their country, fell down in the middle of their journey and gave up the ghost. It was horrific to behold human corpses decaying in the houses, the streets, and the roads, swarming with worms, while they were consuming in corruption with an abominable stench. For no one was left to bury them in the earth, all being cut off either by the sword or by famine, or having left the country on account of the famine. Meanwhile, the land being thus deprived of any one to cultivate it for nine years, an extensive solitude prevailed all around. There was no village inhabited between York and Durham; they became lurking places to wild beasts and robbers, and were a great dread to travellers.

While the king was doing such deeds as these around and near York, Agelwin bishop of Durham, and the chiefs of the people, fearing lest, on account of the slaughter both of the earl and of the Normans at York, the king's sword should include equally the innocent and the guilty in indiscriminate slaughter, with one consent betook themselves to flight,[3] on Friday, the third of the ides of December [11th Dec.], carrying with them the uncorrupted body of the holy father Cuthbert. They made their first stay at Jarrow, their second at Bedlington, the third at Tughall, and the fourth at Holy Island. But about evening, when the full tide would prevent travellers from crossing over, behold by its sudden recess it left the approach clear for them; so that neither when they hurried did the waves of the sea linger behind them, nor when they delayed did they press upon them. But when they reached the land, lo! the sea coming up covered the whole sands as before. In the mean-

[1] See Dugd. Baron. i. 110.   [2] Id. i. 400.
[3] See Simeon's History of the Church of Durham, chap. L.

while the king's army, which had spread over all the places between the Tees and the Tyne, found only one continued solitude; the dwellings being everywhere deserted, and the inhabitants seeking safety in flight, or lying hid in the woods or the fastnesses of the mountains. Then, too, the church of St. Paul at Jarrow was destroyed by fire; the church of Durham, deprived of all care and ecclesiastical service, became a den for the poor, the infirm, and the sick, who no longer being able to fly, there lay perishing of hunger and disease. When spring was at hand, the king returning to the south of the Humber, bishop Agelwin with all the people, having passed three months and some days in Holy Island, returned with the treasure of that sacred body, arranging their resting-places on their return as they had in going; and on the eighth of the kalends of April [25th March], the church being first cleansed from all pollution, and reconciled by the pontifical offices and benediction, making their entrance, they restored the sacred corpse to its place with hymns and praises.

A.D. 1070. By the advice of William, earl of Hereford,[1] and some others, at the time of Lent,[2] king William ordered the monasteries of the whole of England to be searched, and the money which the richer English had there deposited, on account of his harshness and rapacity, to be carried off and stored up within his treasury. Bishop Egelwin returning from flight was contemplating a final escape. For, observing that the affairs of the Angles were everywhere in confusion, and dreading the heavy rule of a foreign nation, whose language and customs he knew not, he determined to resign his bishopric, and provide for himself wherever a stranger might. A ship, therefore, furnished with the necessary supplies, lay ready for him in the harbour of Wearmouth, waiting for a favourable wind. There were also there, at that time, some other ships under the command of Edgar Atheling, with his mother Agatha, and his two sisters, Margaret and Cristina, Siward Barn, Marlesswein, Alfwin the son of Norman, and many others, who, after the storming of the castle of York, (the Danes who had been their auxiliaries, having returned to their own country,) were in dread of the king's indignation against themselves, and were preparing to go as refugees into Scotland, and awaited there a prosperous voyage. During the same time a countless multitude of Scots marched through Cumberland under the command of king Malcolm, and turning to the east, ravaged with fierce devastation the whole of Teesdale, and the parts bordering it on each side. And when they came to the place called in English Hundredeskelde, that is, The hundred springs, having there slaughtered some nobles of the English nation, the king (keeping part of the army), sent part home by the way they came with a vast booty. By this craftiness he designed that when the wretched natives (who, from fear of the enemy, had hid themselves in whatever lurking-places they could find safety) should return to their villages and homes, supposing the enemy to have altogether departed, he might by a sudden inroad come upon them unawares.

---

[1] Dugd. Baron. i. 66.
[2] In 1070, Ash-Wednesday fell upon 17th February.

And this happened accordingly. For having pillaged Cleveland in part, by a sudden foray he seized Holderness, and thence, savagely overruning the territory of St. Cuthbert, he deprived all of their whole property, and some also of their lives. Then he destroyed by fire, under his own inspection, the church of St. Peter, the prince of the Apostles, at Wearmouth. He burnt also other churches, with those who had taken refuge in them. When he was riding along the banks of the river, beholding from an eminence the cruel exploits of his men against the unhappy English, and feasting his mind and eyes with such a spectacle, it was told him that Edgar Atheling and his sisters, who were beautiful girls of the royal blood, and many other very rich persons, fugitives from their homes, lay with their ships in that harbour. When they came to him with terms of amity, he addressed them graciously, and he pledged himself to grant them and all their friends a residence in his kingdom as long as they chose. Amidst these pillagings and depredations of the Scots, earl Gospatric (who, as before has been said, had obtained for money from king William the earldom of Northumbria) having called in some bold auxiliaries, made a furious plundering attack upon Cumberland. Having done this with slaughter and conflagration, he returned with great spoil, and shut himself, with his allies, into the strong fortress of Bamborough; from which making frequent sallies, he weakened the forces of the enemy; for Cumberland was at that time under the dominion of king Malcolm, not held by right, but subjugated by force. Having heard (while still gazing on the church of St. Peter as it was being consumed by the fire of his men) of what Gospatric had committed against his people, scarcely able to contain himself for fury, he ordered his troops no longer to spare any of the English nation, but either to smite all to the earth, or to carry them off captives under the yoke of perpetual slavery. Having received this licence, it was misery even to witness their deeds against the English. Some aged men and women were beheaded with the sword; others were thrust through with pikes, like swine destined for food; infants snatched from their mother's breasts were thrown high into the air, and in their fall were received on the points of lances and pikes thickly placed in the ground. The Scots, more savage than wild beasts, delighted in this cruelty, as an amusing spectacle. These children of the age of innocence, suspended between heaven and earth, gave up their souls to heaven. Young men also and maidens, and whoever seemed fit for toil and labour, were bound and driven before the face of their enemies, to be reduced in perpetual exile to slaves and bondmaids. Some of these females, worn out by running in front of their drivers further than their strength would bear, falling to the earth, perished even where they fell.

Seeing these things, Malcolm was yet moved to pity by no tears, no groans of the unhappy wretches; but, on the contrary, gave orders that they should be still further pressed onward in the march. Scotland was, therefore, filled with slaves and handmaids of the English race; so that even to this day, I do not say no little village, but even no cottage, can be found without one of them.

After Malcolm's return to Scotland,[1] when bishop Egelwin was commencing his voyage towards Cologne, a contrary wind arising soon drove him back to Scotland. Thither also it bore with a favourable course Edgar Atheling, with his companions before named. King Malcolm, with the consent of his relatives, took in marriage Eadgar's sister, Margaret, a woman noble by royal descent, but much more noble by her wisdom and piety. By her care and labour the king himself, laying aside the barbarity of his manners, became more gentle and civilized. Of her he begat six sons, Eadward, Eadmund, king Eadgar, king Alexander, Ethelred, and king David, and two daughters, Matilda queen of the English, and Mary, whom Eustace count of Bologne took in marriage. In Easter-week a great council was held at Winchester, by order and in the presence of king William, and by the consent of the lord pope Alexander, his authority being represented by his legates—Hermenfred, bishop of Sedun [Sion], and John and Peter, presbyter cardinals of the apostolic see.[2] In this council Stigand, archbishop of Canterbury, was degraded for three causes; to wit, because he had unlawfully held the see of Winchester in conjunction with the archbishopric; and because not only had he taken the archbishopric whilst archbishop Robert still lived, but also had for some time, in celebrating mass, used the pall of the latter which had remained at Canterbury, when he was violently and unjustly driven from England; and lastly, because he had received a pall from Benedict, whom the holy Roman church had excommunicated, because that personage had acquired the apostolic see by simony. Several abbots were also there degraded, the king making it his business, that as many as possible of the English should be deprived of their rank, in place of whom he might substitute natives of his own nation, in order to further the establishment of his newly acquired kingdom. For this reason also he deprived both bishops and abbots of their dignities, without any apparent ground of condemnation either by councils or secular laws, and kept them confined in prison to the very end of their lives; actuated, as we have said, merely by mistrust towards his newly acquired kingdom. While other timorous persons in this council, knowing the king's disposition, were trembling lest they should be deprived of their dignities, that venerable man, Wulstan bishop of Winchester, stoutly pleaded for, and demanded the restoration of, several estates of his see, which had been kept in his possession by archbishop Aldred when he was translated from the church of Worcester to York, and which at his decease had come into the possession of the king; and he, therefore, urged that justice should be done both by those who presided at the council and by the king himself. But because the church of York was silent, not having a pastor who could plead in its behalf, it was decided that this suit should remain over until the appointment of an archbishop who could defend the church and answer his suit, so that the trial might be conducted plainly and justly by the opponent and respondent.

On Whitsunday [23d May], the king at Windsor gave the

---

[1] See Simeon's History of the Church of Durham, chap. lii.
[2] See this volume, p. 542, note [2].

archbishopric of York to the venerable Thomas, canon of Bayeux,
and the bishopric of the church of Winchester to Walcelin, his
chaplain.   Immediately by his order on the morrow, the aforesaid
Hermenfrid, bishop of Sion, held a synod; the cardinals John and
Peter, whom we have already mentioned, having returned to Rome.
In this synod Agelric, bishop of the South Saxons, was uncanonically
degraded, and the king, for no crime whatever, afterwards put him
in prison at Marlborough.   Many abbots were also degraded; and
on their deprivation the king gave to his chaplains, Arfast the
bishopric of the East Angles, and to Stigand that of the South
Saxons.   To some Norman monks also he gave abbeys.   And
because the archbishop of Canterbury was deposed, and the archbishop of York deceased, by command of the king, Walcelin was
consecrated in the octave of Whit-Sunday [30th May] by the same
Armenfred, bishop of Sion, the legate of the apostolic see.

Just at the feast of St. John the Baptist [24th June], earl Osbern
went to Denmark with the fleet which had wintered in the river
Humber, but his brother Suane, king of the Danes, outlawed him,
on account of the money which, contrary to the desire of the
Danes, he had accepted from king William.   That very brave man,
Edric, surnamed the Forester, of whom mention has been before
made, was reconciled with king William.

After these things the king summoned from Normandy, Lanfranc,
abbot of Caen, a Lombard by birth, a very learned man in every
respect, well skilled in the knowledge of all liberal arts, and in
divine as well as secular literature; and equally wise in the counsel
and management of worldly affairs.   On the day of the Assumption
of St. Mary [15th Aug.] he appointed him archbishop of the church
of Canterbury, and on Sunday, being the feast of St. John the
Baptist,[1] he caused him to be consecrated at Canterbury.   So he
was consecrated by bishops Gyso of Wells, and Walter of Hereford,
both of whom were ordained at Rome by pope Nicholas, when
Aldred, archbishop of York, had received the pall.   For they
avoided being consecrated by Stigand, who then ruled over the
archbishopric of Canterbury, because they were aware that he had
not canonically received the pall.   Herman also, bishop of Salisbury, with some others, was present at his consecration.   Then
Lanfranc consecrated Thomas archbishop of York.   When these
matters were accomplished, then the suit of the venerable Wulstan,
bishop of Worcester, was again mooted,—for Thomas had now been
consecrated bishop, and could plead for the church of York,—and
was brought to an issue at a council held at Pedreda before the
king, and Lanfranc, archbishop of Canterbury, and the bishops,
abbots, earls and nobles of all England, insomuch that the man of
God, Wulstan, not only recovered the estates sued for and demanded, but also, God granting and the king yielding, received
his church, and with the same liberties by which it had been
enfranchised by its founder and their successors.

A.D. 1071. Lanfranc and Thomas went to Rome, and received
the pall from pope Alexander.   Earls Edwin and Morkar secretly

---

[1] That is, the feast of the Decollation of St. John the Baptist, 29th August.

fled from the court because king William wished to put them in
confinement, and were for some time in rebellion against him.
But when they saw that the undertaking in which they had embarked had not gone prosperously for them, Edwin determined to
go to Malcolm, king of Scots; but on his way, suffering from the
treachery of his own men, he was slain; Morkar, and the very
valiant man Hereward, went by ship with many others to the Isle
of Ely, intending to winter thère.   Agelwin also, bishop of Durham, and Siward, surnamed Barn, sailing back from Scotland had
arrived there.   But hearing of this, the king with his mariners on
the east side of the island debarred them from all exit, and on the
west side he ordered a bridge to be constructed two miles long;
but they seeing themselves thus blockaded ceased from opposition,
and all gave themselves up to the king, except Hereward, who with
a few men made his escape through the marshes.   He soon sent
bishop Agelwine to prison at Abingdon, where he ended his days
that winter. The earl, and the others dispersed throughout England,
he partly placed in confinement, and part he allowed to depart,
having cut off their hands or put out their eyes.   The king
appointed Walcher bishop of the church of Durham, from a clerk
of the church of Liege, (for he had come over on the invitation of
the king himself,) illustrious in birth, upright in character, endowed
with the grace of sacred and secular learning.   Eilaf, the housecarl,
held in especial honour by the king, with many other leading men,
conducted him to York, where, by the king's direction, earl Cospatric met and received the prelate, to accompany him as far as
Durham; and he came to the church of his see at Mid-Lent
[27th March].

    A.D. 1072. After the Assumption of St. Mary [15th Aug.] king
William, having in his company Edric, surnamed the Forester, set
out for Scotland with a force both of sailors and men-at-arms, to
reduce it to subjection.   For the king of Scots, Malcolm, had
grievously offended him, because, as before has been said, he had
in the preceding year furiously ravaged the territories of his kingdom.   But when the king of the English had entered Scotland,
king Malcolm met him at the place called Abernethy, and became
his homager.   William returning thence deprived Cospatric of the
dignity of his earldom, charging him with having afforded counsel
and aid to those who had murdered the earl and his men at
Durham, although he had not been present in person; and that he
had been on the side of the enemy when the Normans were slain
at York.

    But here let us revert a little to the past, mention having been
made of the earls of Northumberland, in order that it may be
known by what earls that province began to be administered when
the line of its kings failed.   The last of the kings of that province
was Eiric,[1] whom the Northumbrians, in violation of the faith
which they had sworn to king Eadred, made their king.   Wherefore
the king, being enraged, ordered that the whole province should be
utterly devastated.   Hereupon the Northumbrians, their king being

---

[1] See A.D. 949.

driven out and slain by Maccus, the son of Onlaf, pacified king
Eadred by oaths and presents, and the province was committed to
earl Osulf.   From that time Osulf administered the affairs on the
north side of the Tyne, and Oslac at York and its territories.   To
them succeeded the elder Walthef, who had his son Uchtred as his
successor.   He, when in the reign of Agelred king Cnut made an
attack upon Northumbria, was compelled by necessity to betake
himself with his men to Cnut; and after having taken an oath and
given hostages, he was slain by a powerful Dane, Thurbrand, surnamed Hold, with the consent of Cnut.   His brother, Eadulf Cutel,
was put in his place.   But earl Uchtred had left three sons, Aldred,
Eadulf, and Cospatric, of whom the first two were successively
earls of the Northumbrians.   The third, who did not attain the
rank of the earldom, had a son named Uchtred, whose son was
Eadulf, surnamed Rus, who afterwards appeared as the leader of
those who murdered bishop Walcher, and he is said to have killed
him with his own hand; but he was himself afterwards slain by a
woman, and was buried in the church of Geddewerde [Jedburgh],
but that corruption was afterwards cast out thence by Turgot, formerly prior of the church of Durham, and archdeacon.   After
Eadulf Cudel, Aldred, son of the aforesaid earl Uchtred, having
obtained the earldom, in revenge for his father's death slew the
murderer Thurebrand.   Carl, the son of this Thurebrand, and
the aforesaid earl Aldred, after plotting each against the life of the
other, were at length reconciled; but not long after, Aldred, suspecting no evil, was treacherously slain in the wood called Risewood
by his sworn brother Carl.   After his brother's death, Eadulf
became earl of the Northumbrians, who, being puffed up with
arrogance, very cruelly pillaged the Britons; but in the third year
after, when he had gone to be reconciled in friendship with Hardecnut, he was put to death by Siward, who then himself held the
earldom of the whole province of the Northumbrians; that is, of
the district from the Humber to the Tweed.   At his death Tosti
succeeded him, who being driven by the Northumbrians from
England, on account of the heavy injuries that he had inflicted
on them, his dukedom was committed to Morkar, first by king
Eadward, and afterwards by king William.   But Morkar being
burdened with other weighty matters, handed over the earldom
beyond the Tyne to the young Osulf, son of the aforesaid earl
Eadulf.   Morkar being subsequently taken and committed to
prison, king William granted the earldom of Osulf to Copsi, who
was on the side of earl Tosti, a man of discretion and skill.   Osulf,
driven by Copsi from the earldom, concealed himself in the woods
and mountains in hunger and want, till at last having gathered
some associates whom the same need had brought together, he surrounded Copsi while feasting at Newburn.   He escaped through
the midst of confused crowds; but being discovered while he lay hid
in the church, he was compelled by the burning of the church to
go out to the door, where at the very door he was beheaded by the
hands of Osulf, in the fifth week of his charge of the earldom, on the
fourth of the ides of March [12th March].   By and by, in the following

autumn, Osulf himself, rushing headlong against the lance of a
robber who met him, was thrust through, and there perished. At
his death, Cospatric the son of Maldred, the son of Crinan, going
to king William, obtained the earldom of the Northumbrians,
which he purchased for a great sum; for the dignity of that earldom
belonged to him by his mother's blood. His mother was Algitha
the daughter of earl Uchtred, whom he had of Algiva, daughter of
king Agelred. This Algitha her father gave in marriage to Maldred
the son of Crinan. He then held the earldom, until the king, for
the causes above named, took it from him. Flying therefore to
Malcolm, he not long after made a voyage to Flanders; returning
after a little time to Scotland, the aforesaid king bestowed upon him
Dunbar, with the lands adjacent in Lothian, that out of these he
might provide for himself and his friends until more prosperous
times should come. This Cospatric was the father of Dolfin,
Walthev, and Cospatric. After Cospatric the earldom was given
to Walthev, the son of earl Siward; but he being afterwards
imprisoned, the charge of the county was committed to bishop
Walcher, until the day of his murder. The king then gave that
honour to Albric, who being of very little use in difficult affairs,
returned to his country; and the king gave the earldom of Northumberland to Robert de Mowbray, but he being taken prisoner,
king William the second held Northumbria in his own hand, as at
this time does king Henry.

Having thrown together these matters in a digression for the
information of my readers, the pen must now return, to resume the
course of its interrupted order.

Cospatric being cast down from his dignity, Waltheov was
raised to the earldom, which was his right by his father's and
mother's descent; for he was the son of earl Siward, by Elfleda,
daughter of earl Aldred.

At that time (namely, when the king had returned from Scotland) he built a castle in Durham, where the bishop might keep
himself and his people safe from the attacks of assailants. Bishop
Walcher and earl Waltheov were very friendly and accommodating
to each other; so that he, sitting together with the bishop in the
synod of priests, humbly and obediently carried out whatever the
bishop decreed for the reformation of Christianity in his earldom.

A.D. 1073. In this year all things connected with the course of
the sun and moon occurred as they had done in the fifteenth year
of Tiberius, in which our Lord was baptized; that is to say, the
day of his baptism, the eighth of the ides of January [6th Jan.],
was on the Epiphany Sunday, and on the Monday was the
beginning of his forty days' fast. From the baptism, therefore, of
our Lord in the fifteenth year of Tiberius, two great cycles have
elapsed,—that is, one thousand and sixty-four years.

William, king of the English, subdued the city of Mans, with
the province belonging to it, having obtained great assistance
from those of the English whom he had brought with him from
England. Edgar Atheling came from Scotland through England
into Normandy, and again reconciled himself with the king. Earl

Waltheov sending a strong band of Northumbrians, cruelly avenged the death of his grandfather earl Aldred, inasmuch as the sword of treachery destroyed the sons of Carl, who had put him to death, while they were feasting at Settrington.

A.D. 1074. Hildebrand, called also Gregory, archdeacon of Rome, was elected and made pope. This pope in a solemn synod, according to the ordinance of St. Peter the Apostle, St. Clement, and other holy fathers, by a decree forbad clerics, especially those ordained to the sacred ministry, to have wives, or to dwell with women, save those whom the Nicene Council or other canons excepted. He decreed also, under the judgment of St. Peter, that not only were they to be condemned with Simon Magus who bought or sold any office, such as that of a bishopric, abbey, priory, or deanery, or the tithes of the church, but those also, whoever they might be, who should consent to it. For the Lord has said, "Freely ye have received, freely give."

Three[1] poor monks setting out from the province of the Mercians, and sent by divine instigation to the province of the Northumbrians, came to York, asking of Hugh the son of Baldric, who at that time filled the office of sheriff, that he would provide a guide for their journey to the place called Monkchester, that is, The city of monks, now called Newcastle. Brought thither by his guidance, they remained there for a time; but finding in that place no trace of the ancient community of servants of Christ, they proceeded to Jarrow, where were to be seen many buildings of the monks with half-ruined churches, of which the remains scarcely indicated what their original condition had been. Bishop Walcher received them with great rejoicing, and supplied their needs. These were their names: first, in years and virtues, was Aldwin; next, Ealfwy; and third, Rinfrid. By these, then, three monasteries were established in the country of the Northumbrians: one at Durham, over the sacred and uncorrupted body of the father Cuthbert, in honour of St. Mary the Virgin; another at York, in honour of the same mother of God, Mary,—where of a little church was made a noble convent, which had for its first abbot, Stephen; its second, Richard; third, Gaufrid; fourth, Severinus; fifth, Clement, the present abbot. The third monastery was at the place formerly called Streneshald, that is, The bay of the watch-tower, now Whitby. There presided as its first abbot, William; the second was Nicholas; the third, Benedict; the fourth, Richard, who yet survives. But, indeed, after the most cruel devastation of the pagans had reduced the churches and monasteries to ashes by the sword and fire, and Christianity had almost perished, scarcely any churches—and those formed of branches and thatch—and nowhere any monasteries, had been rebuilt for two hundred years; the devotion of faith gradually growing cold, and religious worship altogether ceasing, the name of monks was unheard among the inhabitants of these provinces, who were filled with amazement when they saw any one adopting a monkish habit and mode of life. But when the aforesaid three monks took up their dwelling among them, they began to alter their manners for

[1] See Simeon's History of the Church of Durham, chap. lvi.

the better from their savage life, and they employed themselves in the work of restoring the holy places. They repaired and rebuilt of their own accord the half-ruined churches, and even founded new ones in places where there were none before; many also abandoning a worldly life entered upon the monastic warfare. Attracted by their fame, a few of the natives of the provinces, and many from the remoter parts of England, with one mind here joined them. One of these was Turgot, afterwards bishop of the Scots. He, deriving his descent from no ignoble race of the Angles, was one amongst others who, after the conquest of England by the Normans, were kept as hostages for all Lindsey in the castle of Lincoln. Obtaining by money a mitigation of his imprisonment, he at a great risk privily made his escape to the Norwegians, who were then loading a merchant vessel at Grimsby for Norway. In this vessel also certain ambassadors, whom king William was sending to Norway, had procured a passage ; and now when the ship in full sail was out of sight of land, lo! the king's run-away hostage emerging from the hold of the vessel in which the Norwegians had concealed him, astounded the ambassadors and their companions. For when a diligent search had been everywhere made, the king's inspectors had examined this very vessel, but the cunning of the concealers baffled the observation of the searchers. The ambassadors then insisted that they should lower their sails, and should somehow or other take back the ship with the king's fugitive to England. This the Norwegians sharply resisted, as a voyage so well begun would carry the vessel forward prosperously. Such a quarrel of the parties ensued that they betook themselves to arms on both sides ; but since the force of numbers was with the Norwegians, the insolence of the ambassadors was soon repressed, and the nearer they approached the land the more submissive did they become. When they arrived there, the young refugee by his modest and discreet behaviour rendered himself agreeable to the nobles and gentry. He attained also to the acquaintance of king Oláve, who, as he was of a very religious turn, was accustomed to the use of the sacred writings, and cultivated learning amidst the cares of his kingdom ; he was wont also to assist the priest at the altar, and when the latter was putting on the sacred vestments, he would pour the water[1] on his hand, and devoutly perform other offices of this kind. Hearing therefore that a clerk had come from England, (which at that time was reckoned an important event,) he took him as his master in learning psalmody. In this way Turgot had enough and to spare of good things flowing in upon him by the bounty of the king and noblemen. His soul was constantly stirred to contempt of the world ; so that, avoiding festivities whenever he could, he indulged in solitary tears, beseeching God to direct him in the way of salvation. But as religious impulses often change when they are distracted, his soul by degrees declined from that state, attracted in the course of events by the pleasures of the world. But although unwilling of his own accord, he was in time com-

---

[1] See "De manuum lotione," in Durant, De Ritibus Ecclesiæ Catholicæ, lib. ii. cap. xxviii.

pelled to enter the home of his heavenly Father. For after some years, when he was returning to his own country with much treasure, in the midst of the sea the ship was wrecked by a violent tempest, his companions perished, and he suffered the loss of all his property, and with five or six others with much difficulty barely preserved life alone. Coming to Durham for devotion, he told all things concerning himself to bishop Walcher, and showed him that his mind was disposed to embrace the monastic life. The bishop perceived this with much satisfaction, and sending him to bishop Aldwin, of whom mention has been made above, he said, "I pray and desire that you will receive this my son, clothe him with the monastic habit, and teach him to observe also the monastic life." He received him, and duly placed him on his probation; and when he was approved he delivered him the monastic habit; and so instructed him by word and example, that when the same Aldwin died, by order of bishop William, Turgot succeeded him in the priory of the church of Durham, which he ably administered for twenty years all but twelve days. For in the eighth year of the episcopate of Ralph, who succeeded William, at the request of Alexander, king of Scots, he was elevated by Henry, king of the English, to the episcopate of the church of St. Andrew in Scotland, which is the see of the primate of the whole nation of the Scots. But his consecration was deferred for a year or more, on account of dissensions between the church of York and the church of St. Andrew in Scotland. For the former, from some imaginary right, claimed for itself the consecration and subjection of the primate of the Scots; but the latter, on the other hand, repudiated any obligation which might arise from either antiquity or custom. But that the church being deprived of a pastor, might not remain longer in suspense, at the request of the king of Scots, king Henry ordered that Thomas the second, archbishop of York, should consecrate him without any requirement of subjection, saving the authority of each church; so that afterwards, where, when, and by whomsoever the cause should be moved, a due termination might be put to the dispute between the two parties. Going thus consecrated to Scotland, and finding that he could not rightly exercise his episcopal office in difficult causes, he prepared to go to Rome, where he could pass his life under the counsel and advice of the lord pope Paschal [II]. But he was prevented from carrying that into effect, because when the disputes between him and the king came to an issue, through distress of mind he fell into a dispirited state. Having therefore on account of his infirmity received licence to stay for a while at Durham, he went on the vigil of the apostles Peter and Paul [28th June] to Wearmouth, where he had formerly received from Aldwin the monastic habit; having there in the morning celebrated mass as well as he could, he set out for St. Cuthbert's, and there taking to his bed, his end was preceded by febrile attacks, sometimes low, sometimes acute, and this for two months and four days. When the hour of his death came, as he was repeating in prayer as well as he could, "In[1] peace is his habi-

---

[1] Psalm lxxvi. 2, Vulg.; cl. 1.

tation, and his dwelling in Sion;" and, "Praise the Lord in his
holiness," he yielded up his spirit in the presence of his brethren, at
the third hour, on Tuesday, the second of the kalends of April
[31st March]. After an episcopate of eight years, two months,
and ten days, he obtained of God the gift which he had earnestly
sought, that he might breathe his last breath near the sacred body of
Cuthbert. He was buried in the chapter-house, where his body lies
between that of bishop Walcher on the south, and bishop William
on the north. He died in the year of our Lord's incarnation[1] one
thousand one hundred and fifteen.

So much by way of digression; let us now resume the order of
the history.

In the same year in which pope Hildebrand held the aforesaid
council, Roger, earl of Hereford, son of William, earl of the East
Angles, contrary to the command of king William, gave his sister
in marriage to earl Ralph, and celebrated the nuptials with great
pomp, at the place called Yxning, in the province of Cambridge,
where they made a great conspiracy against king William, in
which many joined. They compelled earl Waltheov, who had been
entrapped by their wiles, to enter into the conspiracy. He went,
as soon as he could, to Lanfranc, archbishop of Canterbury, and
received from him a penance for the oath which he had taken,
though unwillingly; and by his advice he proceeded to king
William, who was residing in Normandy; and when he had laid
the whole affair before him, he voluntarily threw himself on his
mercy. But the other nobles above mentioned repaired to their
castles, with the intention of carrying out the conspiracy which they
had commenced; and, with their supporters, began to organize
a rebellion with all their might. But Wulstan, bishop of Worcester,
with a large military force, and Agelwin, abbot of Evesham, with
his men, having summoned to their aid Urso, sheriff of Worcester,
and Walter de Lacy, with their troops and a number of other people,
prevented the earl of Hereford from crossing the Severn, and thus
forming a junction with earl Ralph and with his army at the
appointed place. And then Odo, bishop of Bayeux, the king's
brother, and Geoffrey, bishop of Coutance, who were prepared for
battle, with a large force both of English and Normans encountered
earl Ralph, who had encamped near Cambridge. He perceived
the weakness of his force, and fearing the numbers of his opponents,
he privily escaped to Norwich, and committing the castle to the
care of his wife and his soldiers, embarked in a vessel and fled from
England to Lesser Brittany. The enemy pursued him in his flight,
and either killed, or in various ways disabled all of his men whom
they could catch. The leaders then besieged the castle until,
a treaty being made, by the king's permission the countess was
allowed to depart from England with her people. After these
events, the king returned in the autumn from Normandy, and put
earl Roger in confinement. He also imprisoned earl Waltheov,
although he had petitioned for mercy from him.

---

[1] In A.D. 1115 the 31st March did not fall upon a Tuesday, which, however, it
did in 1114.

Egitha, formerly queen of the English, died at Wilton, in the month of December ; her body was brought to London by the king's order, and honourably buried at Westminster, near the body of her husband, king Eadward. The king held his court thereat the ensuing Christmas, and of those who had raised their heads against him, some he banished from England, some he maimed by putting out their eyes, or cutting off their hands. The earls Waltheov and Roger, who had been condemned by a judicial sentence, he placed in stricter custody.

A. D. 1075. Since the clergy preferred lying under anathema to parting from their wives, pope Hildebrand, in order to punish them if he could by means of others, ordered that no one should hear mass from a married priest, as follows :—

" Gregory, pope, also called Hildebrand, the servant of the servants of God, to those throughout the kingdoms of Italy and Germany who exhibit the obedience due to St. Peter, sends the apostolic benediction.

" If there are any priests, deacons, or subdeacons, who are wallowing in the crime of fornication, we, on behalf of Almighty God, and by the authority of St. Peter, forbid them access to the church, until they repent and amend ; but if any choose to continue in their sin, let none of you presume to listen to the offices which they perform, since their blessing is turned into a curse, and their prayer into a sin, as the Lord witnesseth by the prophet, saying, ' I will curse your blessings.' " (Mal. ii. 2.)

Earl Waltheov, by order of king William, being led without the city of Winchester, was undeservedly and cruelly beheaded by the axe, and his body buried in the same place ; but, in process of time (God so appointing it), his body was disinterred, and with great respect conveyed to Croyland, and reverently buried in the church. Before his death, when he was placed in close confinement, he constantly and bitterly bewailed whatever he had done amiss ; and by prayers, fastings and alms, sought to make his peace with God. Men wished to blot his memory from the earth ; but we believe that he rejoices with the saints in heaven ; for the aforesaid archbishop Lanfranc, of pious memory, from whom after confession he had received penance, was a faithful witness, who both affirmed that he was free from the crime imputed to him—to wit, the aforesaid conspiracy—and that whatever sins he had committed in other respects, he mourned over them like a true Christian, with penitential tears ; and that he himself would be happy if, after the termination of his life, he should share his blessed rest. After him the charge of the earldom was committed to bishop Walcher.

After these things the king, crossing the sea, marched an expedition into Lesser Brittany, and besieged the castle of earl Ralph, called Dol, until Philip, king of the French, drove him from thence.

A. D. 1076. Suane, king of the Danes, died ; a man well imbued with learning. His son Harold succeeded him.

A. D. 1077. Robert, eldest son of king William, (because he did not grant him possession of Normandy, which before his going to

England he had given him, in the presence of Philip, king of the French,) went to France ; and, by the aid of king Philip, constantly committed great depredations in Normandy, burnt the towns, slew the people, and caused his father no little trouble and anxiety.

A.D. 1078. The abbey of St. Mary, at York, was founded.

A.D. 1079. Malcolm, king of Scots, after the Assumption of St. Mary [15th Aug.], devastated Northumberland, as far as the great river Tyne, slew many, took more prisoners, and returned with great spoil. King William, while engaged in battle with his son Robert before the castle of Gerberoy, which king Philip had given him, was wounded by him in the arm, and thrown from his horse ; but as soon as he recognised him by his voice, Robert immediately dismounted and desired his father to mount his own horse ; and so allowed him to depart. He then took to flight ; many of his men being killed and some taken, and his son William, with many others, being wounded. The venerable man Robert, who received the order of priesthood by the ministry of the most reverend Wulstan, bishop of Worcester, was consecrated bishop of the church of Hereford, at Canterbury, by Lanfranc, archbishop of Canterbury, on Sunday, the fourth of the kalends of January [29th Dec.].

A.D. 1080. Walcher,[1] bishop of Durham, a native of Lorraine, was slain, on Thursday, the second of the ides of May [14th May], at the place called Goteshead, (that is, The goat's head,) by the Northumbrians, in revenge for the death of Ligulf, a noble and good thane. This man, by hereditary right, had large possessions spread throughout England. But since at that time the Normans continually gave scope to their ferocity in every quarter, he betook himself with his family to Durham, inasmuch as he loved St. Cuthbert with his whole heart. He had married Algitha, daughter of earl Aldred, of whom he begat two sons, named Uchthred and Morckar. Elfleda, mother of earl Waltheof, was sister of this Algitha. Wherefore that earl gave his little cousin, the aforesaid Morkar, to God, to be educated by the monks of Jarrow. At that time the earl himself was at Tynemouth,[2] which place he had granted along with the aforesaid youth, to the disposal of those monks. The boy's father, Ligulf, was so much beloved by the bishop, that he would by no means carry on or administer the greater matters of secular business without his advice. On this account his chaplain, Leobwin, (whom he had raised so high that scarcely anything could be managed in the bishopric or the county without reference to him,) stimulated by envy, and excessively puffed up with arrogance on account of his own power, insolently set himself up against the aforesaid Ligulf ; wherefore he made light of some of his opinions and counsels, and strove in all ways to render them void. Also he frequently quarrelled with him before the bishop, not without menaces, and he often provoked him to anger by his opprobrious language. So it happened, that one day when this man Ligulf (who was summoned to counsel by the bishop) had

---

[1] See Simeon's History of the Church of Durham, chap. lix.

[2] This incident is illustrated by two charters, printed among the Illustrations appended to this History, letter [A].

decided that certain things were lawful and right, Leobwin obstinately opposed him, and irritated him by his contemptuous speeches;
but as he replied to him more severely than usual, he therefore left
the place of meeting, and calling to him Gilbert, to whom—for he
was a relation—the bishop had under himself committed the
government of the earldom of the Northumbrians, he earnestly
begged that he would avenge him, and hasten to put Ligulf to
death as speedily as possible.   Gilbert readily yielded to his neighbour's request, and gathering together his own soldiers, along with
those of the bishop and Leobwin himself, he marched one night to
the vill where Ligulf was resident, and wickedly slew him, with almost
all his family, in his own house.   When this was known, the bishop
groaned heavily from the bottom of his heart, and tearing the hood
from his head and throwing it to the ground, he in his grief at once
said to Leobwin, who was then present, " These things, Leobwin,
are the result of your grievous doings and most stupid craft ; therefore I would have you to know for certain that by the sword of
your tongue you have destroyed both me, and yourself, and all my
family."   Saying this, he quickly betook himself to the castle, and
sending messengers immediately through all Northumbria, he took
care that all should be informed that he was not privy to the death
of Liulf, but that, on the contrary, he would utterly banish his
murderer, Gilbert, and all his associates from Northumbria, and
that he would be ready to clear himself according to the decision of
the pontiff; then, by sending mediators, he and the relatives of the
slain persons agreed to a truce on each side, and appointed a place
and day where and on which to meet, in order to settle a firmer
agreement between them.   When the time came, they met at the
appointed place ; but, as the bishop would not hold the meeting
in the open air, he went with his clergy and more worshipful knights
into the church there, and a conference being held, he again and
again sent such of his friends as he pleased out of doors to them, for
the purpose of making an agreement.   But they refused to accede
to his requests, since they were fully convinced that Liulf had been
put to death by his order.   For not only had Leobwin, on the night
after the murder of their neighbour, received Gilbert and his associates into his house familiarly and amicably, but also the bishop
himself had received him as before into his favour and society ;
wherefore, they first slew all of the bishop's party who were out of
doors, except a few who escaped by flight.   At sight of this the
bishop, to satisfy the fury of his enemies, ordered his relative, the
aforesaid Gilbert, to leave the church.   The soldiers followed on
his footsteps as he went out, to defend him; but assailed at once on
every side by the swords and lances of their enemies, they perished
in a moment.   Nevertheless, they spared two English thanes, on
account of their relationship.   They killed also Leobwin the dean of
Durham, because he had so often given the bishop many evil counsels
against them, and the other clerics as soon as they came out.
The bishop, when he saw that their fury could by no means be
allayed except by the death of Leobwin, the head and author of
all that disaster, begged him to go out; but as he was altogether

unable to prevail upon him to depart, he himself went to the doors of the church, and begged them that his own life might be spared. When they refused this, he covered his head with the border of his tunic and went out of doors, and immediately fell pierced by the swords of his foes. They then ordered Leobwin to come out; and when he would not, they set fire to the roof and walls of the church; but he, choosing to end his life by burning rather than by massacre, for some time endured the flames. But when he was half burnt he broke forth, and being hewed to pieces, he miserably perished, paying the penalty of his iniquity. In retaliation for this horrible murder, king William the same year ravaged Northumbria; sending thither Odo, bishop of Bayeux, with a large military force. In the autumn of this year, the same king William sent his son Robert to Scotland against Malcholm; but having gone as far as Egglesbreth he returned without accomplishing anything, and built the new castle on the river Tyne. William received the bishopric of Durham on the fifth of the ides of November [9th Nov.]; but was consecrated by Thomas, archbishop of York, on the fourth of the nones of January [2d Jan.], at Gloucester.

The emperor Henry, on Whitsunday [31st May], decreed at Mentz, that pope Hildebrand should be deposed; and on the Nativity of St. John Baptist [24th June], he made Wibert, bishop of the city of Ravenna, pope in his place.

A. D. 1081. King Henry went with a hostile intent against pope Hildebrand to Rome, which he assaulted, but did not enter.

A. D. 1082. Much slaughter and depredation having taken place between king Henry and pope Hildebrand, many men were killed in the night of Palm Sunday [17th April]. King William put his brother Odo, bishop of Bayeux, into confinement in Normandy.

A.D. 1083. King Henry stormed and took the city of Rome, and placed Wibert in the apostolic see. Hildebrand went to Benevento, where he remained until his death; but Henry returned to Germany. An infamous dissension took place between the monks and Turstin their abbot, at Glastonbury, a man unworthy to be spoken of, whom king William had unwisely preferred from the monastery of Caen to be abbot of that place. Amongst other deeds of folly he disdained the Gregorian chant, and began to force the monks to discontinue it, and to learn and sing the chant of one William of Fescamp. As they bore this very ill—for they had now grown old both in that and other ecclesiastical service according to the custom of the Roman church—one day he suddenly rushed upon them unawares into the chapter with an armed military force, and pursued the monks as they were flying in extreme terror into the church, as far as the altar, while the soldiers pierced the crucifixes, and images, and shrines of the saints, with their javelins and arrows, and thrusting through with a pike one of the monks, even while he was embracing the holy altar, they slew him; and they murdered another at the base of the altar, pierced with arrows. The rest, urged by necessity, bravely defending themselves with the benches and candlesticks of the church, although severely wounded, drove back all the soldiers out of the choir. And then it happened that two of the monks were killed and fourteen wounded, as were also some of the soldiers. An action being brought on this account, as it was evident that the abbot was chiefly to blame, the king removed the same abbot, and placed him in a monastery of his own in Normandy. Very many of the monks were dispersed in prisons through the bishoprics and abbeys by order of the king. After his death the same abbot again bought his abbey from his son, king William, for five hundred pounds of silver; and, roving about for some years through the possessions of the church, he ended his life miserably, as he deserved, far from his monastery. Queen Matilda died in Normandy, on Thursday, the fourth of the nones of November [2d Nov.], and was buried at Caen. In this year monks first assembled at Durham.

A. D. 1084. Pope Hildebrand, otherwise called Gregory, died. William, king of the English, received from each hyde of land throughout England six shillings.

A. D. 1085. Eadmund, abbot of Pershore, a man of remarkable goodness and piety, died at a good old age, on Sunday, the seventeenth of the kalends of July [15th June], and was buried by Serlo, the venerable abbot of Gloucester. Turstin, a monk of Gloucester, succeeded him. In the same year the king of the Danes, Cnut the son of Suane, came to England equipped with a powerful fleet, and aided by his father-in-law Robert, count of Flanders, whose daughter he had married. Wherefore king William hired many thousands of mercenary foot soldiers and archers from France; and, taking some from Normandy, he returned to England in the autumn, and having distributed them through the whole kingdom, he ordered the bishops, abbots, earls, barons, sheriffs, and king's officers, to give them provisions; but, on learning that the intentions of his enemies had been delayed, he sent back part of the army, and part he retained with him the whole winter. And at Christmas he held his court at Gloucester; where he gave to his three chaplains, Maurice, William, and Robert, the bishoprics of London, Thetford, and Chester.

A. D. 1086. King William caused the whole of England to be described; how much land each of his barons possessed, how many feudatory soldiers, how many ploughs, how many villains, how many horses, even what quantity of live stock each man possessed, in the whole of his kingdom, from the greatest to the least, and how much tribute each estate could pay; and the land was harassed with much loss resulting from thence. And in Whitsun-week[1] he invested his son Henry with the arms of a knight at Westminster, where he was holding his court. Not long after, he commanded the archbishops, bishops, abbots, earls, barons, sheriffs, with their knights, to meet him on the kalends of August [1st Aug.], at Salisbury. On their coming thither, he made their knights swear fealty to him against all men. At that time Eadgar Atheling, having obtained the king's permission, crossed the sea with two hundred soldiers, and went to Apulia. His sister Christina, a virgin, entered the monastery called

---

[1] Whitsunday fell upon 24th May.

Romsey, and assumed the garb of a nun. In the same year was a plague among cattle, and great severity of weather.

A.D. 1087. In this year the relics of St. Nicolas were translated from Myra[1] to the city of Baris. Aldwin, prior of Durham, died. A furious fire destroyed many cities, also the church of St. Paul the Apostle, with the greater and better part of London. The Danes martyred their sovereign, king Cnut, in a church, on Saturday, the sixth of the ides of July [10th July]. Stigand, bishop of Chichester; Scoland, abbot of St. Augustin's; Alsi, abbot of Bath; and Turstin, abbot of Pershore, died. Before the Assumption of St. Mary [15th Aug.], king William went to France with an army, and burnt the town called Mathun [Mantes], and all the churches in it, and two recluses, and returned thence into Normandy. But on his return he was seized with a severe complaint of the bowels, and grew worse and worse daily; and when, by the increase of his illness, he perceived that the day of his death was at hand, he liberated his brother Odo, bishop of Bayeux, and earls Morkar and Roger, and Siward surnamed Barn, Wulnoth, king Harold's brother, whom he had detained in captivity from childhood, and all whom he had kept in prison either in England or Normandy. Then he gave the kingdom of England to his son William; and to his eldest son Robert (who was then in exile in France) he granted the earldom of Normandy. And so, strengthened with the heavenly viaticum, he gave up at once his life and his kingdom, after ruling over the English nation twenty years, ten months, and twenty-eight days, on the fifth of the ides of September [9th Sept.], and lies buried at Caen, in the church of the protomartyr St. Stephen, which he had built from its foundations and enriched with wealth.

His son William hurried off to England, taking with him Morkar and Wulnoth; but as soon as he came to Winchester he committed them to prison just as they had been before; and on Sunday, the sixth of the kalends of October [26th Sept.], he was consecrated king at Westminster by Lanfranc, archbishop of Canterbury. Then, returning to Winchester, he distributed throughout England his father's treasures, as he had directed; namely, to some principal churches he gave ten marks of gold, to some six, to some less. He ordered also, that sixty pence each be given to such churches as were situated in towns or villages; and among the higher churches and monasteries he distributed crosses, altars, screens, gospels, candlesticks, holy water stoups, pipes, and various ornaments decked with gems, gold, silver, and precious stones. His brother Robert also, on his return to Normandy, bestowed abundantly the treasures which he found on the monasteries and poor churches, for the good of his father's soul; and having freed from imprisonment Ulf, son of Harold, formerly king of the English, and Dunechald, son of Malcolm king of Scots, and invested them with the arms of knighthood, he allowed them to depart.

A.D. 1088. In this year a dissension arose among the nobles of

[1] See Act. SS. Bolland. die nona Maii, p. 359, inter prætermissos.

England; for a small part of the Norman nobility favoured king William, the other and the greater number were in favour of Robert, earl of the Normans, desiring that he would seize the kingdom to himself;—they wished either to betray the one brother alive to the other, or by putting him to death to deprive him of the kingdom. The leaders in this infamous affair were Odo, bishop of Bayeux, who was also earl of Kent; Geoffrey, bishop of Coutance; Robert, earl of Moreton; Roger, earl of Shropshire; and the higher nobles of all England, except archbishop Lanfranc. They secretly concocted this execrable plot during Lent,[1] and immediately after Easter [16th April], each began to ravage all around, to seize and plunder everything, and to fortify the castles with ramparts and provisions. Geoffrey, bishop of Coutance, and Robert de Mowbray went to Bristol, where they had a very strong castle, and they laid waste the entire country as far as the place called Bath. The nobles of Herefordshire and Shropshire, accompanied by a multitude of the Welsh, marched to Worcester, pillaging and burning all before them. They thought also to take the church and the castle, the latter of which was at that time under the charge of the venerable bishop Wolstan. When the bishop heard of these events he was greatly distressed; and, considering what counsel he should adopt under the circumstances, he betook himself to his God, and prayed that He would have respect to his church and his people oppressed by enemies. While he was thus occupied, his retainers sallied from the castle, and they took and killed five hundred of the assailants, and put the rest to flight. Roger Bigot entered the castle of Norwich and conquered all, but to his own damage. Bishop Odo (the originator of these evils) marched to Kent and pillaged the royal vills; moreover, he ravaged the lands of all who continued faithful to the king, and garrisoned the castle of Rochester. When the king heard of this he called an assembly of the English; he showed them the treachery of the Normans, and begged that they would aid him, on condition that, if they would be faithful to him in this his hour of necessity, he would grant them the best laws they could choose for themselves; he forbad all unjust levies, and allowed permission to all persons to use his forests for hunting. But whatever he promised he kept but a very short time; yet the English faithfully assisted him. The king, therefore, levied an army to go to Rochester, where he supposed bishop Odo to be. When they reached Tunbridge they found the castle held out against the king; but the English bravely assaulting it, destroyed the whole castle, and the garrison capitulated. This being accomplished, the king, with his army, directed his march to the castle of Pevensey, for bishop Odo had now retreated to Rochester, and secured himself in that castle. The king pursued him, and besieged the castle with a large army for six whole weeks.

While these things were passing in England, Robert, earl of Normandy, assembled a large army, and prepared to send it to England, intending to follow presently, as if they were secure

---

[1] In this year Ash-Wednesday fell upon 1st March.

of England by means of bishop Odo and the rest of his party there; but king William had now guarded the sea by his marine force, who slew and drowned in the sea so many of those who were coming to England, that no man knew the number of those who perished.

In the meantime, while this was taking place at sea, bishop Odo, and those who were with him, were reduced by famine to yield the castle of Pevensey, and they promised with an oath that they would leave England, and would not again enter it except by permission of king William, and that they would first give up the castle of Rochester. But when Odo came to Rochester with the king's men who were to receive the castle on the king's behalf, the men who held that castle immediately put him in fetters and those who accompanied him: some affirmed that this was done by the bishop's cunning; certainly there were in this castle brave knights and almost all the nobility of Normandy: there was Eustace, the young earl of Bologne, and many noble Flemish.

When this news reached the king he came with an army to Rochester, and besieged the city, and in a short time the garrison surrendered to him, and were driven with disgrace from England; and thus the bishop, who had been almost a second king of England, irrecoverably lost his dignity. But the bishop, on his arrival in Normandy, immediately received from earl Robert the charge of the whole province, the details of which are recorded in a little book which was written for the purpose. Also William, bishop of Durham, (being then in the eighth year of his episcopate,) departed from England, along with many others.

A.D. 1089. Lanfranc, archbishop of Canterbury, died on Thursday, the ninth of the kalends of June [24th May]. In the same year, on Saturday, the third of the ides of August [11th Aug.], a very great earthquake was felt throughout England.

A.D. 1090. William the younger, king of the English, wishing to take Normandy from his brother Robert, and to bring him into subjection to himself, first reduced the castle of Walter of St. Waleric, and the castle called Albamarle, and placed in them troops to devastate Normandy. Seeing this, and knowing the unfaithfulness of his men, earl Robert sent ambassadors to his liege lord Philip, king of the French, and caused him to come into Normandy, and he and the king besieged one of the castles in which his brother's troops were garrisoned. When this was made known to the king, he secretly sent no small sum of money to king Philip, and he entreated him to raise the siege and return home; and in this request he was successful.

A.D. 1091. In the month of February king William the younger went to Normandy, to seize it from his brother. But during his stay there peace was made between them, on condition that the earl of his own consent should yield to the king the earldom of Eu, the abbey of Fescamp, situated on Mount St. Michael, and the castles which had revolted from him. But the king placed under the earl's rule the province of Mans, and the castles which then held out against him in Normandy; that he should restore to

all the Normans the lands which they had lost in England, on
account of their adherence to the earl; and should give to the earl
as much land in England as had been agreed upon between them.
Besides, they settled between themselves that if the earl should
die without a son born in lawful wedlock, the king should be his
heir, and likewise, if the king chanced to die, the earl should be his
heir of the whole. This agreement was confirmed by the oath of
twelve barons on the king's side, and twelve on the earl's. In the
meantime their brother Henry entered Mount St. Michael with all
the soldiers he had at his command, ravaged the king's land, and
took some of his men prisoners, and despoiled others. Wherefore
the king and the earl assembled their army and besieged the mount
for the whole of Lent,[1] and frequently joined battle with him, and
lost some men and horses; so that the king was wearied out by
the length of the siege, and departed unsatisfied.

Not long after this the king deprived Eadgar Atheling of the rank
which the earl had given him, and expelled him from Normandy.
Meanwhile, in the month of May, Malcolm, king of Scots, invaded
Northumbria with a large army, intending to push on further if he
met with success, and to throw his force upon the inhabitants of
England; but God was against him, and therefore his design was
unsuccessful. When the king heard of it, he returned to England
in the month of August with his brother Robert. Not long after,
he set out for Scotland with a considerable fleet and an army
of cavalry, to subdue Malcolm. When he reached Durham he
restored bishop William to his see, on the very day three years
after that on which he had left it, namely, the third of the ides of
September [11th Sept.]. But before the king entered Scotland,
being a few days before the feast of St. Michael [29th Sept.],
almost all his fleet was wrecked, and many of his cavalry perished
of cold and hunger. King Malcolm met him with an army in the
province of Lothian. Earl Robert, when he saw this, summoned
Eadgar Atheling to him, whom the king had expelled from Normandy, and who was then living with the king of Scots. By his
aid he procured a treaty between the kings, on this condition, that
Malcolm should obey William as he had obeyed his father, and
that William should restore to Malcolm the twelve vills which he
had held in England under his father, and should give him twelve
marks of gold each year; but the agreement thus made between
them did not last long. The earl also reconciled Eadgar himself
with king William.

On Wednesday, being the ides of October [15th Oct.], a
vehement flash of lightning striking the tower of the church of
Winchelcombe, went quite through the wall near the top, split one
of the beams, and striking with violence the head of the image
of Christ, threw it to the ground, and broke the right leg. Also
the image of St. Mary, which stood near the cross, was struck by
the flash and fell to the ground. A great smoke ensued, with an
exceedingly unpleasant smell, and filled the church; it continued

---

[1] Ash-Wednesday fell this year upon 26th February.

until the monks of the place went round the buildings with holy
water and incense, and the relics of the saints, chanting psalms.
Moreover on Friday, the sixteenth of the kalends of November
[17th Oct.], a very violent whirlwind, blowing from the south-
west, struck and shattered more than six hundred houses and very
many churches in London.   Rushing into the church of St. Mary,
called Bow, it killed in it two men, and raising aloft the roof with
its beams, it carried them for some time hither and thither in the
air, and at length planted six of the beams, in the order in which
they had before been fixed in the roof, so deep into the earth, that
of some of them a seventh, of others an eighth part only was visible;
they were twenty-seven or twenty-eight feet long.

After this the king returned from Northumbria, through Mercia,
into Wessex, and kept the earl with him till nearly Christmas ; but
he would not fulfil the compact made between them, at which
the earl being incensed returned to Normandy, on the tenth of the
kalends of January [23d Dec.], with Eadgar Atheling.

As was reported in England, there were at this time two persons
who were styled Roman pontiffs opposing each other, and drawing after them God's church, which was divided between them ;
namely, Urban, who had formerly been called Odo, bishop of Ostia,
and Clement, who had been called Wibert, archbishop of Ravenna.
Not to speak of other parts of the world, this matter for many
years occupied the church of England to such an extent, that
from the death of Gregory, called Hildebrand, to this time it
would not be subject or obedient to any one in the place of pope ;
but Italy and France had already received Urban as the vicar of
St. Peter.

A.D. 1092. The city of London was for the most part destroyed
by fire.   Osmund, bishop of Salisbury, consecrated the church
which he had built in the castle at Salisbury, assisted by bishop
Walcelin and John of Bath, on Monday, the nones of April
[5th April].   Bishop Remigius, who by licence of king William
the elder had transferred the episcopal see of Dorchester to Lincoln,
wished to consecrate a noble church built in that latter place,
as the cathedral of his diocese ; for he felt that the day of his
death was drawing near ; but Thomas, archbishop of York, opposed
him, by objecting that it was built within his diocese.   But king
William the younger, for a sum of money which Remigius had
given him, ordered the bishops of almost all England to assemble
together on the seventh of the ides of May [9th May], and to
dedicate the church.   But two days before the day appointed, bishop
Remigius himself departed this life, by the secret counsel of God;
and the dedication of the church was put off on this account.
After this, as the king was going into Northumbria, he restored the
city, which in British is called Cairleil, but in Latin Lugubalia, and
built a castle in it.   For this city, like some others in those parts,
had been destroyed by the Danish pagans two hundred years before,
and had remained uninhabited to this time.

A.D. 1093. King William the younger was seized with a severe
illness at the royal vill called Alvestan, and went in haste to the

city of Gloucester, and there lay sick during the whole of Lent; [1] and supposing himself to be at the point of death, he vowed to God, (as his barons suggested to him,) that he would amend his life, that he would no longer sell or tax churches, but would protect them by his royal authority; and that he would abolish unjust laws, and enact just ones. He gave the archbishopric of Canterbury, which he held in his own hands, to Anselm, abbot of Bec, who was then staying in England; and the bishopric of Lincoln he gave to his chancellor Robert, surnamed Bloet.

The new church was commenced at Durham on Thursday, the third of the ides of August [11th Aug.], by bishop William, of which Malcolm, king of Scots, and prior Turgot, laid the first stones of the foundation. On the day of the feast of St. Bartholomew [24th Aug.], Malcolm, king of Scots, met king William the younger at Gloucester, as had been before agreed between them by ambassadors, for the purpose of renewing and reestablishing a firm alliance between them, according to the wishes of some of the English nobility; but they separated without coming to terms. For William, from his excessive pride and power, disdained to see Malcolm or to hold converse with him; moreover, he wished to compel him to do him right in his own court, according to the judgment of his own barons only; but Malcolm would by no means do that, except within the confines of his own kingdom, where the kings of the Scots were wont to do right to the kings of England, and according to the judgment of the primates of each kingdom.

After this there appeared a very wonderful sign in the sun, and Roger, earl of Shrewsbury, and Wido, abbot of St. Augustin's, and Paul, abbot of the monastery of St. Albans, died. This Paul, having by the aid of earl Robert taken possession of the church of Tynemouth, contrary to the injunction of the monks of Durham, for it belonged to them, was there attacked by illness; and on his journey home, he died at Seterington near York. Malcolm, king of Scots, and his eldest son Edward, with many others, were slain in Northumbria on the day of the feast of St. Brice [13th Nov.], by the soldiers of earl Robert. In his death the justice of an avenging God was plainly manifested; for this man perished in that province which he had often been wont to ravage, instigated by avarice; for five times he had wasted it with a savage devastation, and carried captive the wretched natives to reduce them to slavery. Once in Eadward's reign, when Tosti, earl of York, had gone to Rome; a second time, in William's reign, when he pillaged Cleveland also; thirdly, in the reign of the same king William, when he went as far as the Tyne, and returned with great spoil after massacring the men and burning the dwellings; fourthly, in the reign of William the second, he went with his numberless forces to Chester [le-street], not far from Durham, with the intention of proceeding further; but an inconsiderable military force assembled against him, and caused him speedily to retire, from fear. The fifth time, he invaded Northumbria with as large an army as he could collect,

[1] Ash-Wednesday fell this year upon 2d March, and Easter-day upon 17th April.

intending to bring upon it utter desolation; but he was cut off near the river Alne, with his eldest son Eadward, whom he had appointed heir of the kingdom after him. His army either fell by the sword, or those who escaped the sword were carried away by the inundation of the rivers, which were then more than usually swollen by the winter rains. Two of the natives placed the body of the king on a cart, as none of his men were left to commit it to the ground, and buried it at Tynemouth. And then it happened that where he had deprived many of life, property, and liberty, there he himself lost at the same time his life and his possessions, by the judgment of God. On hearing of his death, Margaret, queen of Scots, was afflicted with so great distress, that she at once fell into a severe illness; and without delay, summoning her priests, she went into the church, and having confessed her sins to them, she caused herself to be anointed with oil and strengthened by the heavenly viaticum, beseeching God with constant and most earnest prayers, that He would no longer allow her to continue in this miserable life. Nor were her prayers long unheard; for three days after the king's death, she was freed from the fetters of the flesh, and passed, as we trust, to the joys of eternal salvation. For while she lived she had devoutly cultivated piety, justice, peace and charity. She was frequent in prayers, and kept under her body by watching and fasting; she endowed churches and monasteries; she loved and honoured the servants and handmaids of the Lord; she divided her bread to the hungry; clothed the naked; gave lodging, garments and food to all wanderers who came to her; and she loved God with her whole heart.

On her death the Scots chose for themselves as king, Dufenald, brother of king Malcolm, and expelled from Scotland all the English who were of the king's court. When this was known, Duncan, son of king Malcolm, besought king William, in whose service he was then fighting, that he would grant him his father's kingdom; which having obtained, he swore fealty to him, and so he hastened to Scotland with a multitude of English and Normans, and drove his uncle Dufenald from the kingdom, and reigned in his stead. Then some of the Scots assembled together and cut off nearly all his men, and he and a few others escaped with difficulty. Nevertheless, after this they permitted him to reign, on this condition, that he should no longer bring into Scotland either English or Normans, or permit them to fight for him. Two suns were seen in the heaven far distant from each other.

The bishops of almost all England assembled together; among whom Thomas, archbishop of York, held the primacy; and they consecrated as bishop, Anselm, abbot of Bec, on the second of the nones of December [4th Dec.]. In the same year William, count of Eu, overcome by great lust of gold, and enticed by the promise of great honours, revolted from his legitimate sovereign, Robert earl of Normandy, to whom he had sworn fealty; and coming to England to king William, he yielded himself to his dominion as his greatest corrupter.

A.D. 1094. Robert, earl of Normandy, announced by ambassadors to his brother king William the younger, that he would no longer observe the peace which they had concluded between them. Moreover, he called him perfidious and perjured, if he would not fulfil the agreement which had been made between them in Normandy. On this account the king went to Hastings, about the kalends of August [1st Aug.]; and while he stayed there he caused the church of Battle to be dedicated in honour of St. Mary; there also he deprived Herbert, bishop of Thetford, of his pastoral staff, because he wished to go secretly to pope Urban to obtain absolution from him for the bishopric which he had bought for himself, and the abbey which he had bought for his father, from this king William for a thousand pounds. Then, in the middle of Lent,[1] the king went to Normandy, in order to hold a conference with his brother under a truce; but left him without coming to an agreement. Lastly, they met in the Campus Martius, where those who had confirmed the treaty between them by their oaths laid all the blame upon the king. But the king would neither acknowledge that he was in fault, nor perform the agreement; therefore, they separated in great wrath without having come to any terms. The earl went to Rouen, and the king returned to Eu, and [remained there; he hired mercenaries everywhere; and gave to some and promised to others of the nobles of Normandy, gold, silver, and lands, that they might leave his brother and yield up themselves with their castles to his dominion. When things had succeeded according to his desire, he distributed his soldiers through the castles of which he had possession before, or which he then obtained. In the meantime he stormed the castle called Bures; part of the earl's soldiers who were taken in it were sent as prisoners to England, part were imprisoned in Normandy; and thus he harassed his brother in various ways, and strove to disinherit him. Compelled by necessity, Robert brought his liege lord Philip, king of the French, with an army into Normandy; where he laid siege to the castle of Argenteuil; and on the very day of the siege seven hundred soldiers of king William, with twice as many squires and all the garrison who were in it, were taken prisoners without bloodshed. He ordered the prisoners to be kept in confinement until each man should ransom himself; and after having done this he returned to France. Earl Robert besieged the castle called Holme, until William Peverel and eight hundred men who defended it capitulated to him. When the king learnt this, he despatched messengers into England, and ordered twenty thousand infantry to be sent to his aid. When they were assembled at Hastings to cross the sea, Ranulf Flambart, by the king's order, took from them the money which had been given them for their provision, namely, ten shillings to each man; and ordered them to return home: this money he sent to the king.

Meanwhile all England was harassed by heavy and continual taxation, and by a mortality of men, during the present and following year. Besides this, the North Welsh first, and then the West Welsh and South Welsh, shook off the yoke of bondage by which

[1] Mid-lent Sunday fell this year upon 19th March.

they had long been oppressed; and raising their heads, strove to maintain their liberty. A multitude of them assembled, and stormed the castles which were fortified in West Wales, and in the provinces of Chester, Shropshire, and Hereford; they continually burnt the vills, committed depredations, and killed many of the English and Normans. They stormed also the castle in the Isle of Anglesea, and subdued it to their power. At this time the Scots, by the persuasion and encouragement of Dufenald, treacherously put to death their king Dunechan, and some others along with him ; they drove all the English from Scotland, and again appointed Dufenald to be king. After this, on the fourth of the kalends of January [29th Dec.], king William returned to England, and led an army into Wales to reduce the Welsh, that is, the Britons; and there he lost many of his men and horses.

A.D. 1095. That venerable man of most admirable life, Wulstan, bishop of the holy church of Worcester, engaged from youth in divine services, after many contests of holy toil, in which, that he might obtain the glory of the heavenly kingdom, he was most intently diligent in serving God with great devotion and lowliness of mind, departed this life, on the eighteenth day of the month of January, being in the eighteenth lustrum of his age, and the third year of the seventh lustrum of his episcopate. At the very hour of his departure, in a miraculous manner, he appeared in a vision to his friend whom he dearly loved, Robert, bishop of Hereford, in the town called Cricklade, and told him to hasten to Worcester, to bury him. Also, God allowed no one to draw from his finger the ring with which he had received the pontifical benediction ; lest after his death the holy man should seem to deceive his friends, to whom he had very often before said, that he would not lose it while he had life, nor even at the day of his burial.

On the day before the nones of April [4th April], stars were seen as if falling from heaven. Walter, bishop of Albano, who had been sent as legate of the holy Roman church from pope Urban, came to England before Easter,[1] bringing to king William the pall for which he had sent the preceding year; which, according to agreement, being laid by him on the altar of the Saviour at Canterbury, on Sunday, which was the fourth of the ides of June [10th June], was taken thence by Anselm, and humbly kissed by all, out of reverence to St. Peter.

Robert, bishop of Hereford, a man of great piety, died on Tuesday, the sixth of the kalends of July [26th June]. The aforesaid Wulstan, bishop of Worcester, on the thirteenth day after he had departed this life, again appeared to him in a vision, and sharply rebuked him for his negligence and indolence ; and admonished him to labour as earnestly as possible for the correction both of his own life and that of those under him; which if he did, he said that he would soon obtain from God the pardon of all his sins ; and he added, that he would not long hold his see, where he now sat, but if he would be more watchful, he should banquet with himself in the presence of God. For both of these, by their exceeding love,

---

[1] It fell this year upon 25th March.

were alike in the love of God, and so united to each other, that we may well believe that he who first departed from this life to God felt deep concern for his best loved friend, whom he had left in this world, and would do what he could that they might soon rejoice together before God.

Robert de Mowbray, earl of Northumberland, and William de Eu, with many others, plotted to deprive king William of his kingdom and his life, and to make his aunt's son, Stephen de Albamarle, king; but in vain. For when the matter was known, the king assembled an army from all parts of England, and besieged the castle of the aforesaid earl Robert, which was situated at the mouth of the river Tyne, for two months. During that time, having stormed a certain outwork, he took almost all the earl's best soldiers, and placed them in confinement. He then besieged the castle itself, and placed in custody the earl's brother, and the knights whom he found therein. After this he fortified a castle before Bebbanbyrig [Bambrough], that is, Queen Bebba's city, to which the earl had fled, and called it Malvoisin, and having placed a garrison in it, he returned to the country south of the Humber. After his departure, those persons who were on the watch at New Castle promised earl Robert, that if he would come there secretly he should be admitted. Highly rejoicing at this, he went out one night with thirty men for this purpose; but when this was known, the knights who kept the castle followed him, and sent messengers to inform the garrison of the New Castle of his departure. Not knowing this, he attempted one Sunday to effect his design, but failed, for he was discovered. He fled, therefore, to the monastery of St. Oswin, king and martyr; when on the sixth day of its blockade, he was severely wounded in the leg while struggling with his foes, of whom many were killed, and many wounded; some of his men also were wounded, all were taken; he fled into the church, being dragged from which he was placed in confinement.

In the meanwhile the Welsh took by storm the castle of Montgomery, and killed in it some men of Hugh, the earl of Shrewsbury. The king, enraged at this, at once ordered an invasion, and after the feast of St. Michael [29th Sept.], he led an army into Wales, and there lost many men and horses. Returning thence, he ordered earl Robert to be taken to Bebbanburgh, and his eyes to be put out, unless his wife and his relative Moreal should surrender the castle. Compelled by this necessity, they delivered it up; the earl was taken to Windsor, to be placed in close confinement. Moreal revealed the origin of this plot to the king.

A.D. 1096. William, bishop of Durham, died at Windsor in the king's court, on Monday, the fourth of the nones of January[1] [2d Jan.], but was buried at Durham. In the octave of the Epiphany [13th Jan.], at a council held at Salisbury, William de Eu being conquered in a trial by duel, they put out his eyes and emasculated him; and the king ordered his steward, William de Aldric, his aunt's son, who was cognisant of his treason, to be hanged. He

---

[1] In 1096 the 4th of the nones of January fell upon a Thursday. See Florence of Worcester, p. 313.

imprisoned Odo, earl of Champagne, father of the aforesaid Stephen; Philip, brother of Roger, earl of Shrewsbury; and some others, who were sharers in the treason.

Pope Urban came into France, and, at a council held at Clermont during Lent,[1] he exhorted the Christians to set out for Jerusalem, to subdue the Turks, Saracens, and other heathens. Through his persuasion, at once, in the very council, Raimond, count of St. Giles, and many others with him, signed themselves with the cross of Christ, and vowed that they would undertake a pilgrimage in God's behalf, and perform what the pope had recommended. On hearing of this, other Christians from Italy, Germany, France, and England, eagerly prepared themselves for the same enterprise;—the leaders[2] and chiefs of whom were the bishop of Puy,[3] with many other bishops; Peter, a monk and a hermit; Hugh the Great, the brother of Philip, king of the French; Godfrey, duke of Lorraine; Stephen de Blanio,[4] count of Chartres; Robert, earl of Normandy; Robert, earl of Flanders; the two brothers of duke Godfrey,—namely, Eustace, count of Bologne, and Baldwin, the aforesaid count Raimond; and Boamund, son of Robert Wiscard.

Samson, bishop of Worcester, was consecrated by Anselm, archbishop of Canterbury, in the church of St. Paul the Apostle, at London, on Sunday, the seventeenth of the kalends of July [15th June].

After this, Robert, earl of Normandy, when he designed to set out with others for Jerusalem, sent ambassadors into England, begged his brother, king William, to restore peace between them, and to lend him ten thousand marks, for which he would give him Normandy in pawn. In order to his request, William enjoined the chief men of England speedily to lend him money to the utmost of their power. Therefore the bishops, abbots, and abbesses, broke up the gold and silver ornaments of the church; earls, barons, sheriffs, plundered their soldiers and villains, and bestowed on the king no small sum of gold and silver. In the month of September he crossed the sea; and having made an agreement with his brother, he gave him six thousand six hundred and sixty-six pounds, and received Normandy from him as a security.

A. D. 1097. William, king of England, returned to England in Lent, and after Easter [5th April] he set out with a second army of cavalry and infantry to Wales, intending to put to death all the male inhabitants; but he could hardly capture or kill any of them, and lost some of his own men and many horses. He then sent Eadgar Atheling to Scotland with an army, that he might make his relative Eadgar, son of king Malcolm, king there, by the expulsion of his uncle Dufenald, who had seized upon the kingdom.

The Christians took the city of Nicea on Saturday, the thirteenth of the kalends of July [19th June]. A star, called a comet,

---

[1] This council, which confirmed the canons of the council of Clermont, held A. D. 1095, was held at Tours, in the third week in Lent. Jaffé, p. 467.
[2] See Guil. Tyrensis, lib. i. c. xvii. p. 23; and Florence of Worcester, p. 318.
[3] Adhemar de Monteil; concerning whom, see Gallia Christ. ii. 701.
[4] Stephen de Blois.

appeared on the third of the kalends of October [29th Sept.], for fifteen days; some affirmed that at that time they saw in the heavens a wonderful sign like a burning cross.

Afterwards a dissension arose between the king and the archbishop of Canterbury, Anselm, because he had not been allowed to hold a synod from the time he was made archbishop, or to correct the evils which had sprung up throughout England, and so he crossed the sea and remained for a time in France, and afterwards went to Rome to pope Urban. About the feast of St. Andrew [30th Nov.], the king himself set out from England to Normandy. Baldwin, abbot of the monastery of St. Edmunds, a Frenchman by birth, a man of exemplary piety, died on the second of the kalends of January[1] [31st Dec.]. The monastery of Citeaux was begun.

A. D. 1098. Walcelin, bishop of Winchester, died on Sunday, the third of the nones of January [3d Jan.]. In this summer William the younger, then king of the English, reduced the city called Mans, and great part of that province, by force. At the same time, Hugh, earl of Shrewsbury, and Hugh, earl of Chester, went with an army to the island of Menavia, commonly called Anglesey, and took prisoners many of the Welsh who were in it, killed some, and blinded some, cutting off their hands or feet, and emasculating them. They dragged from the church a certain priest of advanced age, named Cenred, from whom the Welsh received advice in their proceedings; and, having emasculated him and put out one of his eyes, they cut out his tongue; but, by the mercy of God, speech was restored to him on the third day. At that time, Magnus[2] [III.], king of the Norwegians, son of king Olave, son of king Harold Harvager, having added to his empire the Orkney and Menavian islands, came thither in a few vessels. And when he would have brought the ships to land, Hugh, earl of Shrewsbury, with many armed soldiers, met him on the very shore, and, as it is said, soon was speedily stricken with an arrow, shot by the king himself, on the seventh day after he had practised this cruelty on the aforesaid priest.

The city of Antioch was taken by the Christians on Wednesday, the third of the nones of June [3d June], in which, a few days afterwards, the spear with which the Saviour of the world when hanging on the cross was wounded, was found in the church of St Peter the Apostle, through a revelation of St. Andrew, the most gracious of saints. Cheered by this discovery, the Christians, carrying it with them, issued from the city on Monday, the fourth of the kalends of July [28th June], and engaging in battle with the pagans, put to flight at the point of the sword Curbara, the chief of the soldiery of the sultan of Persia, and the Turks, Arabs, Saracens, Publicans, Azimati, Persians, Agulani, and several other tribes, slaying many thousands of them, and by the goodness of God obtaining a complete victory. An unusual light shone throughout almost the whole night on the fifth of the kalends of October

---

[1] Compare Florence of Worcester, p. 319.
[2] See Anderson's Genealog. Tables, p. 423.

[27th Sept.]. In the same year, the bones of Cnut, king and martyr, were raised from their tomb by the Danes, and reverently deposited in a shrine. Roger, duke of Apulia, having assembled a large army, laid siege to the city of Capua, which had revolted from his authority. Pope Urban, accompanied as he directed by Anselm, archbishop of Canterbury, set out to the council which he had appointed to be held at Bari on the kalends of October [1st Oct.], in which council many matters concerning the catholic faith were debated with eloquent reasoning by the apostolic pope. There also, when the question was mooted on the part of the Greeks, (who wished to prove from the authority of the gospels that the Holy Spirit has procession only from the Father,) the aforesaid Anselm so treated, discoursed, and resolved upon the point, that there was no one in that assembly who did not agree that he was thereby fully satisfied.

A.D. 1099. Pope Urban held a great council at Rome, in the third week[1] of Easter, in which he rescinded what ought to be rescinded, and ordained what ought to be ordained; and then the whole council of the pope pronounced sentence of excommunication on the adversaries of holy church, on all laics who should grant investitures of churches, and on all receiving such investitures at their hands; also on all who should consecrate any person to the office of any such dignity thus given. He bound under an anathema those who became the vassals of laymen for the sake of ecclesiastical preferments, saying: "That it appeared a most accursed thing that those hands which had risen to such an excellency, that (as has been granted to none of the angels) by their consecration they could create God the Creator of all things, and offer His very Self for the redemption and salvation of the whole world, before the eyes of the most high God the Father, should be thrust down to such ignominy as to become the slaves of those hands which day and night were defiled by contact with obscene things, or stained by habits of robbery and unjust shedding of blood." "Amen, Amen," was exclaimed by all; and thus the council was concluded. After this, the archbishop went to Lyons.

William the younger, king of the English, returned to England from Normandy, and on Whitsunday [29th May] he held his court at London; on which occasion he gave the bishopric of Durham to Ralph, whom he had appointed manager of the business of the whole kingdom; Thomas, archbishop of York, presently consecrated him there in the church of St. Peter, on the octaves of Whitsunday, being the nones of June [5th June]. On Friday, the ides of July [15th July], Jerusalem was taken by the Christians; and afterwards, on the eleventh of the kalends of August [22d July], the same day of the week, Godfrey, duke of Lorraine, was elected king by the whole army. Pope Urban died on Thursday, the fourth of the kalends of August [29th July]. On the same day of the week, being the second of the ides of August [12th Aug.], the Christians fought a great battle before the city of Ascalon with Amiraviss, the commander of the army, and second

---

[1] See Jaffé, p. 176. The third Sunday after Easter fell upon 1st May.

in the royal power of the whole dominion of the king of Babylon, and by the favour of Christ obtained the victory. The reverend man Paschal, who had been ordained priest by pope Hildebrand, being elected by the Roman people on the ides of August [13th Aug.], was consecrated pope on the following day, that is, Sunday, the nineteenth of the kalends of September [14th Aug.]. On the third of the nones of November [3d Nov.], the sea overflowed the shore, and submerged vills, and many of the inhabitants, and innumerable sheep and oxen. Osmund, bishop of Salisbury, died on Friday, the third of the nones of December [3d Dec.].

A.D. 1100. Pope Clement, called also Wibert, died. Thirty-three canons were appointed in Jerusalem, in the monastery in which our Lord's sepulchre is contained, by Godfrey, king of the same city, and the patriarch Wibert. On Sunday, the ides of July [15th July], the church at Gloucester, which abbot Serlo of revered memory had built from the foundations, was dedicated with great pomp by bishops Samson of Worcester, Gundulf of Rochester, Girard of Hereford, and Hervey of Bangor. Then, on Thursday, the fourth of the nones of August [2d Aug.], in the eighth indiction, William king of the English was killed whilst engaged in hunting in the New Forest, called in the language of the English, Ytene, being struck by an arrow heedlessly aimed by a certain Frenchman, Walter, surnamed Tirell; and being carried to Winchester, was buried in the Old Monastery, in the church of St. Peter. Nor is it strange, since, as popular rumour affirms, this was undoubtedly an act of the goodness and vengeance of God; for in ancient times (namely, in the times of king Edward, and other kings of England his predecessors), the same district abounded with inhabitants who were worshippers of God, and with churches; but, by the order of king William the elder, the men were driven out, the houses pulled down, the churches destroyed, the land only kept as a habitation of wild beasts; and this, as it is believed, was the cause of this catastrophe. For some time before this, Richard, the brother of the same king William the younger, had perished in the same forest; and, a short time before, his cousin Richard, the son of Robert earl of Normandy, had been killed when hunting, having been pierced by an arrow shot by one of his knights. On the place where the king fell, a church had been built in former times, but, as we have said, it was pulled down in the time of his father.

In the time of the same king (as has been partly noticed before), many signs occurred in the sun, the moon, and the stars; the sea also very often overpassed its bounds, and drowned both men and cattle, and overthrew many vills and houses. Also the devil frequently showed himself in the woods in a horrible shape to many Normans, openly spoke with them concerning the king, and Ralph, and some others. And no wonder; for in their time almost all legal justice was disregarded, and when causes were brought before the courts, money alone governed among the nobles. Lastly, at the same time, as some regarded the king's will more than justice, Ralph—contrary to ecclesiastical law and the order of his rank (for

he was a priest)—received anew from the king, first abbeys, and
then bishoprics, whose rulers had died, and exposed them for sale;
and hence each year he made no small sum of money. His policy
and talent were so serviceable, and he increased so much in a
short time, that the king appointed him administrator and collector
of the whole kingdom. Having received this great authority, he
amerced the richer and more wealthy by the seizure of their
property and lands everywhere throughout England; the poorer he
continually oppressed by heavy and unjust taxation; and in many
ways, both before and during the time of his episcopate, he
harassed both great and small; and this system he continued up
to the time of this king's death. For on the very day when he was
killed, the king held in his own hand the archbishopric of Canterbury, and the sees of Winchester and Salisbury. This king reigned
thirteen years, save thirty-eight days. His younger brother Henry
succeeded him, and afterwards was consecrated king at Westminster, by Maurice, bishop of London, on Sunday, being the nones of
August [5th Aug.]. On the day of his consecration, he set free the
church of God, which had been sold and put to farm in his
brother's time, and abrogated all the bad customs and unjust
exactions by which the kingdom of England had been iniquitously
oppressed; he established secure peace in the whole of his kingdom, and ordered it to be kept; he restored to all alike the law
of king Edward, together with those improvements with which his
father had amended it; but yet he retained and held in his own
hand the forests which he had made. Not long after, he committed
Ralph, bishop of Durham, to prison in the Tower of London; and
recalled from France, Anselm, archbishop of Canterbury. Meanwhile, first the earls Robert of Flanders and Eustace of Bologne
returned home from Jerusalem; and then earl Robert of Normandy returned to his country, with a wife whom he had married
in Sicily. At this time, Henry king of the English assembled the
elders of England at London, and took in marriage the daughter of
Malcolm, king of Scots, and queen Margaret, Matilda by name;
whom Anselm, archbishop of Canterbury, consecrated queen, and
crowned on Sunday, being the feast of St. Martin [11th Nov.].
Thomas, archbishop of York, a man of revered memory and extraordinary piety, affable and kind to all, departed this life at York, on
Sunday, the fourteenth of the kalends of December [18th Nov.].
Gerard, bishop of Hereford, succeeded him.

A.D. 1101. King Henry held his court at London on Christmas-
day, when Louis, the elect king of the French, was present. After
Christmas, Ralph, bishop of Durham, escaped by great cunning
from prison and crossed the sea; he went to Robert, earl of the Normans, and persuaded him to invade England; and besides this, many
nobles of this country sent messengers to him, and begged him to
hasten to England, promising him the crown and kingdom. The
city of Gloucester, with the principal monastery and others, was
consumed by fire, on Thursday, the eighth of the ides of June
[6th June]. Robert, earl of the Normans, collecting a great multitude of horse, archers, and foot, assembled his ships at the place

called, in the Norman tongue, Ultresport.   When the king knew
this, he ordered his sailors to guard the coast, and watch lest any
one from the Norman coast should land in England.   He then
collected an innumerable army from all England, and pitched his
camp in Sussex, not far from Hastings; for he concluded for certain that his brother would effect a landing in that district.   But,
by advice of bishop Ralph, he so seduced some of the king's
sailors, by promises of various kinds, that, laying aside the allegiance which they owed to the king, they fled to him, and became
his pilots to England.   Therefore, when all was ready he embarked
with his army, and about the feast of St. Peter ad Vincula
[1st Aug.] he landed at the place called Portsmouth; and immediately marching his army towards Winchester, he pitched his
camp in a suitable position.   On the news of his arrival, some
of the nobles of England came over to him, as they had before
arranged to do, and some remained with the king, with feigned
regard.   But the bishops, common soldiers, and English, stood by
him with a steadfast determination, unanimously resolving to go
forth with him to battle.   But the more discreet on each side,
taking salutary counsel among themselves, arranged a treaty between
the two brothers, on the condition that the king should pay the
earl yearly three thousand marks of silver, and should freely restore
to all persons their former rank which they had forfeited in England
by their adherence to the earl; and that the earl should restore
without payment their honours to all those from whom they had
been taken away in Normandy on the king's account.   This being
arranged, the king's army returned home; part of the earl's
returned to Normandy, and part remained with him in England.

Godfrey, king of Jerusalem, who had been the most potent duke
of Lorraine, son of Eustace the elder, earl of Bologne, ended his
life, and rests interred in the church of Golgotha.   After his death
the Christians, with one consent, elected his brother Baldwin king.

Robert de Belesme, earl of Shropshire, son of earl Roger, began
to rebuild, with a broad and high wall, the fortress which Agelfled,
the lady of the Mercians, had formerly built on the south side of the
river Severn, at the place called, in the Saxon tongue, Bricge
[Bridgenorth], in the reign of her brother king Eadward, in opposition (as the event proved) to king Henry.   He began, also, to
build another in Wales, at the place called Carrocove.

A.D. 1102.   The aforesaid earl Robert de Belesme (who at that
time also ruled the earldom of the province of Ponthieu, and possessed many castles in Normandy) strongly fortified against king
Henry the city of Shrewsbury and the castle therein, and also the
castles of Arundel and Tickhill, with provisions, munitions of war,
horsemen, and infantry.   He hastened by every means to complete
the walls and towers of the castles of Bridgenorth and Carrocove,
labouring and working day and night.   He incited the Welshmen
also who were under his control, by honours, lands, horses and
arms, and by abundantly bestowing various gifts, in order to render
them more active and faithful to him, and more resolute to accomplish his designs; but his plans and labours were very soon inter-

rupted ; for, his treachery and plots being exposed by clear proofs,
the king pronounced him a public enemy.   Therefore, he speedily
assembled as many Britons and Normans as he could, and he and
his brother Arnold ravaged part of the county of Stafford, and
carried off from thence into Wales many cattle and horses, and
some men.   But the king laid siege without delay, first, to the
castle of Arundel, and having planted fortresses before it, retired ;
he then ordered Robert, bishop of the city of Lincoln, with part of
the army to lay siege to Tickhill ; and he himself beleaguered
Bridgenorth with the army of almost all England, and began there
to construct machines and fortify a castle.   Meanwhile, he easily
corrupted by small bribes the Britons, in whom Robert placed great
confidence, to break the oaths of fidelity which they had sworn
to him, and caused them to revolt from him, and rise against him.
Within thirty days, the city and all the castles having surrendered, he
vanquished his enemy Robert, and ignominiously expelled him from
England ; soon after which, he condemned to a similar fate his
brother Arnold for his treachery.

After this, on the feast of St. Michael [29th Sept.], the king was
in London and Westminster, and all the nobles of the kingdom of
ecclesiastical and secular rank with him.   Here he invested two
of his clerks with two bishoprics ; namely, Roger his chancellor,
with the bishopric of Salisbury, and Roger his larderer, with that of
Hereford.   There also archbishop Anselm held a great council,
about matters which concerned Christianity : there sat with him,
Gerard, archbishop of York ; Maurice, bishop of London ; William,
bishop elect of Winchester ; Robert, bishop of Lincoln ; Sampson,
bishop of Worcester ; Robert, bishop of Chester ; John, bishop of
Bath ; Herbert, bishop of Norwich ; Ralph, bishop of Chichester ;
Gundulf, bishop of Rochester; Hervey, bishop of Bangor; and the
two recently invested bishops named Roger.   Osbern, bishop of
Exeter, could not be present, for he was prevented by illness.   Nor
was Ralph, bishop of Durham, present at this council.   In it many
abbots, as well French as English, were deposed, and deprived
of the rank which they had iniquitously acquired, or in which they
had lived lewdly : to wit, Wido of Pershore ; Aldwin of Romsey ; the
abbot of Tavistock ; Haimo, abbot of Cernel ; the abbot of Michel-
ney ; Agelric, abbot of Middleton ; Godric, abbot of Peterburgh ;
Richard, abbot of Ely ; and Robert, abbot of St. Eadmunds.   Priests
also were forbidden to have concubines ; hereupon many of them
shut the doors of the churches, leaving off all church services.   The
aforesaid Roger, bishop elect of Hereford, was seized with illness
and died ; and the king's chancellor Reinelm was substituted in his
place, with a like mode of investiture.   Henry, king of the English,
gave Mary, sister of queen Matilda, in marriage to Eustace, earl of
Boulogne.

A.D. 1103. A great dissension arose between king Henry and
archbishop Anselm, because the archbishop would not consent that
the king should grant investitures of churches ; nor would he consecrate nor communicate with those persons to whom the king had
already given churches : because the apostolic pope had forbidden

him and all others to do so. Wherefore, the king directed Gerard,
archbishop of York, to consecrate the bishops to whom he himself
had given investitures ; namely, William Giffard, and Roger, who
was the king's chaplain, to whom he had given the church of Salisbury. Gerard undertook what the king ordered; but William spurned
both the king's orders and archbishop Gerard's benediction, having
regard to the righteousness of the matter. Wherefore, he was
stripped of all his property by the king's sentence, and was banished
from the kingdom ; while the others remained unconsecrated. A
short time previously, Reinelm had surrendered up the see of
Hereford to the king, because he perceived that he had offended
God, in having accepted the investiture of a church from the hand
of a layman. At Easter [29th March] following, the king held his
court at Winchester. Archbishop Anselm, after many wrongs and
divers insults which he endured, went to Rome at the king's
desire, on the fifth of the kalends of May [27th April], as had been
agreed upon by him and the king. He took with him William,
bishop elect of the church of Winchester, and the abbots who had
been deposed from their abbeys, Richard elect of Ely, and Aldwin,
abbot of Ramsey. Robert, earl of Normandy, came to England
to confer with his brother ; and before his return, he remitted
the three thousand marks of silver which the king owed him
yearly, by their agreement. In the province called Berkshire, at
the place called Heamstede, blood was seen by many to flow from
the earth. In the same year, on the third of the ides of August
[11th Aug.], a great storm of wind arose, which did so much
damage to the fruits of the earth throughout England, as those who
then lived had never experienced in times past.

A. D. 1104. Two reverend abbots died; Walter, abbot of Evesham,
on the thirteenth of the kalends of February [20th Jan.], and
Serlo, abbot of Gloucester, on the fourth of the nones of March
[4th March]. Henry, king of England, held his court on Whitsunday [5th June], at Westminster. On Tuesday,—that is, the
seventh of the ides of June [7th June],—four circles were seen
around the sun of a white colour, about the sixth hour, each circle
being, as it were, painted under another. All who saw them
were astonished, since nō one had ever seen such appearances
before. William, earl of Moreton, was dispossessed of all the land
which he held in England. The misery which the land of England
at that time suffered from the exactions of the king cannot easily be
described. The body of St. Cuthbert[1] was disinterred, on account
of the incredulity of certain persons, and was exhibited (in the
episcopate of bishop Ralph) in the presence of earl Alexander,
who afterwards became king of Scots, and many others. Ralph,
abbot of Seez, afterwards bishop of Rochester, and ultimately archbishop of Canterbury, and the brethren of the church of Durham,
having examined it closely, discovered that it was uncorrupted, and
so flexible in its joints, that it seemed more like a man asleep than
one dead ; and this occurred four hundred and eighteen years, five
months, and twelve days, after his burial. This happened in the

---

[1] See the illustrative documents at the end of the volume. [B.]

fifth year of king Henry, in the sixth of the episcopate of Ralph, and five thousand three hundred and eight years from the beginning of the world.

A. D. 1105. Henry, king of the English, crossed the sea; almost all the chief of the Normans abandoned the earl, their sovereign, and repudiating the fealty which they owed him, they ran after the gold and silver which the king had brought thither from England, and surrendered their castles, fortified cities, and towns to him. He burnt Bayeux, with the church of St. Mary which was in it, and took Caen from his brother, and then he came back to England (since he was unable to reduce the whole of Normandy), in order that he might return thither next year with a more abundant supply of money, in order to dispossess his brother, and bring the remainder into subjection to himself.

A. D. 1106. Earl Robert of Normandy came to England, to confer with his brother, king Henry, whom he found at Northampton. The earl then begged of him to restore what he had taken from him in Normandy; all which the king refused to do. Thereupon, the earl departed in anger, and crossed the sea. In the first week of Lent, on Friday, the fourteenth of the kalends of March [16th Feb.], an unusual star appeared in the evening, and for twenty-five days was seen shining at the same hour, and in the same manner, between the south and west. For it appeared small and obscure, but the light which proceeded from it was very brilliant, and an effulgence from the north-east like a great beam threw itself upon the same star. Some said that they saw many unusual stars at that time.

On the night of Maundy Thursday [22d March] two moons appeared a little before daybreak, one in the east and another in the west, both being full, and the moon was then fourteen days old. In this year a very abominable contention arose between Henry [IV.] emperor of the Romans, and his son Henry; and in the same year this emperor died, after a reign of fifty years; his son Henry [V.] succeeded him. Henry, king of the English, crossed the sea before the month of August, and went to Normandy; thereupon almost all the chiefs of the Normans yielded to him, except Robert de Belesme, William of Moreton, and a few others who remained firm to earl Robert. On the Assumption of St. Mary [15th Aug.], came to Bec, Henry, king of the English, where he and archbishop Anselm met, and at length all the differences which had kept them asunder were brought to an amicable settlement. Not long after this, the same archbishop returned to England, by the order and at the request of the king. The king, having collected an army, marched to a certain castle of the earl of Moreton, called Tenercebrei, and laid siege to it. While he lay there, earl Robert, the king's brother, came upon him with his army, on the eve of St. Michael [28th Sept.], and with him Robert de Belesme, and earl William of Moreton; but the right and the victory were on the king's side. There were taken prisoners, earl Robert of Normandy, and William earl of Moreton, and Robert de Stutevill; Robert de Belesme took to flight, and William Crispin was captured, and many others with him.　Having accomplished this, the king subdued the whole of Normandy, and governed it according to his own will, and by letters informed the archbishop of this.

A.D. 1107.　Eadgar, king of Scots, died on the sixth of the ides of January [8th Jan.]; his brother Alexander succeeded him. Normandy being brought under the king's rule, and Robert earl of the Normans, and William earl of Moreton, being sent prisoners into England, the king himself returned to his kingdom before Easter [14th April].　On the kalends of August [1st Aug.], an assembly of all the bishops, abbots, and nobles of the kingdom was held in the king's palace at London; and for three days a great debate took place, in the absence of Anselm, between the king and the bishop about the investitures of churches; some striving to bring this about, that the king should act in regard to investitures as his father and brother had done, and not according to the precept and obedience of the apostolic see.　For pope Paschal, while he stood firm in the sentence which had been published on that point, had yet conceded all things which pope Urban had forbidden equally with investitures, and by so doing had brought the king to accordance with him in the matter of investitures.　Then, Anselm being present, the king agreed and ordained before the assembly that, from that time, no one should ever in future in England be invested with a bishopric or abbey by the giving of the staff or ring by the king, or by any lay hand; Anselm also enacted that no one who was elected to a bishopric should be deprived of consecration to the dignity conferred upon him, on account of the homage which he should make to the king.　Gerard, archbishop of York, placing his hand on that of Anselm, promised that he would yield him the same subjection and obedience in his archbishopric as he had promised when consecrated by him as bishop of the church of Hereford.　The bishops elect, William of Winchester, Reinelm of Hereford, Roger of Salisbury, William of Exeter, and Urban of the church of Glamorgan in Wales, came at the same time to Canterbury, and they were consecrated by Anselm on Sunday, which was the third of the ides of August [11th Aug.], the suffragans of his see assisting him in this service.　Also Gerard, archbishop of York, was present at their consecration, at the request of Anselm.　There was certainly no one at that time who remembered so many pastors having been elected and ordained together in England in former days, except in the time of Eadward the elder, when archbishop Plegmund ordained in one day seven bishops to seven churches.

In this year also died Maurice, bishop of London; Richard, abbot of Ely; Robert, abbot of St. Edmunds; Milo Crispin; Robert Fitz Hamo; Roger Bigot, and Richard de Redvers.

A.D. 1108.　Gundulf, bishop of Rochester, died on the nones of March [7th March].　Henry, king of England, having established peace, decreed by a firm law, that any one who was caught in theft or robbery should be hanged.　He also enacted that debased and false money should be amended, and this under so high a penalty

that no ransom should avail any one convicted of coining false
coin, but that they should lose their eyes and the lower limbs of
their bodies. And since it very often happened, that when coin was
examined, they were found to be bent, broken, and refused, he
ordained that no penny or half-penny, (which he also fixed should
be round,) or even any farthing, should be unalloyed. From this
great good arose to the whole kingdom, for the king did this to
relieve the distresses of the land in secular matters.

Gerard, archbishop of York, died; and in his place Thomas, the
provost of the church of Beverley, the cousin of his predecessor
Thomas, was chosen. Philip [I.], king of the French, died, and
his son Louis succeeded him. Henry, king of the English, crossed
the sea. Archbishop Anselm, at the king's request, consecrated
Richard, bishop elect of the church of London, in his chapel at
Paggaham, (having first received from him the usual profession
of obedience and subjection,) four other bishops assisting him in
this office,—namely, William, bishop of Winchester ; Roger, bishop
of Salisbury ; Ralph, bishop of Chichester ; and William, bishop
of Exeter. After this he went to Canterbury, and on the third of
the ides of August [1] [11th Aug.] he consecrated Ralph, abbot of
Seez, a religious man, to the church of Rochester, in the room of
Gundulf. On that day, Richard, bishop of London, showed his
respect to his mother, the church of Canterbury, by a handsome
present, after the custom of his predecessors.

These are the statutes concerning archdeacons, priests, deacons,
sub-deacons, and secular canons, which Anselm, archbishop of
Canterbury, and with him Thomas, archbishop elect of York, and
all the other bishops of England, ordained in the year of our Lord's
incarnation one thousand one hundred and eight, in presence of
the illustrious king Henry, with the assent of his barons.

" It was enacted that priests, deacons, and sub-deacons should
live chastely, and should not have in their houses any women
except those allied to them by near relationship, according to what
the holy Nicene council has decreed. Those priests, deacons, or
sub-deacons, who, after the prohibition of the synod of London,
have retained their wives, or married others, if they wish any more
to celebrate mass, shall put them away from them so entirely, that
neither shall they enter the women's houses, nor the women theirs ;
and neither shall they knowingly meet in any house, nor shall any
women of this sort reside in the territory of the church ; and if for
any proper reason it be necessary to confer with them, they shall
meet out of doors in the presence of two lawful witnesses.

" If any of them shall be accused by two or three lawful witnesses,
or by common report of the parishioners, of having violated this
statute, he shall purge himself by calling fit witnesses according to
his degree ; six, if he shall be a priest,—four, if a deacon,—two,
if a sub-deacon ; but if this purgation shall fail, he shall be judged
as a transgressor of the sacred canon.

" Those priests who, in despite of the divine altar and holy orders,
shall rather choose to dwell with women, shall be removed from

[1] As the 11th August fell upon a Tuesday in A.D. 1108 ; this date is doubtful.

their divine function, and, deprived of every ecclesiastical benefice, shall be put out of the choir and pronounced infamous.

" Those rebellious and contumacious persons, who have not left their wives, and yet presumed to celebrate mass, if they do not appear, on being called to make satisfaction, they shall be excommunicated in eight days.

" The same sentence embraces archdeacons and all canons, both with respect to relinquishing their wives and avoiding their conversation, and the infliction of this censure, in case they shall transgress the statutes.

" All archdeacons shall swear that they will not accept any bribe for tolerating an infringement of this statute; or allow priests, whom they know to have wives, to chant the mass, or put in vicars : deans shall do likewise.

" Any archdeacon or dean who will not take this oath shall lose his archdeaconry or deanery.

" Those priests who give up their wives, and choose to serve God and his holy altars, shall be suspended from officiating for forty days, during which time they may appoint vicars in their room, and shall suffer penance according as their bishops shall see fit."

A.D. 1109. Anselm, archbishop of Canterbury, died at Canterbury, on Wednesday, the eleventh of the kalends of May [21st April], and was honourably buried on the following day, which was Maundy Thursday. Henry, king of the English, returned to England about Rogation week,[1] and at Whitsuntide [13th June] he held his court at Westminster. Thomas, archbishop elect of York, was consecrated at London, by Richard, bishop of London, on the fifth of the kalends of July [27th June] ; and afterwards, on Sunday,[2] the third of the kalends of August [30th July], received at York, from cardinal Ulric, the pall which the pope had sent him. And on the same day he consecrated Turgot, prior of Durham, to the bishopric of St. Andrew's, in Scotland, which is called Cenrimunt. In the same year, the king erected the abbacy of Ely into an episcopal see, and preferred to the same church Hervey, bishop of Bangor. A comet appeared in the month of December about the milky way, pointing towards the southern region of the heavens.

A.D. 1110. Henry, king of the English, gave his daughter in marriage to the emperor Henry ; and sent her, at the beginning of Lent, which was the fourth of the ides of April[3] [10th April], from Dover to Whitsand. In the same year, divers signs appeared throughout England. A great earthquake occurred at Shrewsbury. At Nottingham, the river called the Trent was dried up for the space of a mile, from morning to the third hour of the day ; so that men could go through its bed dryshod. A comet appeared on the sixth of the ides of June [8th June], and shone for three weeks.

A.D. 1111. Henry, king of the Germans, went to Rome, took

---

[1] Rogation Sunday fell upon 30th May.   [2] The 30th of July fell upon a Friday.
[3] Another error; in A.D. 1110 Ash-Wednesday fell upon 23d of February; 10th April was Easter-day.

pope Paschal [II.] and placed him in confinement; but afterwards, at the bridge on the Via Salaria, where they celebrated the Easter festival in the Campus, he made a treaty [1] with him. In this way a reconciliation was effected between the king and the sovereign pope. This is the king's oath :—

"I, Henry, king, will set free, on Thursday or Friday next, the sovereign pope, and the bishops and cardinals, and all the prisoners and hostages which have been taken, either with him or for him, and I will cause them to be safely conducted within the gates of the city, beyond the river Tiber; nor will I again capture, or permit to be captured, those who continue in their fealty to the sovereign pope Paschal : and I will keep peace and quietness by me and by mine, in person and property, with the Roman people, both of the city beyond the Tiber and island, provided they keep peace with me. I will faithfully assist the sovereign pope Paschal to hold the popedom in peace and safety. I will restore the patrimonies and possessions of the Roman church which I have taken away; I will faithfully aid her to recover and hold all things which she ought to have by custom, as my predecessors have done; and I will obey the sovereign pope Paschal, saving the honour of my kingdom and empire, in like manner as the catholic emperors have obeyed the catholic Roman pontiffs. All these things I will observe in good faith, without guile and treachery."

These are the jurors on the part of the king: Frederic, archbishop of Cologne; Gebehard, bishop of Trent; Burchard, bishop of Munster; Bruno, bishop of Spires; Albert, chancellor; earl Herimann; Frederic, count Palatine; earl Berengarius; count Frederic; marquis Boniface; Albert, earl de Blandriac; count Frederic; count Godfrey; marquis Warner.

The second agreement between the pope and the king :—

"The sovereign pope, Paschal the second, will grant to the sovereign king, Henry, and to his kingdom, and will confirm and enforce under anathema, this his privilege; that it shall be lawful for the sovereign king to invest with the ring and staff any bishop or abbot, who shall have been freely elected without simony by the king's consent; and a bishop or abbot so invested by the king shall freely receive consecration by the bishop to whom it belongs. And if any one be chosen by the clergy and people, he shall not be consecrated by any one unless he be invested by the king; and the archbishops and bishops shall have liberty to consecrate those persons so invested by the king. In none of these things shall the sovereign pope Paschal molest king Henry, nor his kingdom, nor his empire."

This is the oath on the part of the pope :—

"The sovereign pope Paschal will not molest king Henry, nor his kingdom, nor empire, on account of the investiture of bishoprics and abbacies, nor on account of the injury inflicted on him and his people; nor will he return evil to him, or to any one, for this cause. And he will not on any account pronounce an anathema on the person of king Henry; nor shall there be any delay in the

---

[1] See Jaffé, p. 521.

sovereign pope in crowning him, as is contained in the ritual. And by the influence of his office he will assist him to the utmost of his ability to hold his kingdom and empire; and the sovereign pope will fulfil this without guile or treachery."

These are the names of those bishops and cardinals who confirmed by oath the grant and amity to the sovereign emperor Henry, by the order of the sovereign pope Paschal the second: Peter, bishop of Porto; Centius, bishop of Sabina; Robert, cardinal of St. Eusebius; Boniface, cardinal of St. Mark; Anastasius, cardinal of St. Clement; Gregory, cardinal of the apostles St. Peter and St. Paul; likewise Gregory, cardinal of St. Chrysogonus; John, cardinal of St. Potentiana; Risus, cardinal of St. Laurence; Reiner, cardinal of St. Marcellinus and St. Peter; Vitalis, cardinal of St. Balbina; Duiuzo, cardinal of St. Martin; Theobald, cardinal of St. John and St. Paul; John, deacon of St. Mary, in the Greek school.

This is the privilege of the sovereign pope, which he made to the emperor respecting the investitures of bishoprics :—

" Paschal, bishop, servant of the servants of God, to his most dearly beloved son in Christ, Henry, the illustrious king of the Germans, and, by the grace of God, august emperor of the Romans, wishes health and apostolic benediction.

" The divine appointment has so ordered it, that your kingdom is very closely connected with the holy Roman church. The predecessors of your excellency, by virtue of superior wisdom, obtained the crown and empire of the city of Rome; to the dignity of this crown and empire the Divine Majesty has advanced your person, most beloved son, Henry, by the ministry of our priesthood. That prerogative of rank which our predecessors conceded to your predecessors, the catholic emperors, and have confirmed by written documents, we also concede to you, beloved friend, and confirm it by the instrument of this present grant; to wit, that you shall freely confer the investiture of the staff and ring upon those bishops or abbots of your kingdom, except those elected by violence or simony; and that, after such investiture, they shall canonically receive consecration from the bishop to whom it pertains. But if any one shall be elected by the clergy and people, without your assent, he shall not be consecrated by any one, unless he be invested by you. The bishops, or archbishops, shall truly have liberty of consecrating canonically such bishops or abbots as are invested by you. For your predecessors have so bountifully furnished the churches of their kingdom with great endowments out of their royalties, that it is especially proper that their empire should be strengthened by the aid of bishops or abbots; and it is necessary that the popular tumults, which often happen in elections, should be restrained by royal authority. Wherefore, you ought all the more earnestly to apply your wisdom and authoritative care, that the dignity of the Roman church, and the safety of others, may be preserved in their benefices and services, under the protection of God. If, therefore, any ecclesiastic or secular person shall audaciously attempt to pervert the import of this our grant, he shall be bound with the chain

of anathema, unless he repent; and shall also incur the loss of his
rank and dignity.   May the divine mercy guard those who observe
it, and grant your majesty to govern happily, to his honour and
glory."

By these agreements and oaths, harmony was restored between
the sovereign pope and the emperor, at the feast of Easter [2d
April].   On the ides of April following [13th April], the emperor
went to Rome, and the pope celebrated mass, and consecrated him
emperor, in the church of St. Peter, and gave absolution to him,
and all his people, and forgave every injury done to himself.
Henry, king of the English, removed into Wales the Flemings who
inhabited Northumbria, with all their implements, and directed
them to dwell in the territory called Ross.   By the agency of
William, bishop of Winchester, the king ordered that the New
Monastery, which was within the walls of Winchester, should be
built outside the walls; and not long after, he crossed the sea.   In
this year occurred a very severe winter, a great famine, a mortality
of men, a murrain among animals, as well in the fields as in the
houses, and a very great destruction of birds.

A.D. 1112. The decision of a council held against the heresy
respecting investiture :—

" In the thirteenth year of the pontificate of the sovereign pope
Paschal the second, the fifth indiction, in the month of March, the
fifteenth of the kalends of April [18th March], a council was held
at Rome, in the Lateran, in the church of Constantine; in which,
when the sovereign pope had taken his seat, with the archbishops,
bishops, and cardinals, and a mixed multitude of clergy and laity,
on the last day of the council, having before them all made profession of the catholic faith, lest any one should doubt his belief,
the pope said: ' I embrace all holy Scripture, to wit, of the Old
and New Testament, the Law written by Moses, and the holy
Prophets.   I embrace the four Gospels, the seven canonical Epistles, the Epistles of the glorious doctor the blessed apostle Paul,
the sacred canons of the apostles, the four general councils (as
I embrace the four Gospels), those, namely, of Nice, Ephesus, Constantinople, and Chalcedon; the council of Antioch, the decrees
of the holy fathers, the Roman pontiffs, and especially those of my
lord pope Gregory the seventh, and pope Urban of blessed memory.
What they accepted, I accept; what they held, I hold; what they
confirmed, I confirm; what they condemned, I condemn; what
they rejected, I reject; what they interdicted, I interdict; what
they prohibited, I prohibit, in all and through all; and in these
things I will always remain constant.' "

When this was done, Gerard,[1] bishop of Engouleme, legate in
Aquitania, rose for all, and, by common consent of the sovereign
pope Paschal and the whole council, he read this writing in the
presence of the assembly :—

" All we who are assembled in this sacred council, with the lord
the pope, do, by canonical censure and ecclesiastical authority, and
by the judgment of the Holy Spirit, condemn and pronounce to be

---

[1] Gerard de Blaye; concerning whom see Gallia Christ. ii. 999.

void and of no effect, that grant (which is no privilege, but ought rather to be called a violation of the law) for the liberation of captives and of the church, extorted from the sovereign pope Paschal by the violence of king Henry; and we utterly anathematize it, so that it may have no authority nor effect. And it is condemned on this account, because in that grant is contained the clause, that one elected by the clergy and people shall not be consecrated by any one unless he be first invested by the king, a thing which is contrary to the Holy Spirit and to canonical order."

This charter being read through, the whole council exclaimed, "Amen, Amen! So be it, So be it!" These are the archbishops who were present, with their suffragans : John, patriarch of Venice ; Senues, of Capua ; Landulf, of Benevento ; the prelates of Almafi, Reggio, Otranto, Brindisi, Capsa, Geronto ; and the Greeks, Rosanus, and the archbishop of St. Severino ; also bishops Peter, of Porto ; Leo, of Ostia ; Cono, of Prenesti ; Gerard, of Engouleme ; Galo, of Leon ; the legate for the archbishops of Bourges and Vienne ; Roger, of Volaterra ; Ganfrid, of Sienna ; Rolland, of Populonia ; Gregory, of Terracina ; William, of Traia ; Gibinus, of Syracuse, the legate for all the Sicilians ; and about a hundred other bishops. Siguin, and John of Tusculum, bishops, although they were at Rome on that day, were not present at the council ; but, after having read the condemnation of the iniquitous decree, they assented and approved.

In this year (namely, 1112), archbishop Thomas mourned over the church of Hexham ; for it was almost reduced to a desert, and it had been given as the portion of a certain prebend of the church of York. In order to grace it by the concourse of the devout, he placed in it canons regular, on the kalends of November [1st Nov.], over whom there presided, as first prior, Aschatil, a canon of Huntingdon, a man kind to all. Sampson, bishop of Worcester, died on the third of the nones of May [5th May]. Henry, king of the English, having captured count Robert de Belesme, in the month of October, put him in confinement in Carisbrook.

A.D. 1113. The monks of Tyron came to England ten years before the monks of Savigni came. The monks of Tyron came to Selkirk in the country of David, king of Scotland, and remained there for fifteen years. The city of Worcester, with the cathedral church and all the others, and the castle, was consumed by fire on Thursday, the thirteenth of the kalends of July [19th June]. One of the most useful monks in the monastery, with two servants and fifteen of the citizens, perished in the fire. Henry, king of the English, returned to England in the month of July, and placed in the closest confinement at Wareham, earl Robert de Belesme, whom he brought over from Normandy. Teulf, the king's chaplain, received the bishopric of Worcester at Windsor.

A.D. 1114. Matilda, the daughter of Henry, king of the English, was married to Henry, emperor of the Romans, at Mentz on the eighth of the ides of January [6th Jan.], and was consecrated empress. Thomas, archbishop of York, a man of exemplary piety, died on Tuesday, the sixth of the kalends of March [24th Feb.]. Besides his other deeds of holy virtues, he went to the Lord in the purity of virginity. With how great uprightness of character and innocent purity of life he was adorned, both before and during his episcopate, cannot, I think, be expressed by any human language. Ralph, bishop of Rochester, was elected to the archbishopric of Canterbury, at Windsor, on Sunday, the sixth of the kalends of May [26th April]. The city of Chichester, with the principal monastery, was consumed by fire, through culpable carelessness, on Tuesday, the third of the nones of May [5th May]. Turstin, the king's chaplain, was elected at Winchester to the archiepiscopate of York, on the day of the Assumption of St. Mary [15th Aug.], and Arnulf, abbot of Peterborough, was elected bishop of the church of Rochester. Henry, king of the English, after he had marched an army into Wales, crossed the sea before the feast of St. Michael [29th Sept.]. On the sixth of the ides of October [10th. Oct.], the river called the Medway became so low for some miles, that the smallest boats could not possibly keep afloat in the middle of its bed, on account of the deficiency of water. And the same deficiency of water appeared the same day in the Thames ; for between the bridge and the king's Tower,[1] likewise under the bridge itself, the water of that river was so shallow that an innumerable multitude of men and boys, not only on horseback but even on foot, crossed it, the water scarcely reaching their knees. This want of water lasted from the middle of one night to the middle of the following night. We have learnt by trustworthy report, that a similar want of water occurred on the same day at Yarmouth, and in other places throughout England.

A. D. 1115. In this year there was a very hard winter ; so much so, that almost all the bridges throughout England were broken by the ice. The emperor Henry, after having long besieged Cologne, and lost many of his men on the field of battle, made peace with the city, which was confirmed and certified by oath. On Sunday, the fifth of the kalends of July [27th June], Ralph, archbishop of Canterbury, received the pall from Anselm, legate of the holy Roman church, at Canterbury, where were assembled the bishops of all England. And on the same day, Teoulf, bishop of the church of Worcester, was consecrated with great pomp. Wilfrid, bishop of St. David's in Wales, died. The British bishops continued till his time. In the octaves of the apostles,[2] a great council was held at Châlons, by Cono, cardinal of the Roman church ; in which he excommunicated the bishops who were not present at the council ; some he degraded ; and many abbots were deprived of their staffs, deposed from their seats, and forbidden to exercise their ecclesiastical functions. Henry, king of the English, returned to England in the middle of the month of July. Turgot, formerly prior of the church of Durham, but at this time bishop of the Scots, returning to Durham, there ended his life. Bernard the queen's chancellor was elected bishop of the church of St. David in Wales ; Reinelm, bishop of Hereford, died about the feast of All Saints [1st Nov.] ; and Gosfrid, the king's chaplain, was

---

[1] Compare Florence of Worcester, p. 334.
[2] Namely, St. John and St. Paul [6th July].

elected in his place. On the day of St. Stephen, martyr [26th Dec.], in Christ's church, Canterbury, Ralph, archbishop of Canterbury, ordained Arnulf, abbot of Peterborough, as bishop of the church of Rochester, and Gaufrid to the see of Hereford.

A.D. 1116. In the spring time, Griffin ap Res committed depredations, and burnt castles in Wales, because Henry, king of England, would not give him any portion of the land of his father. An assembly of the nobles and barons of all England took place at Salisbury, on the fourteenth of the kalends of April [19th March]; and there, in the presence of king Henry, they did homage to his son William, and swore fealty to him. The cause was tried respecting the dispute which had been carried on for a whole year between Ralph, archbishop of Canterbury, and Turstin, archbishop elect of York. The latter, being admonished by the archbishop himself, upon his election, to perform what was due to the church of Canterbury, and to receive his blessing, according to ecclesiastical prescript, replied, that he would indeed willingly receive his blessing, but would on no account make the profession which he demanded,[1] beyond that which the blessed pope Gregory had appointed. For he had laid down this rule between the two archbishops of England, and morever, after him, pope Honorius [VI.] had done the same in like manner, that neither of them should make profession of subjection to the other, save only that he who was first consecrated should be reckoned the superior during his own life; an arrangement well becoming the servants of God, that in true humility they should be lowly the one to the other, and no one should desire to exercise lordship or authority over the other, as our Lord, the preacher and lover of true humility, when rebuking his disciples who were striving about this very thing, said to them, "Whosoever will be chief among you shall be servant of all." (St. Mark x. 43.) And of a truth, none of the archbishops of Canterbury after the blessed Augustine (who should be called not so much the archbishop, as the apostle of the English) presumed to claim the primacy of all England down to the time of archbishop Theodore, to whom, on account of his extraordinary skill in ecclesiastical discipline, all the bishops of England agreed to submit, as Beda,[2] in his Ecclesiastical History of the Angles, testifies, thus writing of him: "He was the first among the archbishops to whom all the bishops of Britain consented to yield obedience." Wherefore Turstin would make no other profession of subjection to the archbishop of Canterbury, except that which the blessed pope Gregory had appointed. But king Henry, when he found that Turstin stood to his resolution, openly declared that he should either follow the custom of his predecessors, both in making the profession, and in all other things appertaining of ancient right to the dignity of the church of Canterbury, or should altogether lose the episcopate of York, and the benediction also. On hearing this, he, hastily yielding to the impulse of his own will, renounced the archbishopric, promising the king and the archbishop that, as long as he lived, he would not claim it, nor would he raise any cavils whoever should be appointed.

---

[1] Compare Florence of Worcester, p. 334.   [2] Eccl. Hist. § 256.

Owen, king of the Britons, was slain; and Henry, king of the
English, crossed the sea, Turstin, archbishop elect of York, accompanying him, in the hope that he might recover the investiture
of his archbishopric, and obtain the benediction from the archbishop by the king's order, without the exaction of the profession.
About the month of August, Anselm, who had brought the pall to
the archbishop of Canterbury from Rome, coming again from
Rome, went to king Henry in Normandy, bearing letters from the
apostolic see, which granted him the administration of affairs as
the pope's legate in England. This speedily became known in the
kingdom of England; wherefore, by the united advice of the queen
and some of the nobles of England, Ralph, archbishop of Canterbury, after the feast of the Nativity of St. Mary [8th Sept.],
crossed the sea and went to the king, whom he found staying at
Rouen; and, having earnestly discussed with him the business
about which he had come with reference to the state of affairs, by
his advice he set out on his journey to Rome.

A. D. 1117. According to the order of king Henry, the new
building was commenced at Cirencester. A great earthquake took
place in Lombardy, and, as those who know have affirmed, it continued for the space of forty days, and destroyed many houses;
and, what appears wonderful to see or to tell, a certain very large
town was suddenly removed from its situation, and in the sight
of all stopped at a place far remote. Whilst some men of patrician
rank at Milan, occupied in affairs of state, were assembled in a
tower, a voice without sounded in the ears of all, calling one of
them by name, and begging him to go out quickly. On his delay-
ing, a certain form appeared before them, and by entreaty induced
him to depart. On his going out, the tower suddenly fell, and
crushed by its unhappy fall all who were there present. On the
kalends of December [1st Dec.] there was excessive thunder and
lightning, which was followed by a great inundation of rain and
hail; and on the third of the ides of December [11th Dec.] the
moon appeared as of a bloody colour, and afterwards was obscured.
Robert, bishop of Chichester,[1] died, and Gilbert, abbot of Westminster.[2]

A.D. 1118. Pope Paschal, of blessed memory, died on the fourteenth of the kalends of February [19th Jan.], and in his place
one John, a native of Gaeta, succeeded, and, changing his name, was
called Gelasius. He was brought up from infancy as a monk, in
the monastery of Monte Cassino, and when grown up had been
constant in the service of the venerable apostolic popes, Desiderius,
Urban, and Paschal, discharging the office of chancellor. The
German king, who is also emperor of Rome, on hearing that the
pope had departed this life, hastened to Rome, and driving Gelasius
from the city, appointed as pope the bishop of Braga (who in the
preceding year had been excommunicated at Benevento by the late
pope), and changed his name from Burdinus to Gregory. Matilda,

---

[1] Compare Florence, p. 335, and Hardy's Le Neve, i. 543.
[2] Here ends the Chronicle of Florence of Worcester; but Simeon was acquainted with the continuation of that work, a few extracts from which follow.

queen of the English, died on the kalends of May [1st May], at
Westminster, and was honourably interred in that monastery. Earl
Robert de Mellent died. Many of the Normans set aside the
allegiance which they had sworn to king Henry, and went over to
his enemies, Louis king of France and his nobles, disregarding the
claims of him, their legitimate sovereign. The aforesaid pope
Gelasius came by sea to Burgundy, and his arrival was personally
known to all France. This is his epistle which he sent into
Gaul:—

"Gelasius, bishop, servant of the servants of God, to the
venerable brethren, archbishops, bishops, abbots, clergy, nobles,
and other faithful throughout Gaul, sends health and the apostolic
benediction.

"As you are members of the Roman church, we have made it
our care to notify to you, beloved ones, what things have lately been
transacted in it; inasmuch as after an election the sovereign emperor secretly, and with thoughtless haste, came to Rome, and
compelled us to depart. Afterwards, with threats and menaces, he
demanded an agreement, saying he would do what lay in his power
as soon as we had given him certainty of peace by oath. To which
we thus replied: 'Respecting the variances between the church
and the kingdom, we readily agree either to a convention or to a
judicial sentence, at a fitting place and time, that is to say, either at
Milan or Cremona, on the following feast of St. Luke [18th Oct.],
and this with the judgment and counsel of our brethren, who are
by God constituted judges in the church, and without whom this
cause cannot be handled. And since the sovereign emperor requires
security from us, we, by word and writing, promise these things;
provided he does not himself oppose any obstacle in the meanwhile;
for neither the honour of the church nor custom permits us to give
other security.' On the forty-fourth day after an election, he invaded the rights of mother church, and thrust in the bishop of Braga,
who had been excommunicated last year by our sovereign predecessor, pope Paschal, at the council of Benevento, who also when he
formerly received the pall by my hands, swore fealty to the same
our sovereign and his catholic successors, of whom I am the first.
In this great iniquity the emperor had, God be thanked, no associate
among the Roman clergy; but the Guibertines alone, Romanus de
St. Marcello, Centius, who is called the cardinal of St. Chrysogonus,
and Euzo, who for a long time committed excesses in Dacia; and
these are the persons who have made themselves notorious by this
exploit. We therefore command your wisdom, by the precept of
these present letters, to take these matters into your common
deliberation by the grace of God, and so you apply yourselves, as
you know it behoves you to do, to the avenging of mother church
under God's favour by your united aid.

"Given at Gaeta, on the seventeenth of the kalends of February[1]
[16th Jan. 1119]."

When these had passed throughout all the provinces, the nobles

[1] This letter, although it occurs here and in Malmesbury's Hist. of the Kings,
§ 431, has escaped the researches of Jaffé. See his Regesta Pontiff. Rom. p. 525.

and those of inferior rank were aroused, and came to the assistance
of the apostolic pope, and eagerly prepared themselves to take part
in the council which he decided should be held at Rheims at Midlent.

In this year, at the consecration of a certain church at a village
called Momerfeld, in England, as those who had come to the
dedication were returning home, after great calmness of weather
which had previously existed, suddenly a violent storm arose with
thunder; some were stopped, being struck by lightning on the road,
and unable to move from the spot which they had reached. They
were five in number, three men and two women; one of the
women was struck by the thunderbolt, and died; the other perished
miserably, struck and burnt from the middle to the feet, the men
alone barely escaping with life. Their five horses also were killed
by the lightning.

A.D. 1119. Pope Gelasius died at Clugni, and was there buried.
In his place the other Roman cardinals who had followed him
there, substituted Guido, archbishop of Vienne, and named him
Calixtus; and while these things were passing, the apostolate of the
Roman church was administered by the aforesaid Gregory. Between
these two thus raised to the papacy, the world was inflamed by
party spirit, and was divided; some favouring one, some the other;
and so the church was injured by this great scandal. Goffrid,
bishop of Hereford, died on the fourth of the nones of February
[2d Feb.], and Herbert, bishop of Norwich, on the eleventh of the
kalends of the same [22d Jan.]. On Sunday, the fourth of the
kalends of October [28th Sept.], about the third hour of the day,
an earthquake occurred in many places throughout England. Pope
Calixtus held a general council at Rheims, on the thirteenth of the
kalends of November [20th Oct.]. At this council there assembled
a numerous concourse of archbishops, bishops, abbots, and nobles,
from various provinces, with a great multitude of clerics and laymen.
The staffs of persons of pastoral rank numbered four hundred and
twenty-four; amongst whom went Turstin, archbishop elect of the
church of York, having after some time with difficulty obtained the
king's leave, for the settlement of his own private affairs. But the
king had already despatched his legate to the apostolic pope, to tell
him this amongst other things, that he should not either himself
consecrate the archbishop elect of York, or authorize or permit any
one else to consecrate him, except the archbishop of Canterbury;
as was conformable to custom. To which the apostolic pope
replied, " Let not the king suppose that I will act otherwise
than reason demands, in the matter of which he treats; nor, moreover, have I any desire to lower the just dignity of the church
of Canterbury." But on the morning of the Sunday immediately
preceding the day on which the council was summoned, when
Turstin was prepared to receive consecration to his archiepiscopal
see, the legates of the archbishop of Canterbury presumptuously
objected, that the consecration of the archbishop of York ought to
be performed by the archbishop of Canterbury; to which the apostolic pope replied, " We wish to do no injustice to the church of
Canterbury; but, saving its dignity, we will carry out what we have

proposed. He was, therefore, consecrated[1] by the pope. On the following day, while the persons of ecclesiastical rank were sitting in order in council, (Lewis, king of the Franks, also attending, and many other principal men,) by the consent of all, the statutes of the fathers were renewed in such matters as ought to be decreed, and repealed, where repeal was necessary. The five chapters are as follows:—

1. Those things which have been established by the decrees of the holy fathers respecting simoniacal pravity, we also confirm, by the judgment of the Holy Spirit and the authority of the apostolic see. If any one, therefore, shall buy or sell, either by himself or by any agent, a bishopric, abbey, deanery, archdeaconry, presbyterate, provostship, prebend, altars, or any ecclesiastical benefices, preferments, ordinations, consecrations, dedications of churches, clerical tonsure, stalls in the choir, or any ecclesiastical offices whatsoever, both buyer and seller shall be subject to the loss of his dignity, office and benefice. And, unless he repent, smitten with the sword of anathema, he shall be cut off in every way from the church of God which he has injured.

2. We utterly prohibit investiture of bishoprics, abbacies, or any other ecclesiastical possessions from being made by a lay hand. Whosoever, therefore, of the laity shall henceforward presume to confer investiture, he shall incur the vengeance of an anathema. Moreover, he who shall have been invested shall be altogether deprived, without hope of recovery, of the dignity with which he shall have been invested.

3. We decree, that all the possessions of the churches, which have been granted them by the liberality of kings, the bounty of princes, or the offerings of any person, shall remain for ever untouched and inviolate. And if any one shall seize, invade, or withhold them by the right of the stronger hand, he shall be struck by a perpetual anathema, according to the decree of the blessed Symmachus.

4. No bishop, nor priest, nor any one whatever of the clergy, shall bequeath, as by hereditary right, dignities or benefices to any one. Besides this, we command, that no fee at all shall be demanded for baptisms, chrisms, receiving the holy oil and burial, nor for the visitation or anointing of the sick.

5. We altogether forbid priests, deacons, and sub-deacons, from keeping company with concubines and wives. Whoever shall be found living in this manner shall be deprived of their ecclesiastical offices and benefices; and, if they do not reform their uncleanness by this means, they shall be deprived of Christian communion.

These decrees of the council were transmitted to the emperor Henry, as he was at no great distance from the meeting, first through honourable personages, and at length by the apostolic pope himself, in order that the council, before the breaking up of it, might know, whether he would yield to the churches throughout his kingdom, and each separate province subject to him: 1st, Canonical elections; namely, that bishops and abbots should be elected by the

---

[1] 19th Oct. A. D. 1119. See Hardy's Le Neve, iii. 98.

church; 2d, Free consecration, that the elect should be consecrated where and by whom it was proper; 3d, Investiture of churches, that they might enter through Christ the door, by investiture of the pastoral staff and ring; and 4th, Investiture of ecclesiastical property, that no lay person should demand anything of the property belonging to the churches. To these demands the emperor replied, that he would not forego anything in these matters which the ancient custom of his predecessors had bestowed on him as of his own right. Yet after a while he yielded to the authority of the general council, and granted the first three, but would not concede the last, namely, the investiture of ecclesiastical property; wherefore, when the pope returned to the council, he was pronounced to be excommunicate. When some of the council were displeased at this, the pope gave his opinion, that those who took offence in this matter should go out and be separated from the fellowship of their brethren; giving as an instance [1] those of the Seventy who, when they were offended about eating the flesh of the Lord and drinking his blood, went back and walked no more with Him. "And since," said he, "he who gathereth not with the Lord scattereth; and he who is not with Him is against Him; by thus differing from us, you are striving to rend that coat without seam, woven from the top throughout; to wit, the holy church, which you will not keep undivided by agreeing with us." By the pope discoursing to them in this manner, all of them were forthwith brought to the same mind as the rest, and they launched the sentence of excommunication against the emperor Henry. The council being at length dissolved, after some days, the king of the English, offended with archbishop Turstin, because he had got himself consecrated by the pope without his consent, forbade his return to any part of his dominions. After this pope Calixtus went to Gisors, where the king of the English met him at a conference; many things were settled between them of sufficient consequence to warrant the meeting of two such important personages. Amongst these the king obtained from the pope, that he would concede to him all the customs which his father had held in Normandy and in England, and, especially, that he would allow no one at any time to discharge the office of legate in England, unless he himself should require this to be done by the pope, under pressure of some special difficulty, which could not be settled by the bishops of his kingdom. All these matters being thus far settled, the pope begged the king to be reconciled to Turstin, and to restore him to the archbishopric, to which he himself, out of his regard for him, had consecrated him. The king declared, that he had vowed on his faith that he would not do so as long as he lived. He replied, "I am the pope; and if you will do what I require, I will absolve you from that vow." "I will consider the matter," said the king, "and will inform you of the result of my deliberation;" and with that he left the pope; and then, by a deputation, he made him this answer: "Making that concession to you which you so earnestly desire, I admit Turstin to his prelacy, on this condition, that he makes the submission which his predecessors made to the church of Canterbury; otherwise, during

---

[1] See St. John vi. 66.

my reign he shall never preside over the church of York." Matters
being brought to this conclusion, the pope departed, and Turstin
remained in France. William, son of king Henry and queen
Matilda, took to wife the daughter of the count of Anjou.

A.D. 1120. Henry, king of the English, and Lewis, king of the
French, after many losses on both sides, held a conference on an
appointed day, which ended in a treaty of peace; and by order of
king Henry, when his son William had done homage to the king
of the French, he received the principality of Normandy, to hold
under him. Thus the kings returning in peace, the whole rebellion
of mutinous Normandy was repressed, and those who had taken up
arms against their sovereign, king Henry, came once more under
his dominion in submissive manner. In arranging the agreement
between the kings, archbishop Turstin had showed himself wary
and active; and so, by this ability of his, he disposed the king's
mind to receive him more readily. Further, the pope, by an
epistle addressed to the king, (who was now preparing to return to
England,) recommended him to receive archbishop Turstin, to lay
aside every pretext, and to restore him to his church. But the
king delayed sending any definite answer to this recommendation,
until his return to England, where, calling a council, he might
maturely consider what was requisite to be done. The nobles
of Normandy, at the king's command, did homage to his son
William, then eighteen years of age, and by oaths gave security for
their fidelity. The king, then, having either subdued or made terms
with all who had rebelled against him; having prosperously completed everything according to his wish, in unusual gladness returned to England with a large fleet, the fifth year of his departure
having not yet come to a close. He had furnished to his son and
the whole of his suite a vessel, than which none in all the fleet
seemed better; but, as it proved, none was more unlucky. The
father sailed first; the son followed somewhat later, but with ill
speed; for when not far from the land, by the very force of its
sailing, the ship was driven upon the rocks as it left the harbour, and
was shattered; and the king's son with all who were with him
perished; this occurred on Thursday,[1] the sixth of the kalends
of December [26th Nov.], in the evening, at Barbaflot. In the
morning the king's treasure, which was in the ship, was found on
the sands; but none of the bodies of the sufferers were recovered.
With the king's son perished his brother, earl Richard the Bastard,[2]
with the king's daughter,[3] who was the wife of Rotro; and Richard,[4]
earl of Chester, with his wife, the king's niece, sister of earl
Theobald, the king's nephew. There perished, also, Othoel,[5] tutor
to the king's son; and Geoffrey Ridel,[6] and Robert Malduit, and

---

[1] The accident having occurred during the night, is sometimes ascribed to the
twenty-fifth of November, sometimes to the twenty-sixth. Thursday, however, was
the twenty-fifth of the month. See Will. Malmesb. Hist. of the Kings, § 419.

[2] See Anderson's Genealog. Tables, p. 741.

[3] Maud, wife of Rotroc, earl of Perch. Anderson, ibid.

[4] Richard, earl of Chester, married Maud, daughter of Stephen, earl of Blois,
by Adela, one of the daughters of William the Conqueror. See Dugd. Baron. i. 36.

[5] This Othoel was natural brother to the last-named Richard, earl of Chester.
Dugd. Baron. ibid.   [6] Id. i. 555.

William Bigot,[1] with many other chief men; also, many noble women, with not a few of the children of the royal family; one hundred and fifty soldiers and fifty sailors, with three captains of the ship.   A certain butcher, clinging to a plank, was the only one who escaped the shipwreck.   The king reached England with a prosperous voyage, and imagined that his son had put into some other port; but on the third day he was afflicted with the news of his sad end.   At first, hearing of this sudden calamity, he fainted like a man bereft of strength; but soon hiding his grief, he resumed his royal courage, as in scorn of fate.   For he had appointed this William (the only one of his sons begotten in lawful wedlock) to be the heir to the kingdom after himself.

A.D. 1121.   A council of all England being assembled at Windsor, before the Purification of St. Mary [2d Feb.], king Henry took in marriage Adelina, daughter of Godfrey, duke of Lovaine. Richard, the king's chaplain, was elected to the bishopric of Hereford; and Robert Peccator, his other chaplain, to that of the church of Coventry.   Herbert, almoner of St. Peter at Westminster, was elected abbot of the same place; Edmer, monk of the church of Canterbury, (who had been elected the preceding year to the bishopric of the church of St. Andrew, of the nation of the Scots,) abandoned his intention of ruling the bishopric, and returned to his place.   William de Campellis,[2] bishop of Châlons, died, on the fifteenth of the kalends of February [18th Jan.], having taken the habit of a monk eight days before his death.   In the same year, king Henry cut a large canal from Torksey to Lincoln, and by causing the river Trent to flow into it, he made it navigable for vessels.   Ralph, bishop of Durham, began a wall from the northern part of the choir of the church, and carried it on to the keep of the castle:—he then began also the castle of Norham, on the banks of the Tweed, at the place called Ethamesford.

The monks at Durham brought an action in the chapter of St. Peter's at York, (in the presence of bishops Turstin aforesaid, Ralph of Durham, and Homo de St. Evroul, and many others,) respecting the church at Tynemouth,[3] alleging that it was theirs by right of a grant from earl Waltheof, when he committed to their care his cousin (the son, namely, of his aunt), the boy Morkar, then a little child, to be educated by them for God in the monastery of Jarrow.   When he had been thus entrusted to them in that church of Tynemouth, the monks took him by ship to Jarrow, and had bestowed great pains in bringing him up and educating him for the service of God. " From that time," said they, " our brethren, the monks of Jarrow, have taken charge of that place; their monks, Edmund, and afterwards Eadred, served that church along with the priest Elwald, who was also a canon of the church of Durham, and regularly went from thence to Durham, as often as his turn of duty occurred, to celebrate mass for the week.   We remember also Wulmar, a monk of our convent, and other brethren in their turns, being sent thither from Jarrow, to perform the divine services there.   The

---

[1] Dugd. Baron. i. 132.   [2] See Gallia Christ. ix. 877.
[3] See Simeon's Hist. of the Church of Durham, chap. lxiii.

bones of St. Oswin, also, were translated by our brethren to Jarrow, as seemed good to them at the time; and they carried them back when they thought fit, from thence to their former place of deposit. Lastly, when Albrius received the dignity of the earldom, he also bestowed the same place upon us, when we were translated to Durham; from which place our monk, Turchil, was sent thither by the common resolution of the whole chapter; and he restored the roof of that church and dwelt there for a long time, until afterwards he was violently driven out by earl Robert de Mowbray, through his ministers, Gumer [1] and Robert Taca, on account of the hatred which he had against bishop William. Not long after this, Paul, abbot of the monastery of St. Albans, obtained the aforesaid church from the earl; but when he came to York to visit it, Turgot (who then held the priory of Durham) sent thither monks and clerks; and, in the presence of archbishop Thomas the elder, and many other very reverend persons, he forbade him by his canonical authority to usurp a place under the jurisdiction of the church of Durham, and thus become a violator of the sacred canons and of brotherly charity. But he, replying with disdain, set at nought that prohibition; and having gone thither, was seized with illness on his return, and ended his life at Setterington, not far from York. Thus we lost the church of Tynemouth."

This cause, being commenced at York about the middle of Lent,[2] was heard again at Durham, on the Wednesday in Easter week, being the ides of April [13th April], before a large assembly of the principal men who happened to have met there at that time about some business; namely, Robert de Brys, Alan de Percy, Walter Espec, Forno the son of Sig:, Robert de Whitwell, Odard, sheriff of the Northumbrians, with the nobility of this county, and many others. When the monks laid their case before this assembly, lo! Arnold de Percy, a man of well-known rank and wealth, and of unshaken adherence to truth, rose up, and stated before all, in evidence of the truth, that he had both heard and witnessed how the earl had repented on account of this injustice which he had violently inflicted on St. Cuthbert. "When," said he, "the earl was taken prisoner at the place which he had seized from St. Cuthbert, and was brought to Durham in a litter, on account of the wounds which he had received, he begged that he might be allowed to enter the church to pray; this not being permitted by the barons, he burst into tears, and, looking towards the church, he exclaimed, 'O holy Cuthbert, I justly suffer these calamities, because I have sinned against thee and thine; this is thy vengeance for my iniquity. I pray thee, O saint. of God, have mercy on me.'" On hearing this, all pronounced that injustice had been done to the church of Durham; and although the matter could not at that present time be set right, yet, careful for their future interests, they providently recorded that this action had been tried before such a numerous assembly.

An epistle of pope Calixtus, concerning Turstin, addressed to king Henry, and Ralph, archbishop of Canterbury, interdicted him

---

[1] Gunner (?)   [2] Mid-lent Sunday fell upon 20th March.

from exercising either the episcopal or the sacerdotal office, as well in the mother church of Canterbury as in that of York, and prohibited the celebration of all divine offices, with the burial of the dead, except the baptism of infants and absolution of the dying, unless within a month after the receipt of that epistle, Turstin should be restored to his church, without the exaction of the profession. Wherefore, he was recalled by the king to England, and was presently restored to his archbishopric.

This year, after the feast of Easter, pope Calixtus, marching from the city [of Rome] with a large force, laid siege to the city of Sutri, until he took both Burdin and the place ; as the subjoined epistle [1] informs us :—

" Calixtus, bishop, servant of the servants of God, to his beloved brethren and sons, the archbishops, bishops, abbots, priors, and other faithful of St. Peter, both cleric and lay, resident throughout France, sends health and the apostolic benediction.

" Since the people has forsaken the law of the Lord, and does not walk in his judgments, the Lord has visited their iniquity with a rod, and their sins with stripes. But, still preserving the bowels of his fatherly affection, He doth not abandon those who put their trust in his mercy. For a long time, indeed, as their sins demanded, the faithful of the church have been disquieted by that puppet of the king of the Germans, to wit, Burdin ; and some have been taken prisoners, and some have been harassed even to death by the torments of imprisonment. But lately, after the celebration of the Easter festival, when we could no longer endure the crying of the stranger and the poor, we set out from the city, with the faithful of the church, and besieged the city of Sutri, until at length God's power delivered both the aforesaid enemy of the church, Burdin, who had there made a nest for the devil, and the place itself into our hands. We therefore entreat you, of your love, that you will render thanks with us to the King of kings for so great benefits, and will steadfastly continue in the catholic obedience and service, that you may receive due reward, now and hereafter, from Almighty God, by his grace. We beg also that you will cause these our letters to be forwarded from one to another, without any neglect. Given at Sutri, on the sixth of the kalends of May [26th April]."

The widow of William, king Henry's late son, who was drowned, (the daughter of Foulke, count of Anjou,) at the request of her father, was sent back to her own country by the king. The sons of the king of the Welsh, having heard that Richard, earl of Chester, was drowned, burnt two castles and slew many persons, and grievously pillaged many places in that county. The king was enraged at this, and, having levied an innumerable army from the whole of England, he marched to ravage Wales ; but when he had proceeded as far as Snowdon, the king of the Welsh made peace with the king of the English, by pacifying him with the gifts and hostages which he demanded ; and the army was presently sent home.

---

[1] See Malmesbury's History of the Kings, § 433 ; and Jaffé, p. 537.

A.D. 1122. On Christmas-eve [24th Dec.], an unusually strong
wind threw down not only houses, but even towers of stone.
Archbishop Turstin demanded profession and submission from
John, bishop of Glasgow; and as he would not yield this, he suspended him from his episcopal office. The bishop presently went
to Rome; whereon, perceiving that his cause did not succeed, he
went on to Jerusalem, and stayed there for some months, under the
courteous hospitality of the patriarch, and often officiated in his
stead in his episcopal duty.

Pontius, abbot of Clugni, who had taken the government of the
monastery by divine call, (a man, as is reported, of unblemished
life,) being accused before the pope, Calixtus, by the convent
under his charge, very readily allowed himself to be deposed from
his government; but another abbot being ordained in his place, he
then voluntarily purged himself by oath, thereby convincing his
accusers, before the sacred body of St. Peter, of having brought
false charges against him. The pope was much distressed that so
good and so innocent a man had been rashly deposed, and speedily
ordered that he should resume his authority, and return to the
government of the monastery, as heretofore. But he replied, that
he would rather die than resume the charge of the monastery of
Clugni. Attended by the pope's regrets, he went to Jerusalem,
where he was respectfully received by all with much joy; and there
making himself a residence over the gate called The golden gate,
he delighted to spend a retired life in divine meditation. Afterwards, he who had been substituted in his place as abbot died, not
long after he came to Clugni. Pontius was then ordered, by messengers and letters sent by the pope, to return to the government
of his monastery; but he could by no means be withdrawn from
his solitary mode of life. Sibilla, queen of Scots, daughter of king
Henry, died suddenly, on the fourth of the ides of July [12th
July].

Pope Calixtus and the emperor Henry were reconciled by the
mediation of sensible and faithful men, (after long dissensions,
which inflicted great injury to their affairs,) as letters sent through
the kingdoms and provinces testify, copies of which are here
given :—

" I, Calixtus, bishop, servant of the servants of God, grant to
you, my beloved son Henry, by the grace of God, the august
emperor of the Romans, that the elections of such of the bishops
and abbots of the kingdom of Germany as belong to that kingdom
may be made in your presence, if they be done without simony or
any violence ; and that if any discussion shall arise between the
parties, you, by the judgment and advice of the metropolitan and
principals, may afford your consent and aid to the sounder party.
The elect shall receive the regalia from you, and shall perform
what by right is due to you on account of them. And one consecrated in other parts of the empire shall, within six months, receive
the regalia from you by the sceptre, and shall perform what by
right is due to you on account thereof, saving all things which are
known to belong to the church of Rome. In those matters wherein

you have made complaint to me, and begged my aid, I will afford you assistance, according to the duty of my office. I give you true peace, and to all who are, or have been, on your side during the period of this dissension."

" In the name of the holy and undivided Trinity, I, Henry, by the grace of God emperor augustus of the Romans, for the love of God, and of the holy Roman church, and of the sovereign pope Calixtus, and for the good of my soul, give up to God, and to God's holy apostles Peter and Paul, and to the holy catholic church, all investiture by ring and staff, and grant that canonical election and free consecration shall be allowed to all the churches which are in my kingdom or empire.   Such of the possessions and royalties of blessed Peter, which, from the beginning of this dissension until yesterday, have been taken away, either in my father's time or mine, if they are in my hands, I restore them to the same holy Roman church.   Those which I do not hold, I will faithfully endeavour to cause to be restored.   The possessions, also, of all other churches and princes, and of others, both clerical and lay, which have been lost in this strife, by the counsel or judgment of the princes, such as I have, I will restore ; what I have not, I will faithfully endeavour to cause to be restored.   And I give true peace to the sovereign pope Calixtus, and to the holy Roman church, and to all who are, or have been, on its side ; and in those things in which the holy Roman church shall demand aid, I will faithfully assist ; and in those matters in which it has made complaint to me, I will do it due justice."

All these things were arranged by the consent and advice of the princes whose names are subscribed: Albert, archbishop of Mentz; Frederic, archbishop of Cologne ; Bruno, archbishop of Treves ; Ardwin, bishop of Ratisbone ; Otto, bishop of Bamberg ; Bruno, bishop of Spires ; and many other persons, ecclesiastical and secular.

This agreement being everywhere published throughout the nations and people ; letters were also sent by the pope to all archbishops and bishops throughout the regions and provinces, to the effect that, setting aside every other plea, they should meet without delay at the council which the sovereign pope was about to hold at Rome, on the fifteenth of the kalends of April [18th March].

In this year king Henry entering the districts of Northumberland crossed over from York, towards the western sea, after the feast of St. Michael [29th Sept.], that he might examine the ancient city, which in the language of the Britons is called Cairliel; now, in English, Carleol [Carlisle]; and in Latin is named Lugubalia. He gave a sum of money, and ordered the place to be fortified with a castle and towers.   From thence he went back to York, and after important meetings of the citizens and men of the province, he returned to the country south of the Humber. Ralph, archbishop of Canterbury, died on the thirteenth of the kalends of October [19th Sept.].

A.D. 1123. Stephen, earl of Bologne, afterwards king of England, gave to Gaufrid, abbot of Savigni, the vill of Tulket, in the province called Agmundernes, on the bank of the river Ribble, to build an abbey[1] of his order, in the time of pope Calixtus, and there they continued for nearly three years. Baldwin, the second king of Jerusalem, was captured at Antioch by the pagans, by stratagem, and was kept in confinement nearly three years. Fulke, earl of Anjou, demanded from Henry, king of the English, the lands, towns and castles which had been given as a dowry to the daughter of that earl, when the king's son, who was now drowned, had taken her to wife. Since the king was not willing to assent to this, he gave his other daughter in marriage to William, son of Robert, earl of Normandy, the king's brother, promising his aid to the young man, that he might be inheritor of some part of his father's dignity. Lest anything adverse to him should result from this, the king held counsel with his friends at Woodstock, (The place of woods,) and sent his illegitimate son Robert, and Ralph, earl of Chester, into Normandy to guard that territory.

John, bishop of Bath, was suddenly attacked after dinner on Christmas-day by disease of the heart, and died on the following day. Not long after, that is, the third day after Epiphany [9th Jan.], Robert Bloet, bishop of Lincoln, while the king was riding in company with him, in sound health, and apart from the others, (for they were engaged in conference about state affairs,) suddenly fell from his horse like a dying man; the king caught him in his fall; every one ran to the spot, and the bishop, unable to speak a word, was carried to the guest-chamber, and died the next day.

After this, when the king held his court at Gloucester, on the Purification of St. Mary [2d Feb.], the appointment of an archbishop of Canterbury was taken into consideration by the king's command; but, since several persons proposed different men for this dignity, the dissension caused a delay in the election; for there was present the prior of the church of Canterbury, with some persons of dignity, who declared that the choice of the church had fallen upon some persons of the monastic order, and demanded that whosoever of these was agreeable to the king and his council should be appointed over the church. But the bishops of all England, who were all of the clerical order, crying out, that they would not have a monk as primate, when they had clerics equally good and fit for the government of the church, the delegates of the men of Canterbury replied, " From the time of St. Augustine (who certainly was a monk), the first prelate of this church, until now, monks have always been chosen to govern it as its archbishops up to the present time. Henceforward, also, by God's favour, the ancient custom shall be preserved." But the king sided with the bishops, and decreed that monks should not be elected; whereupon four clerics were proposed to the meeting, with the understanding that upon whomsoever of these the choice of the men of Canterbury should fall, he should be raised to the archiepiscopate,

---

[1] The Cistercian monastery of Furness, in Lancashire

by the king's order. Therefore, since they were not allowed to observe the ancient custom of election, they were compelled by necessity to give their adherence to one of the four clerics, namely, William de Corbel, whom they knew to be a man of sober life and well skilled in learning, inasmuch as he had frequent and familiar intercourse with archbishop Anselm of pious memory. He had been first a clerk of bishop Ralph at the church of Durham, afterwards, for the sake of bettering his life, he became a regular canon of Chich, and now he was promoted to the archbishopric. Being elected, therefore, by the monks, Turstin, archbishop of York, offered to ordain him according to custom. "If," said he, "you choose to ordain me as primate of all England, I will willingly receive imposition of your hands; but if not, I will not inconsiderately be ordained contrary to ancient custom." Not long after, that is, on the fifth of the kalends of March [25th Feb.], by the king's order he was consecrated at Canterbury by his suffragans. Immediately afterwards, both he and Turstin set out for Rome, each to plead his own cause. And the king sent Bernard, bishop of St. David's; and Anselm, abbot of St. Eadmund's monastery, (nephew to archbishop Anselm;) and Polochinus, abbot of Glastonbury, (brother to archbishop Ralph,) along with archbishop William, —both as his embassy to the pope, and in order that, if anything should arise adverse to the archbishop, they might take his part. Meanwhile John, bishop of Glasgow, was recalled by the pope from Jerusalem to Rome, and ordered to return to his bishopric. Godofrid, the queen's chaplain, (who had come with her from Germany to England,) was elected by king Henry bishop of the church of Bath, and Alexander, (nephew of Roger, bishop of Salisbury,) to the church of Lincoln.

A council of three hundred bishops was held at Rome, on the fifteenth of the kalends of April [18th March], pope Calixtus the second presiding. There the decrees of the fathers were confirmed respecting positive and negative duties; the heads of which, those who wish to know will find here annexed:—

1. Acting upon the obligations entailed upon us by our office, and following the example of the holy fathers, we altogether forbid, by the authority of the apostolic see, any one to be ordained or promoted for money in the church of God. If any one shall obtain ordination or promotion in the church, in this way, he shall be deprived of the dignity so acquired.

2. We utterly prohibit those who are excommunicated by their bishops, from being received into communion by other bishops, abbots, or clergy.

3. No one, unless canonically elected, shall be consecrated bishop; and if such a thing shall be attempted, both the consecrator and the consecrated shall be deposed, without hope of restoration.

4. No archdeacon, or archpriest whatever, whether provost or dean, shall give to any one cure of souls, or prebends in a church, without the decision or consent of the bishop; or rather, as is decreed by the sacred canons, the cure of souls and the manage-

ment of ecclesiastical affairs shall continue under the judgment and authority of the bishop. If any one shall act contrary to this, or shall presume to claim for himself the power which belongs to the bishop, let him be debarred from the threshold of the church.

5. We judge the ordinations made by Burdin the heresiarch, after he was condemned by the Roman church, to be null; as also those made by the pseudo-bishops, after having been ordained by him. No one but a priest shall be ordained to the office of a provost, or an archpriest, or a dean; nor any one but a deacon to be an archdeacon.

6. We altogether prohibit priests, deacons, and sub-deacons from having connexion with concubines and wives, and dwelling with other females, except those whom the Nicene council allows, on account of necessity alone; namely, a mother, sister, aunt, or such like; respecting whom no suspicion can justly arise.

7. Furthermore, we decree, according to the statute of the most blessed pope Stephen, that laics, although of a religious order, shall have no power of ordering anything in ecclesiastical matters; but, according to the canons of the apostles, the bishop shall have the charge of all ecclesiastical affairs, and shall administer them as in the sight of God. If any one, therefore, whether prince or other layman, shall claim to himself the disposal or donation of ecclesiastical property or possessions, let him be judged sacrilegious.

8. We prohibit the marriage of kindred, since both the divine and secular law prohibits them; for the divine laws not only cast out, but pronounce accursed the contractors of such marriages, and the offspring of them. We, therefore, following our fathers, mark them with infamy, and pronounce them abominable.

9. To those who journey to Jerusalem, and strenuously afford their aid to defend the Christian people, and destroy the tyranny of the infidels, we grant remission of their sins; and we take their houses, their families, and all their possessions, into the protection of St. Peter and the Roman church, as was decreed by our sovereign pope Urban. Whosoever, therefore, shall venture to delay or hinder them, while engaged in that journey, shall be punished by the vengeance of anathema. Those who have placed the cross upon their garments, either for the expedition to Jerusalem or to Spain, and have afterwards drawn back, we charge by apostolic authority to resume that cross, and perform their journey, between this present Easter and the Easter ensuing; otherwise, from that time, we debar them from admission to the church, and interdict them all divine offices, in all lands, except the baptism of infants, and the shriving of the dying.

10. Whosoever shall knowingly coin or designedly utter false money, shall be separated from the fellowship of the faithful, as one accursed, and as an oppressor of poor men, and a disturber of the state.

11. If any one shall attempt to seize pilgrims journeying to Rome, or those frequenting the thresholds of the apostles, or the oratories of other saints, or shall plunder them of the property they carry, or shall harass the merchants by new exactions of taxes and

payments, let him be deprived of Christian communion, until he has made satisfaction.

By these synodal decrees, so subscribed and confirmed, the sentence of the general council absolved the emperor Henry, by its legates and writings, from the chain of excommunication by which he had been bound at the council of Rheims; and he, according to the tenor of the writings given before, promised that he would preserve the rights of the holy Roman church.

The council being over, the two aforesaid English archbishops went to Rome; but the archbishop of York arrived before the archbishop of Canterbury. He, on his arrival a few days after, had difficulty in obtaining a hearing for his petition for the pall, being obstructed by what had there been alleged against him: namely, that he had been elected in the court called " the court of blood," because sentences of death were there decreed; that he had not been promoted by general consent of the church of Canterbury to the government of that church; that he would not allow himself to be consecrated by Turstin, archbishop of York; that he was the first of the clerical order who had consented to be preferred over the monks of that church (for the successors of Augustine, who was himself a monk, were all of them monks down to this William): but these objections were at length set aside, by the favour of the aforesaid emperor, and Henry, king of the English, who, by their ambassadors, were vigorous mediators in his behalf; and, having formally received the pall, he complained, in the audience of the whole senate of the Roman church, that the church of Canterbury had been lowered from its dignity, through the undermining of the archbishop of York; it having, from the first bishop, Augustine, down to Ralph, who preceded him, enjoyed the primacy of all England, which now he urgently begged for that church, to which both ancient custom and the authority of privileges, preserved for so many years, had yielded it. To this Turstin discreetly replied, that, since he (having been summoned to Rome) had not been able to be present at the council, he could not fitly reply at that time to a matter of which he had not been forewarned, especially since he had not there with him the charters of the church of York, without which the nature of the dispute would not allow him on that occasion to enter into the matter. Therefore, having finished their business, both of the archbishops returned home; and, by order of the sovereign pope, legates of the Roman church followed them to England; in whose presence, at a council assembled from all England, the aforesaid archbishops brought forward the charters of their respective churches; and then, justice deciding between the two parties, their rights were re-established. William consecrated, at Canterbury, Alexander, bishop elect of Lincoln, and Godefrid, elect of Bath.

King Henry on Easter Monday [15th April] crossed into Normandy, in order that, should any opposition arise through William, his brother's son, (as he was told would be the case,) he might repress it by his royal authority. Four months having not quite elapsed, Galeran, earl of Meulan, and all his allies, deserted the king, and garrisoned their castles, and held them against him. The king levied an army; and having burnt the earl's town, called Brionne, leaving a single tower which he could not take, he committed to the flames his other town, (namely, the bridge of Audomar, commonly called Pontaudomar,) and ravaged and burnt all within a circuit of twenty miles and more, that the enemy might not be able to do any mischief. One hundred and forty soldiers held the castle of that besieged town for seven weeks against the king's army. The king, perceiving that he was not succeeding as he expected, erected a wooden tower, which they call Berfreit. This being brought to the castle by mechanical skill, the besiegers showered down from it, from above, arrows and great masses of stone. This fabric from which the archers and slingers fought, towered twenty-four feet in height above the wall of the fortress. The besieged, no longer able to withstand the force of these fighting from above, made a surrender, and marched out, the king permitting each man to go where he chose. The soldiers whom the king had brought from Lower Brittany, having burnt the aforesaid town, dug up the earth, and found chests containing many things which the citizens (foreseeing the danger) had hidden underground; such as gold, silver, valuable garments, palls, spices, ginger, and other goods of that kind; loaded with which, they took their departure. When the inhabitants of the place, having now made peace with the king, had begun to rebuild the ruins of the town, the aforesaid earl, suddenly setting fire to what had been done, reduced it to ashes. Besides these individuals mentioned above, others also, some of them nobles, revolted from the king, and strengthened their castles against him with a stronger power and number of fighting men. The king, attacking some, took six of them; but some he left as impregnable. He sustained several attacks from William, his brother's son, who was supported rather by the forces of his father-in-law, Fulko, earl of Anjou, than by his own. The king was more in doubt of the treachery of his subjects, than in dread of the inroads of foreigners. On account of these struggles, and the scarcity of means, England was worn down by exactions of money, which were imposed upon all the people to carry on the king's affairs. Teodulf, bishop of Worcester, and Ralph, bishop of Chichester, died. A council was held at Bordeaux, on the fifth of the ides of December [9th Dec.].

A.D. 1124. Alexander, king of Scots, died on the sixth of the kalends of May [26th April], after having reigned eighteen years and three months; his brother David succeeded him; and the kingdom, which his brother had held with great trouble, he received without opposition, and it afterwards continued entirely obedient to him, and in quiet. In this year Alexander, four months before his death, caused Robert Prior, of the regular canons at Scone, to be elected to the bishopric of St. Andrew's in Scotland; but his consecration was delayed for some time, on account of the submission which Turstin, archbishop of York, demanded as due from him according to custom. The Scots asserted, with absurd prating, that there was neither authority nor custom for this demand.

The aforesaid earl of Meulan, while incautiously making the circuit of the castles which he had garrisoned against the king, was captured by an ambuscade, with many of his followers, and was put in close confinement.   Pope Calixtus [II.] died on the ides of December [13th Dec.], and in his room the bishop of Ostia was raised to the popedom, who, according to the custom of his predecessors, changed his name from Lambert to Honorius [II.] A great famine prevailed throughout England, so that everywhere in the cities, villages, and road-sides, dead bodies lay unburied and falling to corruption, a wretched and horrid spectacle.

A.D. 1125. The emperor Henry [V.] died, leaving no sons, after having ruled for twenty years.   Wherefore three candidates were proposed by the chiefs of the kingdom, that one of them should be elected to the government; Leopold, brother-in-law of the deceased emperor, and his nephew Frederick, and Lothaire, duke of the Saxons.   Leopold refused the government, urging his age and the number of his sons, lest if he were raised to the throne some division of the kingdom might arise through them.   Frederick, who put himself forward as the rightful heir of the kingdom, was rejected the more on that account, since his uncle had been held in detestation by all.   Lothaire then was peaceably elected by all ; and though he strove to resist by argument and even by tears, he was anointed king at Aix-la-Chapelle, and after having put to flight Frederick, who waged war against him with great violence, and taken some of his fortresses, he ruled the kingdom and empire with great moderation and justice.   The empress, on the death of her husband, having lost certain fortresses which she had received as a dowry, returned to her father in Normandy.

John of Crema having received from the pope a legation to Britain, after having been a long time kept in Normandy by the king, at length received permission to cross into England; and was reverentially welcomed by the churches, since he had received from the pope commendatory letters to them to this effect, of which copies are here subjoined.

" Honorius, bishop, servant of the servants of God, to his beloved son John, priest, cardinal, legate of the apostolic see, wisheth health and the apostolic benediction.   As it is the duty of good sons to obey their fathers with the lowly humility of devotion, so it is the part of fathers kindly to provide for their sons with the feelings of affection.   We commit therefore to your thoughtful love the care and charge entrusted to you by our predecessor, pope Calixtus, of blessed memory, in the kingdom of England.   And we pray in the Lord that, as a wise and prudent son of the Roman church, you may earnestly labour in those things which pertain to the honour of God and the dignity of the apostolic see.   Given at the Lateran, on the ides of April [13th April]."

" Honorius, bishop, servant of the servants of God, to his brethren and sons, the archbishops, bishops, abbots, nobles and others, clergy and laity, residing in England, wisheth health and the apostolic benediction.   Although you are situated on the extremity of the earth, yet the catholicity of the Christian faith causes you to belong to the church of Peter the Apostle. For since it was said to Peter, 'Feed my sheep; feed my lambs,' truly not one of the sheep, not one of the lambs belonging to the fellowship of Christ, is excluded as not committed to the pastorate of Peter. Besides this, the authority of our most holy father pope Gregory, and the mission of the blessed Augustin, show that the kingdom of England belongs in a special manner to blessed Peter and the Roman church. We are incited by the duty resulting from this cause to watch over you, although situated so far off, with a more anxious care. Wherefore summoning our dearly beloved son John, cardinal, priest of the holy Roman church, to share this our anxiety, we have committed to him the office of our vicar in your territories; that by the aid of your love and the assisting patronage of the holy apostles, he may truly treat of matters concerning the correction of what is amiss, or the enforcing of what is correct within the churches, the spread of religion, and other things which shall seem worthy of praise or censure. We beg therefore, and admonish and charge you, that you reverently receive him as the vicar of St. Peter, hearken to him with humility, and at his summons duly hold with him synodal assemblies, so that by his and your diligence whatever in your kingdom needs to be reformed may be reformed, and whatever should be confirmed may be confirmed, by the inspiration of the Holy Spirit. Given at the Lateran, on the second of the ides of April [12th April]."

The same John received also the office of legate over the kingdom of Scotland; the pope on that account sending this letter to the king of that nation:—

"Honorius, bishop, servant of the servants of God, to his beloved son David, the illustrious king of the Scots, wisheth health and the apostolic benediction. It behoves the devout and humble sons of the blessed Peter to take heedful care in things which they know concern the honour of the holy Roman church. Wherefore we by our entreaty charge your eminence to receive and honour our beloved son John, cardinal, to whom we have entrusted the office of our vicar in these territories; and that you will cause the bishops of your land to assemble in council when summoned by him. The controversy which has been carried on between Turstin, archbishop of York, and the bishops of your land, we commit to the same our legate, to be carefully investigated and discussed, but we reserve the final sentence for the decision of the apostolic see. Given at the Lateran, on the ides of April [13th April]."

With this authority the aforesaid John, making the circuit of England, came to the king of Scots at the place called Roxburgh, on the river Tweed, which separates Northumbria from Lothian. Having there completed the business of his legation, he held a council at London on his return, the particulars of which are stated under the heads subjoined.

A.D. 1126. In the year of our Lord's incarnation one thousand one hundred and twenty-six, in the first year of the pontificate of the sovereign pope Honorius the second, in the reign of the most pious and glorious Henry, king of the English, and in the twenty-fifth year of that his reign, a synod was held at London, in the church of blessed Peter, prince of the apostles, at Westminster, in the month of September, on the ninth day of the month, where (after the discussion of many questions) these chapters, seventeen in number, were published and confirmed by all. Over that council presided John de Crema, (a presbyter cardinal of the holy Roman and apostolic church, by the title of St. Chrysogon,) legate in England of the aforesaid sovereign pope Honorius, with Turstin, archbishop of York, and William of Canterbury, and with bishops of different provinces twenty in number, and abbots about forty, and with a countless multitude of clergy and people.

1. Treading in the footsteps of the holy fathers, we by apostolic authority forbid any one to be ordained in the church for money.

2. We forbid also any fee whatever to be demanded for chrism, for oil, for baptism, for penance, for visitation or unction of the sick, for communion of the body of Christ, or for burial.

3. We enact, and by apostolic authority decree, that in the consecrations of bishops and abbots, in benedictions and dedications of churches, no cope, nor carpet, nor towels, nor vessels, nor anything whatever shall be exacted by compulsion, but it shall be freely offered.

4. No abbot, no prior, no monk, or cleric whatever, shall receive a church, a title, or any ecclesiastical benefice whatever, by the gift, or from the hand of a layman, without the authority and consent of his own bishop; and if this shall be attempted, the donation shall be void, and he shall be subject to canonical punishment.

5. We decree further, that no one shall claim any church, or prebend, by paternal inheritance, or shall appoint a successor to himself in any ecclesiastical benefice. If this shall be attempted, we allow it to have no force, saying with the psalmist, " My God, make them like unto a wheel, who say, Let us possess the sanctuary of God for our inheritance."[1]

6. Furthermore, we enact, that clerks who have churches or benefices of churches, and refuse to be ordained when invited by the bishop, in order that they may live more freely, if they shall disdain to be advanced to orders, shall be deprived at once of their churches and benefices.

7. None but a priest shall be promoted to be a dean or prior; none but a deacon to be an archdeacon.

8. No one shall be ordained to the priesthood, nor to the diaconate, unless to a certain title; and he who shall have been ordained without a title shall be deprived of the rank which he has assumed.

9. No abbot, nor any one at all, cleric or lay, shall presume to eject any one ordained by a bishop to a church without the decision of his own bishop. He who shall dare to do this shall lie under excommunication.

10. None of the bishops shall presume to ordain or to judge the parishioners of another diocese; for to his own master each one

See Psalm lxxxiii. 13.

stands or falls, and no one shall be bound by a sentence pronounced by one who is not his judge.

11. No one shall presume to receive into communion a person who has been excommunicated by another; he who shall knowingly do so, shall himself be deprived of Christian communion.

12. We order, also, that archdeaconries or plurality of honours be not given to one person in the church.

13. We prohibit by apostolic authority priests, deacons, sub-deacons, and canons from haunting the company of wives, concubines, or any females whatever, except a mother, a sister, or aunt, or those women to whom no suspicion can attach. He who shall be acknowledged to be a convicted transgressor of this decree, shall suffer the loss of his rank.

14. We prohibit usury and filthy lucre to clerics of all classes. Whoever shall be known or convicted of such a crime shall be degraded from his rank.

15. Sorcerers, soothsayers, and practisers of any divinations, and those who consult them, we order to be excommunicated and condemned to perpetual infamy.

16. We forbid the contract of marriage between relations, or near of kin, to the seventh degree; if any such shall have been united let them be put asunder.

17. We prohibit the receiving of the testimony of such men as accuse their own wives of being too near of kin, or those whom they produce as witnesses; but in all things let the ancient authority of the fathers be preserved.

These things being thus settled by the synod, Turstin, archbishop of York, and William of Canterbury, were summoned by this John, and they accompanied him on his return to Rome, to plead their causes in the audience of the pope.

The principal coiners of all England being detected in having made alloyed pieces—that is, not wholly of silver—were, by order of the king, summoned to attend at Winchester, on a specified day; and their right hands being cut off, they were emasculated.

A.D. 1127. King Henry, with his daughter the empress, returned to England the third of the ides of September [11th Sept.]. Archbishop Turstin of York, and William of Canterbury, returned from Rome. William returned in the character of the pope's legate for England; but Turstin exactly as he had set out.

A.D. 1128. The abbey of Selkirk was transferred to Kelso near Roxburgh, and the church of St. Mary was founded by the aforesaid monks of the Tyronensian order, and then the pious king David enriched it with great gifts, decorated it with many embellishments, and endowed it with ample estates and possessions. Henry, king of the English, held his court at Windsor at Christmas. Thence he removed to London, where, on the Circumcision of our Lord [1st Jan.], by his order the archbishops, bishops, abbots, David king of Scots, and the earls and barons of all England, swore that they would keep their fealty, and would secure to his daughter, the empress, the kingdom of England by hereditary right after himself, unless at his death he should leave behind him as his heir, a son born in lawful wedlock. They swore, also, to the queen, that whatever the king bestowed on her they would preserve constant and unchanged.

Charles, earl of Flanders, whilst kneeling in prayer, hearing mass in Lent, was surrounded by traitors and slain, before he could recognise his murderers. King Henry's nephew, William, his brother Robert's son, succeeded him in the dignity of his earldom : having been favoured by the utmost aid of Louis, king of the French. Before this, Fulko, earl of Anjou, had espoused his daughter to the youth aforesaid, but a divorce having been pronounced between them, on account of the consanguinity which king Henry had caused to be sworn to exist between them, the king of the French took up the cause of the young man, who was afraid of the snares of his uncle, the king of the English, and contracted an alliance with him, by giving him in marriage the queen's sister; and on this account he raised him to the aforesaid earldom, which of right belonged to him from the side of his paternal grandmother. For king William had married the daughter of Baldwin, earl of Flanders, and of her begot kings William and Henry, and Robert, earl of the Normans, whose son the aforesaid William was. King Henry had set his heart upon obtaining the aforesaid earldom, as due to himself by hereditary right; but was anticipated, as we have just said, by his nephew. Wherefore, lest some mischief should occur to himself from his nephew, he sought the friendship of the earl of Anjou, to whom he had previously been opposed, wishing to unite his daughter, the former empress, in marriage to his son. This at length being satisfactory to both parties, a little afterwards, on the seventh of the kalends of September [26th Aug.], he followed his daughter, whom he had sent before himself into Normandy, and brought the affair to a conclusion, on this condition, that if the king at his death had not an heir born in lawful marriage, his son-in-law should succeed him in the kingdom.

A.D. 1128. The aforesaid earl of Flanders, twice in one week encountering his enemies, with a small force overcame numbers. But soon after, besieging a castle of his opponents, whilst, flushed with the success of victory, he was too hotly pursuing the conquered and flying, he was mortally wounded in the region of the arm and hand, and after surviving three days he died, on the sixth of the kalends of August [27th July]. By favour of the king of the French, king Henry being made his heir by right of relationship, gave the earldom (to be held under him) to Theodore, who derived his descent from the earls of Flanders. Ralph, bishop of Durham, having spent twenty-nine years, three months, and seven days, in his see, ended his life on the nones of September [5th Sept.].

A.D. 1129. William Giffard, bishop of Winchester, died. King Henry liberated from captivity Gualaran, earl of Meulan, and restored him all that had been his except the fortresses; he concluded a peace between himself and the king of the Franks; he received the earldom of Flanders; he also married his daughter, the ex-empress, to the earl of Anjou; his enemies on every side were either conquered or reconciled; prosperity everywhere smiled on him, as he returned to England with a large fleet,

on the ides of July [13th July]. A few days had passed, when
lo! it was told to the king that his daughter was repudiated by
her husband, and cast off without respect, and had returned to
Rouen with a very few attendants. This matter grievously an-
noyed the king's mind. After the feast of St. Michael [29th
Sept.], accompanied by the archbishops, bishops, abbots, and nobles
of almost all England, he came to Winchester; and there gave
the bishopric of the church of Winchester to his sister's son
Henry, who had been brought up from infancy as a monk at
Clugni; the abbey of Glastonbury, the charge of which he had
previously received from the king, being joined to the bishopric
in augmentation of his dignity. Also the bishopric of Coventry,
which is that of Chester, was given to Roger, nephew of Geoffrey
Dedinton; and in order that he might be more fit for such a rank,
his uncle bestowed on him a present of three thousand marks. They
were consecrated on the fifteenth of the kalends of December
[17th Nov.], by William, archbishop of the church of Canterbury.

Here ends the history of Simeon, of sweet and holy memory,
     monk and precentor of the Church of St. Cuthbert, at
     Durham, embracing a period of four hundred and twenty-
     nine years and four months.

This book has been produced in a limited print-run of only
300 copies.

Readers who wish to follow up certain points in the preface,
or certain references in the footnotes, should consult the
original series 'The Church Historians Of England' (1850's).